PROTECTING OUR PORTS

Homeland Security Series

Series Editors:
Tom Payne, University of Southern Mississippi, USA
Tom Lansford, University of Southern Mississippi, USA

This series seeks to provide a body of case studies to explore the growing importance and prominence of homeland security to national defence policy and to examine the development of homeland security within the broader context of national defence policy in the United States and other major developed states. This series will identify and analyze the major threats that are particular to homeland security, as well as those that affect broader national security interests. Comparative studies will be used to elucidate the major similarities and differences in how states approach homeland security and works which advocate new or non-traditional approaches to homeland security. The series aims to integrate information from scholars and practitioners to provide works which will influence the policy debate and examine the ramifications of policy.

Also in the series

Power Plays
Enriched Uranium and Homeland Security
Christopher Hubbard
ISBN 978-0-7546-7693-5

Calculated Risks
Highly Radioactive Waste and Homeland Security
Kenneth A. Rogers and Marvin G. Kingsley
ISBN 978-0-7546-7133-6

The State and Terrorism
National Security and the Mobilization of Power
Joseph H. Campos II
ISBN 978-0-7546-7192-3

Comparative Legal Approaches to Homeland Security and Anti-Terrorism
James Beckman
ISBN 978-0-7546-4651-8

To Protect and Defend
US Homeland Security Policy
Tom Lansford, Robert J. Pauly, Jr and Jack Covarrubias
ISBN 978-0-7546-4505-4

Protecting Our Ports
Domestic and International Politics of Containerized Freight Security

SUZETTE R. GRILLOT
University of Oklahoma, USA
and

REBECCA J. CRUISE
University of Oklahoma, USA
with

VALERIE J. D'ERMAN
University of Oklahoma, USA

LONDON AND NEW YORK

First published 2010 by Ashgate Publishing

Published 2016 by Routledge
2 Park Square, Milton Park, Abingdon, Oxon OX14 4RN
711 Third Avenue, New York, NY 10017, USA

Routledge is an imprint of the Taylor & Francis Group, an informa business

Copyright © 2010 Suzette R. Grillot and Rebecca J. Cruise with Valerie J. D'Erman

Suzette R. Grillot, Rebecca J. Cruise and Valerie J. D'Erman have asserted their right under the Copyright, Designs and Patents Act, 1988, to be identified as the authors of this work.

All rights reserved. No part of this book may be reprinted or reproduced or utilised in any form or by any electronic, mechanical, or other means, now known or hereafter invented, including photocopying and recording, or in any information storage or retrieval system, without permission in writing from the publishers.

Notices:
Product or corporate names may be trademarks or registered trademarks, and are used only for identification and explanation without intent to infringe.

British Library Cataloguing in Publication Data
Grillot, Suzette.
  Protecting our ports : domestic and international politics
  of containerized freight security. -- (Homeland security series)
  1. Container terminals--Security measures. 2. Container
  ships--Security measures. 3. Harbors--Security measures.
  4. Terrorism--Prevention--Government policy.
  5. Terrorism--Prevention--Government policy--United
  States. 6. Terrorism--Prevention--International
  cooperation.
  I. Title II. Series III. Cruise, Rebecca J. IV. D'Erman,
  Valerie J.
  363.3'2593875442-dc22

Library of Congress Cataloging-in-Publication Data
Grillot, Suzette.
  Protecting our ports : domestic and international politics of containerized freight security / by
  Suzette R. Grillot, Rebecca J. Cruise, with Valerie J. D'Erman.
    p. cm. -- (Homeland security)
  Includes index.
  ISBN 978-0-7546-7789-5 (hbk)
  1. Container terminals--Security measures. 2. Container ships--Security measures. 3. Harbors--
  Security measures. 4. Terrorism--Prevention--Government policy. 5. Terrorism--Prevention--
  Government policy--United States. 6. Terrorism--Prevention--International cooperation. I. Cruise,
  Rebecca J. II. D'Erman, Valerie J. III. Title.
  HE566.C6G75 2010
  363.325'938710973--dc22

                                                                                    2010006876

ISBN 9780754677895 (hbk)

Contents

List of Tables		*vii*
Acknowledgements		*ix*
List of Acronyms		*xi*

1	Introduction	1
2	The Domestic Politics of Freight Security	17
3	Building on the Past: From National Security and Nonproliferation Policy to Containerized Freight Security	43
4	The International Politics of Container Security	65
5	Global Governance and an International Maritime Security Regime	91
6	Balancing National and Economic Security	117
7	Assessing Seaport and Container Security Around the World	137
8	Conclusion	165

Index	*179*

List of Tables

4.1	Secure Freight Policies and Programs	76
5.1	Port Security Programs/Policies and International Support Since 2001	102
7.1	Elements of a Secure Containerized Freight System in Brief	147

Acknowledgements

This book is certainly a result of team effort, and we are extremely grateful to the many officials, representatives, analysts, colleagues, students, family and friends that have supported, assisted and encouraged us along the way to this final product. Many thanks to Sridhar Radhakrishnan, Professor of Computer Science and Tom Landers, Dean of Engineering at the University of Oklahoma (OU) who invited us to participate in the Inter-modal Freight Security project that provided us the purpose and funds necessary to conduct this research. We also thank the other members of the Center for Infrastructure Protection and Hardening Through Education and Research (CIPHER) team at OU for listening to our research presentations and providing important feedback. Our colleagues in the School of International and Area Studies, Department of Political Science, and International Programs at OU have also been instrumental in supporting our research efforts. Numerous individuals have helped to facilitate our research program in the form of arranging, scheduling or providing personal interviews and port visits, which were indispensable to our study. Specifically, we thank officials and representatives at a number of US government agencies, private enterprises, international organizations, foreign governments, and domestic and international seaports. Particular thanks go to Bill Anthony of the US Customs and Border Protection agency who provided tremendous assistance with interviews and contacts. Without a doubt, the on-the-ground field research we conducted for this book, and the people we met throughout the process, was the most rewarding aspect of this endeavor.

Beyond conducting the research, we owe thanks to those who have commented on various portions of our research. We thank the editors and reviewers for Ashgate Publishing, editors and reviewers for the *Journal of Homeland Security and Emergency Management*, Rachel Stohl, Jacque Braun, Cassady Craft, Eric Heinze, and Zach Messitte. This project could have never been completed, however, without the work of outstanding research assistants that have provided crucial assistance and feedback. Specifically, we thank Brooke Hammer, Lessa Keller-Kenton, Holly Presnell, and James Roberson for their indispensible work. We also thank our students at the University of Oklahoma for listening to endless stories and examples about port and container security.

Finally, without the avid support of our family and friends, this book would have never seen the light of day. From the bottom of our hearts, therefore, we thank Pat Lannon, Hannah Grillot, Karen Saunders, Jim Grillot, the Beliveau family, the Atkinson family, Mike and Melissa Cruise, Mary Cruise, Stephanie Starr, AJ Kirkpatrick, and Richard and Enzo Marcy for their love, patience, friendship and understanding, and ultimately for reminding us what is really important.

List of Acronyms

AAPA	American Association of Port Authorities
ACE	Automated Commercial Environment
AEO	Authorized Economic Operator
AIS	Automatic Identification System
ANOA	Advance Notice of Arrival
APEC	Asia-Pacific Economic Cooperation
ASEAN	Association of Southeast Asian Nations
ATA	American Trucking Association
ATS	Automated Targeting System
BEET	Business Executives Enforcement Team
CARICOM	Caribbean Community
CBP	Customs and Border Protection
CBSA	Canadian Border Services Agency
CIA	Central Intelligence Agency
CITS	Center for International Trade and Security
COCOM	Coordinating Committee for Multilateral Export Controls
CSI	Container Security Initiative
C-TPAT	Customs-Trade Partnership Against Terrorism
DHS	Department of Homeland Security
DPW	Dubai Ports World
DNDO	Domestic Nuclear Defense Office
DOC	Department of Commerce
DOD	Department of Defense
DOE	Department of Energy
DOS	Department of State
DOT	Department of Transportation
EU	European Union
EXCOMM	President's Executive Committee
FAA	Federal Aviation Administration
FAST	Free and Secure Trade Program (Canada-US)
FBI	Federal Bureau of Investigation
FDA	Food and Drug Administration
FEMA	Federal Emergency Management Agency
GAO	Government Accountability Office
GDP	Gross Domestic Product
HEU	Highly Enriched Uranium
IATA	International Air Transport Association

ICE	Immigration and Customs Enforcement
ICMTS	Interagency Committee on Marine Transportation System
ILWU	International Longshore and Warehouse Union
IMO	International Maritime Organization
IMPACS	Implementation Agency for Crime and Security
IMSR	International Maritime Security Regime
IOs	International Organizations
IPSLO	International Port Security Liaison Officers
ISF	Importer Security Filing
ISPS	International Ship and Port Security
IR	International Relations
MA	Maritime Administration
MDA	Maritime Domain Awareness program
MERCOSUR	Southern Common Market
MTS	Marine Transportation System
MTSA	Maritime Transportation Security Act
MTSNAC	Marine Transportation System National Advisory Council
NAFTA	North American Free Trade Agreement
NATO	North Atlantic Treaty Organization
OPEC	Organization of the Petroleum Exporting Countries
PIP	Partners in Protection
PSI	Proliferation Security Initiative
RFID	Radio Frequency Identification Devices
RPM	Radiation Portal Monitors
SAFE	Security and Accountability For Every Port
SBI	Secure Border Initiative
SFI	Secure Freight Initiative
SOLAS	International Convention for the Safety of Life at Sea
TSA	Transportation Security Administration
TWIC	Transportation Worker Identification Credential
UAE	United Arab Emirates
UNASUR	Union of South American Nations
UNCLOS	United Nations Convention on the Law of the Sea
UPS	United Parcel Service
USCG	United States Coast Guard
VACIS	Vehicle and Cargo Inspection System machine
WCO	World Customs Organization
XLA	Express Delivery and Logistics Association

Chapter 1

Introduction

The sea is a place where many go to enjoy sun, sand and surf, but it is also the location of much commerce and occasional crime, death and destruction. In November 2008, for example, Indian and other citizens and tourists in Mumbai became the target of terrorists who entered the city by sea. After sailing from Pakistan on a cargo vessel, the terrorists overtook an Indian fishing boat and murdered its crew before boarding small inflatable boats and landing in two different places south of Mumbai. Entering the city by sea meant the terrorists could avoid encountering Indian security officers stationed at border points and air ports of entry. And because they entered Indian waters on an Indian fishing vessel, the terrorists did not raise any concern with the Indian coast guard. The armed gunmen proceeded to kill approximately 200 people and held the city of Mumbai hostage for nearly 60 hours before Indian commandos were able to bring the deadly event to an end (Rabasa, Blackwil, et al. 2009). Fearing similar attacks in the United States, port and police authorities from New York City traveled to Mumbai in December 2008 to study the terrorist attacks and strategize on how to prevent such incidents ("Lessons from the Mumbai Terrorist Attacks" 2009; Lubold 2009).

India is not alone in its experience with maritime or seaport centered violence. The possibility of a seaport attack became a reality at Israel's Ashdod port in the spring of 2004. On March 14, two suicide bombers breached port security by hiding behind fake walls placed in freight containers. While the terrorists' explosions missed the fuel and chemical tanks held at the port, ten people were killed and 16 injured. In fact, Israel has experienced numerous maritime terrorist attacks and has detected and prevented many terrorist plots involving its coastline (Lorenz 2007). Additional examples abound. Rebels in Somalia, for example, have targeted ships – particularly fuel tankers – with mortar attacks at Mogadishu's seaport, leaving port authorities and police forces scrambling to enhance security in and around the port area ("At Least Six Rockets Fired" 2007). Moreover, cargo containers have been used to traffic not only weapons and explosives, but drugs, humans, including terrorists themselves, and contraband of all sorts (Turnbull et al. 2006; "Stowaway Terrorists Steal Into America" 2002; "Colombian Coffee Comes with Smuggled Cocaine" 2009). While these types of attacks and misuses of cargo containers are really nothing new, they have seemingly increased in recent years and are leading to more significant concern and more targeted action.

Greatest attention has been focused on the use of seaports and cargo containers to transport, deliver, and even detonate nuclear or other weapons of mass destruction. Terrorist and other violent groups have certainly tried to acquire weapons of mass destruction, and certainly could use the global system of international trade and the ubiquitous cargo container to transfer and ultimately explode such dangerous weapons. Such an incident could be catastrophic. If a 10- to 20-kiloton nuclear weapon – about the size of the bomb used in Hiroshima, Japan in 1945 and approximately the equivalent of 15,000 tons of TNT – were exploded in a large seaport, one organization estimates that somewhere between 50,000 and 1 million people would die, approximately $50 to $500 billion of property would be damaged, trade losses would add up to about $100 to $200 billion, and the overall "indirect costs" of the incident would be around $300 billion to $1.2 trillion (ABT Associates as cited in Medalia 2003, 7). With such large and varied damage estimates being offered, it is no surprise that government authorities in particular, but the general public as well, have become concerned.

Cargo Containers, International Trade and Global Security

To be sure, cargo containers and seaports, in particular, are essential to global commerce. Although maritime merchants have traversed the world's waterways for centuries, trading goods at ports of call on nearly every continent, the shipping container is a much more recent addition to global trade – and has contributed significantly to its tremendous growth. Before the1960s when the 20- and 40-foot standard cargo containers and trans-Atlantic container ships were introduced to international trade, intermodal transportation of cargo was far more difficult. Although improvements in intermodal transshipments were evident in the late 19th and early 20th centuries – particularly between rail and road transportation – the time it took to successfully transfer goods was significantly longer than what could be accomplished after the container was introduced (Rodrigue and Notteboom 2009, 2). In the early 20th century, the pallet was considered the first important unit contributing to the enhanced intermodal transportation of goods. Primarily made of wood, a pallet or skid is a flat set of planks on which boxed or otherwise packaged goods can be stably placed and moved using a forklift or some other lifting device. Before the pallet it would take approximately three days to unload more than 10,000 cases of canned goods from a railcar. Once pallets and forklifts were introduced, the same 10,000 cases could be transferred in only four hours (Leblanc 2002). The development of the pallet, therefore, was a revolution in intermodal transportation itself, but nowhere near as revolutionary as the creation of the cargo container where goods could easily be transferred between ship, rail and truck for quick transport between producers, exporters, importers and consumers. The lack of standardization in container sizes and ships specifications hampered the fast flow of goods initially – particularly inland transfers – but by the 1970s maritime and inland transportation standards were set and the smooth and seamless movement of goods around the world has sailed forward ever since (Rodrigue and Notteboom 2009, 3-4).

With this transportation revolution in mind, it is clear that global ties – both economic and political – widened and deepened, allowing commercial relationships and related governmental regulations to expand and solidify. In fact, this revolution in transportation significantly affected what many refer to as "globalization," particularly as markets opened and American and European companies continued their search for cheaper labor, raw materials and finished goods (Schulte 2005; Bryan and Farrell 1996). However, due to the end of the Cold War, the development of East European and Asian markets, and the resulting expansion of the free flow of goods, capital, labor and knowledge, a subsequent rise in transnational crime became evident (Kaplan 1994; Shelley 1995, 463-489; Williams 1994, 96-113). Difficulties in monitoring, policing, prosecuting and punishing global criminals that operate across borders provide significant challenges to US and international security environments. The primary concern prior to September 11, 2001, however, was with corruption, fraud, theft, and illegal trafficking of illicit goods and materials most likely to be used for personal gain. In the post-9/11 environment, authorities and citizens alike have become more concerned with terrorist exploitation of the globalized environment to perpetrate transnational terrorist violence. Concerns with corruption and the trafficking of dangerous and illegal goods, such as drugs, weapons, stolen property, and laundered money, as well as the trafficking of people – whether they are immigrants, slaves or terrorists – continue (Naim 2003). However, many public officials and private individuals in the United States consider international terrorism to be most problematic.

Even before September 11, 2001 authorities in the United States were concerned with security at ports of entry and exit and the misuse of or interference with cargo containers. In April of 1999, for example, President Bill Clinton established the Interagency Commission on Crime and Security in US Seaports and tasked the Commission with conducting "a comprehensive review of the nature and extent of seaport crime and the overall state of security in seaports" (Report of the Interagency Commission on Crime and Security in US Seaports 2000, iii). In its September 2000 report to the President, the Commission found that seaport security in the United States ranged from poor to fair at best, and only in a few cases was the state of seaport security considered good (Report of the Interagency Commission on Crime and Security in US Seaports 2000, v). This may be the case because prior to 9/11 aviation security was typically the only mode of transportation that received attention to any significant degree – and even then the attention was "sporadic" and "reactive" (Szyliowicz 2004, 355-356). After airplane hijackings, the Federal Aviation Administration (FAA) would employ additional screeners to prevent weapons from being carried on board – and after a bomb destroyed Pan Am 103 in 1988 killing 270 people, the FAA focused its attention on screening suitcases and checked baggage (Ibid. 2004, 355-356).

In 1995 the US Department of Transportation (DOT) did state that they should undertake a review of maritime vulnerabilities and threats to both passengers and cargo, but nothing of significance emerged. Moreover, prior to 9/11, concerns with transportation security focused primarily on one form of transportation at a time

− air, sea or land, and most often on air − rather than concentrating on intermodal security and the real possibility that terrorists could exploit the global system of containerized freight movements to wreak havoc and cause damage, destruction and death (Ibid. 2004, 356-357). It was not until after the terrorist attacks in New York City and Washington, DC in 2001 that the vulnerabilities of global intermodal forms of transportation were highlighted. Since that time a number of measures have been developed, agencies have been created, agreements have been signed, programs have been implemented, and resources have been spent worldwide to minimize the economic, political and human impact of terrorist activity using the world's containerized freight chain.

September 11 and the Heightened Port Security Concern in the United States

In the United States there are approximately 7,000 miles of land border and 95,000 miles of shoreline. The country is therefore particularly concerned about the potential movement of dangerous weaponry into and throughout the country. With approximately 15 million cargo containers moving via sea vessel, train and truck each day − and with additional cargo entering the country by air − the probability that cargo containers may be used to transport and even detonate explosives, dirty bombs, or some other kind of weapon of mass destruction is very real. Ports of entry, particularly seaports, are viewed by some as one of the most vulnerable targets for a terrorist attack. A large percentage of cargo entering the United States flows through the nation's seaports (Hillyard 2005). Between 1999 and 2004, container traffic at the ten busiest seaports in the United States grew from 10% to 110%. Overall during that period, imports of containerized freight increased nearly 50% while exports grew at a rate of around 20% − and much of this growth has occurred since September 11, 2001 (Christopher 2009, 13).

Because of the significant threat that hidden bombs or explosives in cargo containers poses to the United States, the country has taken the lead in developing a number of port security initiatives and policies. For example, the United States government created the Department of Homeland Security (DHS) after the 9/11 terrorist attacks to bring together and centralize a number of agencies working on domestic or homeland security issues. Regarding port and container security, the basic US approach has been to employ "a layered defense" (Regenold 2007). A layered defense requires that multiple policies, programs, and actors function together to provide the most secure ports possible − the purpose being to identify, neutralize and eliminate breaches of security as containers are monitored from one layer to the next. The more overlapping, effective and consistent security layers are, the more protected US ports will be. In an effort to enhance policy and agency cooperation and to minimize inconsistencies in security programs and their implementation, the Department of Homeland Security was created to provide a framework and structure to share intelligence and enhance security

Introduction 5

activities (Szyliowicz 2004). To accomplish its goals, DHS must also work in close connection with other governmental departments on security issues, and naturally on port security. DHS should, therefore, establish and maintain open lines of communication with the Department of State (DOS), Department of Energy (DOE), Department of Defense (DOD), Department of Commerce (DOC), Department of Transportation and all other relevant actors and parties involved and interested in port and container security.

In addition to developing layered defenses, there has been a conscious effort in the United States to "push borders out." The best response to potential US vulnerabilities it to detect nuclear weapons and other dangerous materials in containerized freight before it reaches an American port. Binnendijk suggests that "the first and most important line of defense against container terrorism, therefore, is at the foreign port of origin" (Binnendijk et al. 2002, 1). This requires the United States to work with international organizations, foreign governments, and foreign enterprises to scrutinize containers when in foreign ports. Ultimately, US citizens are safest if an overseas counterpart can detect a dirty bomb or some other dangerous material or explosive before it is shipped to the United States. Because containerized freight is the central component of global trade, it is necessary for the US government to incorporate and include public and private actors in both a domestic and international setting into its national security strategy (Ibid.).

Shortly after 9/11 the United States began working with international counterparts to strengthen the use of nuclear detection and other equipment at ports overseas that ship goods to the United States. Although it is recognized that securing the world's containerized freight supply line is an enormous undertaking requiring a great deal of cooperation among actors internal and external to all countries involved in global trade, the task is not easily accomplished. In today's international system there exists no formal global agreement or organization that governs the international movement of containerized freight and the security measures that ports of entry and exit must develop and implement. Instead, a number of actors, agencies, businesses, industries, agreements, and legal frameworks affect port and container security operations. From the United States Customs and Border Protection (CBP) and Coast Guard (USCG), to the European Union's Freight Security Directive, the International Maritime Organization (IMO) and World Customs Organization (WCO), numerous efforts have been made to secure the international transport of containerized freight. With so many and varied actors involved in and concerned about containerized cargo, there is great potential for disagreements and difficulties, but also significant need and opportunity for collaboration and cooperation.

The General Port, Container and Maritime Security Literature

Without a doubt there has been a tremendous surge in maritime security publications in recent years. These books, of course, build on a very large body of literature on the subject of terrorism that grew significantly after September 11, 2001 (Kegley 2002; Sageman 2004; Mahan and Griset 2007; Hoffman 2006; Combs 2008; Howard, Sawyer and Bajema 2008; Simonsen and Spindlove 2009). In general, while pre-9/11 maritime security studies tended to focus primarily on the issue of piracy (Gray, Monday and Stubblefield 1999), post-9/11 literature highlights the threat of terrorist activity using ocean-faring vessels and their ports of call (Richardson 2004). Many contemporary studies, however, connect the two issues and suggest that pirates, as modern day terrorists, remain of significant concern across the world's oceans (Burnett 2003; Chalk 2008; Lehr 2006; Murphy 2007; Sekulich 2009). The increase in recent years in piracy near Somalia illustrates such concerns (The Editors of Mid-East Business Digest 2009).

Studies that focus specifically on port and container security are, however, relatively few – and those that exist range from stressing the threat to and vulnerabilities of US ports to providing "how to" manuals for strengthening port operations. One of the most visible and more alarmist in nature is Stephen Flynn's (2004) *America the Vulnerable: How Our Government is Failing to Protect Us from Terrorism*. In his work Flynn presents a worst-case scenario situation regarding the use of the global transportation system to transport, deliver and detonate a radiological weapon. Ultimately, Flynn argues that the United States government is ill prepared to prevent or respond to such an incident. A number of other studies are equally alarming, highlighting the threat of terrorist activity on the high seas as well as via global seaports (David 2008; Frittelli 2003; Vesky 2008). This growing concern with maritime security has also opened a market for volumes presenting training materials and technical descriptions relevant for those working in transportation security (Evans 2004; Sweet 2005; McNicholas 2007; Christopher 2009). Moreover, the business community has been a target of this growing literature as private enterprises and their reliance on the global system of trade has been and may continue to be significantly effected by maritime, port and container insecurity (Ritter and Wilson 2006).

In addition to the general literature on these issues, there exist a number of official and other technical reports presented by governmental and nongovernmental agencies. The Congressional Research Service and the Government Accountability Office alone have published hundreds of reports on maritime security – and port and container security more specifically – since 2001 (US GAO Container Security 2003; US GAO Homeland Security 2004; US GAO Maritime Security 2004; Frittelli 2009; Parfomak and Frittelli 2007). US governmental agencies such as the Department of Homeland Security and the Transportation Security Administration (TSA) have also made public hundreds, if not thousands, of statements, reports, fact sheets and updates regarding the issue (US Department of Homeland Security 2004). There have also been countless hearings on maritime, port and container security on Capitol Hill, and nongovernmental organizations such as the RAND Corporation have offered their expert assessment and advice regarding these issues (Martonosi, Ortiz and Willis 2004; Subcommittee on Coast Guard and Maritime Transportation 2002). The existing literature on these significant security concerns, therefore, is plentiful. However, existing publications, reports, news and analysis tend to be rather alarmist, pessimistic or political on the one hand, or technical and descriptive on the other hand. There seems, therefore, to be a significant gap in the literature regarding more systematic and academic research that provides more nuanced views of these important security matters. We seek to remedy this deficiency.

About this Book

Considering the global importance of port and container security issues, it is not surprising that there has been a significant growth in attention, policy, and resources focused on these security related problems. It is surprising, however, that little academic research and systematic analysis has emerged regarding domestic and international activities to ensure the security of ports and containerized freight movements around the world. In the literature there exist few attempts to fuse the political and practical policies of port security with an analytical discussion regarding actual implementation and the real world effects of such policies.

Our book investigates a number of issues surrounding the port and container security discussion. We focus on a range of relevant concerns from the numerous policies that have been advanced in the United States and abroad to address port and container security measures to the political consequences of the US leadership role. The book examines port and containerized freight issues at both international and domestic levels, and from both practical and theoretical perspectives. The study analyzes cooperation between US agencies and among the US government and its overseas counterparts, explores the domestic and international politics of port security, evaluates a number of the world's seaports based on a list of elements determined to be requirements for port and container safety, and examines the oftentimes difficult process of balancing economic and national security as it relates to the global supply chain. Ultimately, we shed light on the container security threat and the domestic and international responses that have emerged as well as those steps that still must be taken.

The book is the result of three years of extensive research on the security of containerized freight and the ports (air, sea, land) that these containers traverse. Secondary source research, such as news and expert analyses, journal articles, official government statements and other sources, served as the initial basis for an understanding of the process of containerized freight movements. This has also included review of the various programs, partnerships, policies and laws that have been created and implemented to address the issue since 9/11. We also include extensive primary source research with dozens of interviews with officials from all major US agencies involved in port security, as well as officials and representatives from the United States Congress, the US Chamber of Commerce, the Association of Port Authorities, UPS and FedEx, and former government officials (see Appendix for the complete list of interviews and site visits). We targeted domestic officials and companies for our interviews to get a complete picture of the port and container security situation and to hear the concerns of a variety of interested parties. US counterparts in Asia and Europe were also interviewed to add an important international perspective. With this research complete, we developed a list of 12 elements officials and representatives believed to be crucial for the operation of safe ports and the secure movement of containerized freight. Using these elements we toured a number of seaports in the United States, Asia and Europe to assess their level of port and container security. After personal observations and the collection of relevant documentation, we completed an assessment questionnaire and ranked the crucial elements along a continuum of development (see Chapter 7).

These primary and secondary sources provide a basis from which we make observations about the current state of port and container security as well as present policy prescriptions for improving security of the entire containerized freight chain. Admittedly, this book is heavily focused on containerized freight that flows through the world's seaports. We do include air and land-based freight movements in our study, but the overwhelming majority of containerized cargo is transported by sea and is transshipped via seaport. Moreover, there has been an overemphasis on airport security in the past – and some argue that national attention to airport security is misplaced and should be altered significantly (Smith 2009). Therefore, an emphasis on seaport security and the safe flow of containerized freight via international waterways are of primary concern.

The following chapters address a number of important issues relevant to port and container security. Chapter 2 highlights the domestic politics of freight security in the United States. After the attacks of 9/11 President Bush experienced a significant and persistent increase in popularity, which allowed his administration to advance a number of security related policies with minimal obstruction. The administration, and others, realized that they could use the nation's unease and insecurity to maintain and increase public support. The result was a number of important developments to enhance national security. However, due to the manipulation of the country's post-9/11 fears, a variety of possible, though highly unlikely, threats have been highlighted at the expense of attention on more probable security concerns. Many issues relating to domestic defense have been affected by this 9/11 politicking, including the issue of containerized freight security. In this chapter we assess the post-9/11 domestic political environment in the United States and explain how fear and insecurity have driven freight policy. Specifically, we provide evidence of instances, for example the 2006 Dubai Ports World sale, where port and container security decisions became obstructed by political gaming. Ultimately we contend that substantial progress has been made to secure ports of entry in the United States, but that the issue of freight security has become highly politicized at the potential cost of continued progress.

Chapter 3 focuses on the many lessons learned from national security policy-making, particularly after World War II and more specifically in the post-Cold War period regarding nuclear nonproliferation issues in the 1990s, and their impact on cargo security in the post-9/11 atmosphere. Lessons from nonproliferation policy and related security programs have informed US bureaucratic politics in the development of container security initiatives. This chapter outlines and examines the significant need for and effectiveness of interagency communication, coordination, cooperation and collaboration concerning port and container security policies.

Chapter 4 moves from the domestic to the international setting with a focus on the international politics of port and container security. Following the events of 9/11 the US government began focusing on the issue of port security in an international context, realizing that US containerized freight security was heavily reliant on international activities. Therefore, Customs and Border Protection (CBP) adopted a policy of "pushing borders out." The United States has since initiated, encouraged, and incentivized programs with international partners, which requires foreign ports to undergo a number of security-related measures. From the American initiated International Ship and Port Security (ISPS) amendment to the International Convention for the Safety of Life at Sea (SOLAS) in 2002, to its advancement of the Container Security Initiative (CSI), Customs-Trade Partnership Against Terrorism (C-TPAT) and Megaports, the United States has actively worked with foreign partners to strengthen the global supply chain. US policy in this area has in many ways dictated international policy and action. This chapter examines the US lead role on port security and explores how its programs are being implemented at ports around the world.

Chapter 5 focuses on the development of an International Maritime Security Regime. Since 2001, new norms and rules regulating international port and container security have resulted in a nascent regime advanced and molded by the United States. In this chapter, we initially outline the tenants of international relations and regime theory to understand the inherent challenges associated with international regime creation, development and persistence. We also examine the motivations of the United States and international actors to participate in this new regime. The United States, in its capacity as regime leader, is interested in enhanced power and influence. On the other hand, international partners are influenced by economic considerations. However, the international environment is changing. International partners (e.g. the European Union) are beginning to challenge the dominance of the United States in the International Maritime Security Regime as they are becoming dissatisfied with new policies that operate to primarily protect the national security interests of the United States.

Chapter 6 addresses one of the most perennial sources of tension regarding the issue of containerized freight security – finding a reasonable balance between heightened security and economic efficiency. The volume of trade that flows in and out of US seaports on a daily basis raises concerns about the security of cargo and the potential for a large-scale threat to enter the United States via containers. At the same time, security measures that impede the flow of trade or slow down the movement of the supply chain have enormous ramifications for all areas of the US economy. Acknowledging this fine line is crucial in any policy formulation, innovation and implementation. As such, our research includes numerous interviews with officials from the private sector, including UPS, FedEx, the American Trucking Association (ATA), the Express Delivery and Logistics Association (XLA), Amtrak, Lockheed Martin, and the US Chamber of Commerce Transportation Research Board. These interviews inform our discussion of security pitfalls and areas in need of improvement in the area of port and container security, and simultaneously highlight the cooperative, inter-modal and layered nature of securing the supply chain. While any sort of threat to the infiltration of containerized freight trade is critical to US security, a discussion of national security measures must necessarily include economic security for port operations to remain effective.

In Chapter 7 we present our unique assessment tool for the evaluation of seaport security around the world. Given the transnational nature of the issue and the importance of international compatibility, it is crucial that port security issues are understood in a multilateral and interdependent framework. Ultimately, US policy on seaport security cannot be understood in isolation from the port practices in operation at other ports around the world. Based on our research on the politics and practices governing US container security at home and international security protocols abroad, we devised a list of 12 elements we believe are crucial for the development of safe ports and for the secure movement of containerized freight. The elements focus on infrastructure, documentation and coordination and are scored on a scale of 0-3. Adherence to these elements by all relevant parties helps synchronize global port policy and ensures that all actors are working towards the same security goals. Overall, this global assessment tool allows us to compare ports and assess strengths and weaknesses.

The final and concluding chapter outlines the general findings of our study and highlights the strengths and weaknesses in current container security policies. This includes analyses of interagency cooperation, the results of new programs and protocols, the depth and effectiveness of collaboration with other governments and foreign ports, and public-private sector cooperation on policy formulation and implementation. In addition, Chapter 8 examines the practical and theoretical implications of current and future regulations for US national and economic security and reveals where gaps in container security policy may remain. Finally, the chapter offers policy recommendations that attempt to strengthen security measures at home and abroad that consider the pragmatics of implementation.

We demonstrate throughout this text that the port and container security issue is one that is most certainly caught in the midst of both domestic and international politics. There is much, however, to be optimistic about regarding the current security situation and the future of its development. Most ports we visited receive very high marks for their security measures. Nonetheless, there are a number of concerns about areas that are in need of improvement. It is the purpose of this book to offer a deeper understanding of the domestic and international political climate as it relates to port and container security, as well as to offer significant insight into the actual secure operations of ports around the world. Although research in this area is growing and should continue, the hope is to offer solid and concrete advice

Introduction 11

for the future of policymaking and academic debate on the important issues of port and container security. A rather wide audience is, therefore, the target of this work. Public authorities, port officials, industry representatives, private enterprises and interested citizens may find something of interest in this study regarding their particular concerns and activities. Moreover, a number of academic, theoretical implications emerge as we situate the port and container security issue in a broader theoretical context. Scholars and analysts therefore, should also find this subject appealing. Ultimately, it will be with the collective actions of varied and numerous audiences that we can successfully address port and container security issues and enhance our overall security environment.

Bibliography

ABT Associates. 2003. "The Economic Impact of Nuclear Terrorist Attacks on Freight Transport Systems in the Age of Seaport Vulnerability," executive summary, 30 April 2003, available at http://www.abtassociates.com/reports/ES-Economic_Impact_of_Nuclear_Terrorist_Attacks.pdf.

Bryan, Lowell and Diana Farrell. 1996. *Market Unbound: Unleashing Global Capitalism* (New York: John Wiley).

Burnett, John S. 2003. *Dangerous Waters: Modern Piracy and Terror on the High Seas* (New York: Plume).

Chalk, Peter. 2008. *The Maritime Dimension of International Security: Terrorism, Piracy, and Challenges for the United States* (Santa Monica, CA: RAND).

Christopher, Kenneth. 2009. *Port Security Management* (Boca Raton, FL: Auerbach).

Colombian Reports. 2009. "Colombian Coffee Comes with Smuggled Cocaine," 9 July 2009, available at http://colombiareports.com/colombia-news/news/4925-colombian-coffee-comes-with-smuggled-cocaine.html.

Combs, Cynthia C. 2008. *Terrorism in the 21st Century* (New York: Longman Publishers).

David, Anthony M. 2008. *Terrorism and the Maritime Transportation System* (California: Wingspan Press).

DEBKAfile. 2002. "Stowaway Terrorists Steal Into America by Sea Container," 18 June 2002, available at http://www.debka.com/article.php?aid=272.

Eaglin, Nina. 2003. "US Seaports May Be The Biggest Terrorist Threat," *On the Waterfront*, 3 August 2003, available at http://www.cbsnews.com/stories/2003/07/25/60minutes/main565180.shtml.

The Editors of Mid-East Business Digest. 2009. *Somali Piracy Yearbook for 2008: A Compendium of Seaborne Attacks, Rescues and Analysis* (Scotts Valley, CA: CreateSpace Publishers).

Evans, Fred. 2004. *Maritime and Port Security: Securing the Nation* (New York: Chelsea House Publications).

Flynn, Stephen. 2004. *America the Vulnerable: How Our Government is Failing to Protect us from Terrorism* (New York: HarperCollins).

Frittelli, John F. 2003. *Port and Maritime Security: Background and Issues* (Hauppauge, NY: Novinka Books).

Frittelli, John F. 2009. "Port and Maritime Security: Background and Issues for Congress," *CRS Report for Congress*, July 2009, available at http://www.fas.org/sgp/crs/homesec/RL31733.pdf.

Gray, Jim, Mark Monday and Gary Stubblefield. 1999. *Maritime Terror: Protecting Your Vessel and Your Crew Against Piracy* (Boulder, CO: Paladin Press).

Hoffman, Bruce. 2006. *Inside Terrorism* (New York: Columbia University Press).

Howard, Russell, Reid Sawyer and Natasha Bajema. 2008. *Terrorism and Counterterrorism: Understanding the New Security Environment* (New York: McGraw-Hill).

Kaplan, Robert D. 1994. "The Coming Anarchy," *Atlantic Monthly*, Vol. 273, No. 2, February 1994, available at http://www.theatlantic.com/doc/199402/anarchy.

Kegley, Charles W. 2002. *The New Global Terrorism: Characteristics, Causes, Controls* (New York: Longman Publishers).

Kelly, Raymond W. 2009. "Lessons from the Mumbai Terrorist Attacks," Testimony of Police Commissioner Raymond W. Kelly, Senate Committee on Homeland Security and Homeland Affairs, January 8, 2009, available at http://www.nyc.gov/html/nypd/html/pr/lessons_from_mumbai_terror_attacks.shtml.

Leblanc, Rick. 2002. "Pallet Evolved Along with Forklift," *Pallet Enterprise*, 2 December 2002, available at http://www.palletenterprise.com/articledatabase/view.asp?articleID=821.

Lehr, Peter. 2006. *Violence at Sea Piracy in the Age of Global Terrorism* (New York: Routledge).

Lorenz, Akiva J. 2007. *The Threat of Maritime Terrorism in Israel* (International Institute for Counter-Terrorism), available at http://www.ict.org.il/Articles/tabid/66/Articlsid/251/currentpage/6/Default.aspx.

Lubold, Gordon. 2009. "Mumbai Attacks Refocus US Port Security Reform," *Christian Science Monitor*, January 15, 2009, available at http://www.csmonitor.com/2009/0113/p02s03-usmi.html.

Mahan, Sue G. and Pamela L. Griset. 2007. *Terrorism in Perspective* (Thousand Oaks, CA: Sage Publications).

Martonosi, Susan E., David S. Ortiz and Henry H. Willis. 2004. "Evaluating the Security of the Global Containerized Supply Chain," (Santa Monica, CA: RAND Corporation), available at http://www.rand.org/pubs/technical_reports/2004/RAND_TR214.pdf.

McNicholas, Michael. 2007. *Maritime Security: An Introduction* (Burlington, MA: Butterworth-Heinemann).

Medalia, Jonathan. 2005. "Terrorist Nuclear Attacks on Seaports: Threat and Response," Congressional Research Service :CRS Report for Congress, available at http://fpc.state.gov/documents/organization/13840.pdf.

Murphy, Martin N. 2007. *Contemporary Piracy and Maritime Terrorism* (New York: Routledge).

Naim, Moises. 2003. "The Five Wars of Globalization," *Foreign Policy*, January/February 2003, available at http://www.foreignpolicy.com/Ning/archive/archive/134/5wars.qxd.pdf.

Parfomak, Paul W. and John F. Frittelli. 2007. "Maritime Security: Potential Terrorist Attacks and Protection Priorities," *CRS Report for Congress*, May 2007, available at http://assets.opencrs.com/rpts/RL33787_20070514.pdf.

Rabasa, Angel, Robert D. Blackwil, Peter Chalk, Kim Cragin, C. Christine Fair, Brian A. Jackson, Brian Michael Jenkins, Seth G. Jones, Nathaniel Shestak and Ashley J. Tellis. 2009. *The Lessons of Mumbai* (Santa Monica, CA: RAND Corporation).

Regenold, Michele. 2007. "All Hands on Deck: Securing Overseas Freight," *Exploring the World of Transportation*, November/December 2007, available at http://www.go-explore-trans.org/2007/nov-dec/secure_freight.cfm.

Report of the Interagency Commission on Crime and Security in US Seaports, Fall 2000. Interagency Commission on Crime and Security in US Seaports (Washington, DC).

Richardson, Michael. 2004. *A Time Bomb for Global Trade: Maritime-related Terrorism in the Age of Weapons of Mass Destruction* (Singapore: Institute of Southeast Asian Studies).

Ritter, Luke, Michael J. Barrett and Rosalyn Wilson. 2006. *Securing Global Transportation Networks* (New York: McGraw-Hill).

Rodrigue, Jean-Paul, and Theo Notteboom. 2009. "The Geography of Containerization: Half a Century of Revolution, Adaptation and Diffusion," *Geo Journal*, Vol. 74, No. 1, February 2009, 1-5.

Sageman, Marc. 2004. *Understanding Terror Networks* (Philadelphia: University of Pennsylvania Press).

Schulte, Jan Aart. 2005. *Globalization: A Critical Introduction*, 2nd Edition (New York: Palgrave Macmillan).

Sekulich, Daniel. 2009. *Terror on the Seas: True Tales of Modern-Day Pirates* (New York: Thomas Dunne Books).

Shabeelle Media Network. 2007. "At Least Six Rockets Fired at Mogadishu Seaport," 5 February 2007, available at http://www.benadir-watch.com/2007%20News/0205_Rockets_fired_at_seaport.pdf.

Shelley, Louise. 1995. "Transnational Organized Crime: An Imminent Threat to the Nation-State?" *Journal of International Affairs*, Vol. 48, No. 2, Winter 1995, 463-489.

Simonsen, Clifford E. and Jeremy R. Spindlove. 2009. *Terrorism Today: The Past, the Players, the Future* (Upper Saddle River, NJ: Prentice Hall).

Smith, Patrick. 2009. "Are Passengers Safe From Terrorists? The TSA Wastes A Lot of Time and Money on an Inefficient Fight Against the Wrong Enemy," *Salon.com*, 28 August 2009, available at http://www.salon.com/tech/col/smith/2009/08/28/askthepilot332/index.html.

Subcommittee on Coast Guard and Maritime Transportation. 2002. "Hearing on Port Security: Credentials for Port Security," 107th Congress [2001-2002] House Committee Meetings, February 2002, available at http://www.lib.ncsu. edu/congbibs/house/107hdgst2.html.

Sweet, Kathleen. 2005. *Transportation and Cargo Security: Threats and Solutions* (Upper Saddle River, NJ: Prentice Hall).

Szyliowicz, Joseph S. 2004. "International Transportation Security," *Review of Policy Research*, Vol. 21, No. 3, 355-356.

Turnbull, Lornet, Kristi Heim, Sara Jean Green and Sanjay Bhatt. 2006. "15 Days in a Metal Box, To Be Locked Up," *The Seattle Times*, 6 April 2006, available at http://seattletimes.nwsource.com/html/localnews/2002914004_smuggling. html.

US Department of Homeland Security. 2004. "Secure Seas, Open Ports: Keeping Our Waters Safe, Secure and Open for Business," 21 June 2004, available at http://www.dhs.gov/xlibrary/assets?DHSPortSecurityFactSheet-062104.pdf.

US Government Accountability Office. 2003. "Container Security: Expansion of Key Customs Programs Will Require Greater Attention to Critical Success Factors," July 2003, available at http://www.gao.gov/new.items/d03770.pdf.

US Government Accountability Office. 2004a. "Homeland Security: Summary of Challenges Faced in Targeting Oceangoing Cargo Containers for Inspection," March 2004, available at http://www.gao.gov/new.items/d04557t.pdf.

US Government Accountability Office. 2004b. "Maritime Security: Better Planning Needed to Help Ensure an Effective Port Security Assessment Program," September 2004, available at http://www.gao.gov/new.items/d041062.pdf.

Vesky, Jonathan P. (ed.) 2008. *Port and Maritime Security* (New York: Nova Science Publishers).

Williams, Phil. 1994. "Transnational Criminal Organisations and International Security," *Survival*, Vol. 36, No. 1, Spring 1994, 96-113.

APPENDIX

List of Interviews and Site Visits

Government and Public Agencies

Customs and Border Protection
Department of Commerce
Department of Defense
Department of Energy
Department of Homeland Security
Department of State
Department of Transportation
Domestic Nuclear Detection Office

Immigration and Customs Enforcement
Office of the Deputy Under Secretary of the Navy
United States Coast Guard
United States Congress: House Committee on Homeland Security

Business and Private Agencies

American Association of Port Authorities
American Trucking Association
Express Delivery & Logistics Association
FedEx
Lockheed Martin
United Parcel Services
United States Chamber of Commerce: Transportation Research Board

US Ports

Port of Los Angeles/Long Beach
Port of New Orleans
Port of New York/New Jersey
Port of Seattle

International Agencies and Offices

European Union Commission: Maritime Affairs
International Maritime Organization
World Customs Organization

International Ports

Port of Antwerp (Belgium)
Port of Athens (Greece)
Port of Duress (Albania)
Port of Gdansk (Poland)
Port of Hamburg (Germany)
Port of Hong Kong
Port of London (UK)
Port of Rotterdam (Netherlands)
Port of Singapore
Port of Taicang (China)
Port of Thessaloniki (Greece)
Port of Tokyo (Japan)
Port of Yangshan (China)

Chapter 2
The Domestic Politics of Freight Security

Introduction

After the Japanese attack on Pearl Harbor, Americans from all corners of the country supported President Roosevelt's decision to enter World War II and willingly bought war bonds and accepted rationing. Likewise, during the Cuban Missile Crisis, the invasion of Panama and Operation Desert Storm, citizens provided not just popular support, but also incredible policy discretion to the country's leaders to begin military operations, to strengthen US agencies, and to enhance funding for security technologies. This was never more evident than the days and months following September 11, 2001. At that time, the country sought comfort, reassurance and action. Just as with previous national and international crises, American citizens, the media and members of Congress rallied behind the most physical embodiments of American unity – in particular they rallied behind the US President. Americans "Rallied 'Round the Flag" in support of their leader, trusting that the President would enact policies to enhance domestic security and prevent further terrorist attacks.

In this chapter we argue that the 9/11 rally led to an environment where the nation's hypersensitivity resulted in relatively unchallenged adjustments to past procedures and the introduction of new policies and programs relating to all areas of homeland defense, including containerized freight security. Though taking impressive and in many ways positive strides to better secure our domestic points of entry, at times the nation's fear was manipulated, and the issue of freight security politicized. Initial acquiescence in Congress turned into jockeying for advantage, with both parties attempting to present themselves as tough on national security long after the 9/11 rally ended.

What follows is a theoretical discussion of the "Rally 'Round the Flag" effect as well as a look at what made the 2001 rally so unusual. We then turn to the issue of containerized freight and provide a brief overview of containerized freight security issues before September 11, 2001, and address the many changes that occurred after that date. From there, we provide detailed information about the actors, agencies, programs and policies that govern US freight security today and provide a description of the security processes currently in practice for containers arriving via sea, land or air ports. After explaining current procedures, there is a presentation of a number of instances (e.g. the Dubai Ports World sale and the 100% foreign container scanning requirement) where domestic freight security issues were used to heighten fear and advance personal and political agendas. Finally, we address the implications of the politicization of this issue.

The Rally 'Round the Flag Effect

The Rally 'Round the Flag phenomenon was first articulated by John Mueller in 1973. Since then, his observation that leaders, particularly Presidents, experience a popularity boost following instances of national crisis has been well studied. From available statistics, we know that US citizens support their Presidents, even if just for a short time, during crisis situations. This generally occurs in instances where there is a dramatic, international event that involves the President (Mueller 1973). In times of imminent external threat, the population intuitively attempts to show a united front, lining up behind their President (Siegelman and Conover 1981). Mueller and others have examined military events such as the Cuban Missile Crisis, the Iranian Hostage Crisis and the Gulf War and found that in each instance, the rally was markedly apparent (Mueller 1973; Hetherington and Nelson 2003).

Hetherington and Nelson argue that the President experiences the effects of a rally at times of crisis, because one of his many roles is that of Head of State – the symbol of the nation. Therefore, a jolted population initially feels closer affinity and perhaps patriotism for the President. After the initial event, the President must continue his additional duties as Head of Government, media attention moves on to the next big story and the importance of the President's symbolic status diminishes as does his escalated popularity. For example, President George H.W. Bush enjoyed a very large rally during the 1991 Gulf War. His job approval reached 89% in the early months of that year – higher than any of his predecessors.[1] However, despite the success of the first Gulf War, six months later his numbers returned to more modest levels. A year and a half later, the elder President Bush lost his 1992 re-election bid (Hetherington and Nelson 2003).

We generally think of the President as experiencing the rally. However, studies show that trust in government in general also increases. It is somewhat unclear if there is an individual rally for members of Congress, though they certainly benefit from the improved perception of government. Conversely, we do know that the rally can adversely affect legislators. Members of Congress are susceptible to negative perceptions if they oppose the President during the weeks or months of his increased popularity. In fact, Regens et al. (1995) found that there was an apparent electoral consequence for members of Congress who failed to support the President in times of crisis or war. The issue becomes one of patriotism, so that those who fail to support the President are "un-American." Most members of Congress, whose livelihoods depend on re-election, shun even the possibility of an unpatriotic label. Therefore, members of Congress will generally also support the President or will remain silent during a rally event for fear of constituency retribution (Stoll 1987).

The media also joins the rally both by enforcing support for the President and by highlighting the importance of the crisis and providing cues for national unity.

---

1   Presidential approval figures were first collected in the 1930s (Feldman 2007).

News shows often bring experts, policy makers and other elites into our living rooms for discussion about the crisis event. These sources often indicate their support for the President, as they too are displaying "crisis unity," further signaling to the population that their leader is taking the proper course (Brody 1991). Media members also appear to elicit further emotions by focusing on the victims of the event and by often using the term "we" to imply that everyone has been jointly victimized (Altheide 2006). This is likely more significant today in the era of 24-hour news cycles. Therefore, after a crisis not only does the President enjoy greater public popularity, but he is also usually granted a period of bi-partisan support from the legislative branch as well as the media. This allows the President to push through initiatives with little to no opposition.

Security and the 9/11 Rally

A Rally Like No Other

On the evening after the terrorist attacks, President Bush told the nation:

> This is a day when all Americans from every walk of life unite in our resolve for justice and peace. America has stood down enemies before, and we will do so this time. None of us will ever forget this day, yet we go forward to defend freedom and all that is good and just in our world (Bush 2001).

The President attempted to calm the citizenry after the attacks, and in return the country gave him unprecedented support. The rally experienced after September 11 proved to be the largest and longest rally in recorded history. A day before the attacks, 51% of the population indicated approval for President Bush's job performance. Five days later, Bush had an 86% approval rating. On September 20 President Bush addressed the nation from the Oval office to explain the country's course of action, at which time pollsters reported a 90% approval rate for the President. Not only is 90% the highest approval rating of any US President, the increase from 51% to 90% is the largest jump in approval ever recorded. His rally bump was significantly higher than the second largest increase, his father's in early 1991[2] (Hetherington and Nelson 2003). Generally rallies are rather short lived, but the 9/11 rally was unique in that it extended into years rather than weeks or months. Though not as persistent, evidence also suggests that trust in government levels increased substantially. Six months later, trust levels had moderated to previous figures, but when trust on security matters was separated, high approval continued (Hetherington and Nelson 2003; Schubert et al. 2002).

---

2   George H.W. Bush experienced a jump from 61% to 89%, a 28% increase. His son's increase of 39% was much higher.

Support for the administration and, by association, the Republican Party continued through the 2002 and 2004 election cycles.[3] The 2002 election led to Republican gains in both the Senate and the House of Representatives. This was the first time since 1934 that the party of the President gained seats in both houses during a mid-term election. In 2004, President Bush promoted the security issue and gained reelection by a greater margin than in 2000. Due to the 9/11 rally and subsequent events that will be addressed shortly, foreign policy, generally an insignificant electoral issue (Page and Brody 1972), became one of the centerpieces of 2002, 2004 and even to some extent the 2006 elections. After the summer of 2001, national security garnered the attention of the American public as it had not since the hottest days of the Cold War.

As theorized, the 9/11 rally created an atmosphere where opposition was unwelcome. The unique strength and duration of public support of the President made protest rare. Even when resistance did occur it was rather hesitant. Support became associated with patriotism. And such comments as "you are either with us or you are against us" and claims of "un-American" behaviors further solidified the connection between support for security measures and patriotism. Sometimes the very language used made opposition next to impossible. Few members of Congress would have the political courage, less than two months after 9/11, to vote down a bill called the Uniting and Strengthening America by Providing Appropriate Tools Required to Intercept and Obstruct Terrorism Act of 2001, or its more familiar name; the PATRIOT Act.[4] During the rally a few public personalities and academics were shouted down in the media as unpatriotic for expressing any disapproval of the Bush administration's military policy, and in Washington, policymakers went through a temporary period of silence and hesitation before bringing forth any less than supportive evaluations of domestic security or military policies (Balz 2002).

Events Extending the 9/11 Rally

The initial strength of the 9/11 rally certainly comes from the unprecedented nature of the terrorist attacks. The persistence of the rally was helped along by

---

3   Though President George W. Bush's popularity decreased from its high point of 90%, it remained above the previous 51% for a significant stretch of time. During a few months in 2003 and 2004, approval moderated back around the pre-rally percentage, only to jump back up as events, such as the capture of Saddam Hussein, resulted in additional spikes. Some could argue that this is actually a series of rallies, but it is appropriate to categorize this as an extended rally due to the fact that the compounding events were inextricably linked to 9/11 and the "War on Terror." Though questions remain about the existence of the 9/11 rally in 2003 and 2004, by 2005 it was quite clear that the rally was over, and President Bush (43) would never again see approval figures near 50%.

4   As it turns out, only one member of Congress, Barbara Lee (D-CA) voted against the bill.

The Domestic Politics of Freight Security

the depth of national unease and by a series of events that exacerbated our fears. Within days of 9/11, the country was further on edge when it was discovered that letters laced with the deadly anthrax toxin were travelling through the arteries of the US postal system, eventually contaminating a dozen citizens and claiming five lives ("Amerithrax Investigation" 2001). The United States also began its mission in Afghanistan and the President declared an ambitious "War on Terror." In the following months and years, a "shoe bomber" was found boarding an airplane, the US invaded Iraq, and terrorist incidences occurred in Madrid (2004) and London (2005). All of these things reinforced the country's apprehensions and served to prolong President Bush's rally.

Politicization and Fear

However, it was not simply the above mentioned events that contributed to the President's support. There were also those who, whether maliciously or not, manipulated and exacerbated the nation's anxiety for their own benefits. The White House, Congress, so-called risk entrepreneurs, and the media helped extend the 9/11 rally by focusing on US vulnerabilities, insecurities, and the threats posed by terrorism. These efforts were effective. As John Mueller aptly explains, "Most Americans seem to have developed a false sense of insecurity about terrorism" (Mueller 2006, 3).[5] At a time of frayed nerves, fear facilitated and prolonged the rally event (Chanley 2002; Huddy et al. 2005).

The constant focus on potential threat and national insecurity led to what some have called the "politics of fear," which came to predominate the post-9/11 environment. This involves not just an overreaction towards perceptions of threat. More importantly, it is also about exploiting public fears as a means of garnering political support – though, as will be demonstrated, this is not only a tactic employed by politicians. In fact:

> ...fears and anxieties created by the 9/11 experience have been so deftly orchestrated and overblown by members of the terrorism industry: politicians, experts, the media, academics, the bureaucracy, and risk entrepreneurs who profit in one way or another by inflating the threat international terrorism is likely to present (Mueller 2006, 6).

This can happen because the population feels vulnerable and is susceptible to such behavior because they seek "protection, policing, and intervention to prevent further victimization" (Altheide 2006, 423). Even after the 9/11 rally ended, security had become so politicized, and fear seen as an effective tool to garner support, that the approach continued.

---

5 As Mueller and others have shown, the threat of terrorism is quite minor. An American is more likely to die of drowning in the bathtub or being struck by lightning than to be a victim of a terrorist incident (Mueller 2006).

President Bush, in particular, received unprecedented popular and political support after the terrorist attacks. Though his concern for national security is likely genuine, prolonging his popularity through a focus on threat and domestic security also greatly benefited his administration's goals. At least in some instances it appears to have been an intentional tactic by the administration to manipulate fear for support (Lemann 2002; Mueller 2006). One example comes from the recollections of Tom Ridge, first Secretary of Homeland Security. In his 2009 memoirs Ridge describes how political considerations played a large role in shaping the familiar color-coded terror alert system. He explains that he was often asked to increase the terror alertness level at times when the administration needed to boost public support (Ridge 2009). Bush, his advisors (particularly Karl Rove) and the Republican Party, knew that if they focused on national insecurity, they would have an electoral advantage – an effective tactic in the short term (Mueller 2006).

However, it was not just the Republicans that focused on fear and insecurity. The Democrats also saw the benefits of focusing on the terrorist threat, though they were perhaps less able to capitalize upon it due to their position as the minority. 2004 Democratic Presidential hopeful John Kerry, for example, commented "I do not fault George Bush for doing too much in the War on Terror, I believe he's done too little" (UCLA Address 2004). The Democrats were finally able, after victory in the interim elections of 2006, to more effectively use the terrorist threat to their advantage. This was perhaps most evident in the way they addressed the security of containerized freight, which is detailed later in this chapter.

Politicians, however, were not alone in their use of national anxiety. News outlets, with their constant stories of 9/11 loss, and later discussion of possible, but in many cases improbable, terrorist targets and means, also contributed to the nation's anxiety. The media, often through their interaction with politicians, set the political agenda and indicate what issues the public should care about (Altheide 2006). The media response to 9/11 and the initial "War on Terror" was interesting. They simultaneously pointed out potential threats and highlighted the lurking dangers that came from the unknown "other" (usually manifest in Islamic fundamentalism). At the same time, they elicited symbols of "we" by presenting unifying cues such as flag pens, bumper stickers and media stories with headings like "America Under Siege" (Mueller 2006). The reaction was compounded by the 24-hour news cycle and increased news source competition. It was also likely furthered by the fact that a number of the 2001 anthrax letters were addressed to high profile media personalities – most notably Tom Brokaw. The news industry also used fear to elicit viewership emotion and increase ratings (Schubert et al. 2002). Mueller reports that between 2001 and 2004, Tom Ridge's Department of Homeland Security issued 23 terror alerts. All 23 alerts ran as lead stories. When the alerts expired to more moderate levels, only 13% of the reductions were even reported (Mueller 2006). Negative news tends to get more interest, and so the media focused on the alerts.

Others sought advantage too. Early in this decade there was also an explosion in the number of private entities who saw terrorism fears as a means by which to increase their profits. All sorts of devices were crafted that would parachute people from high-rises, should a 9/11 like event occur again. New and improved technologies were introduced to monitor subways, to track persons and to protect homes and offices. Some of these were important devices, such as enhanced baggage technology at airports that contributed to national security. Others had little value. However, it is important to remember that it is in the interest of these entrepreneurs and companies to "push" fear because it increases demand for their products or expertise. Indeed, the post-9/11 environment altered our perceptions.

It is clear that a significant and extensive rally event occurred after 9/11 and that it has been bolstered by additional events (Anthrax, "War on Terror," Iraq). Evidence also suggests that the rally was purposefully extended. Taking the opportunities presented, a number of interested parties used fear to advance their own personal agendas. One area of interest sparked from a national security perspective has been attention to large cargo containers that bring goods to the United States through sea, land and air ports of entry. We now turn to containerized freight, an issue area that received only minimal attention before 9/11, yet today serves as an example of domestic security politicization.

Domestic Attention to Port Security Prior to 9/11 Rally

In August 2001, our national borders and ports of entry were regulated, but still relatively easy to cross with evidence of US citizenship or other documentation. It is only recently that US citizens needed a passport to travel to and from Canada or Mexico. In the summer of 2001, passengers could take water bottles and knitting needles through airport security and sweethearts could hold hands all the way to the airplane gate before their tearful goodbyes. At that time, officials also monitored the passage of containerized freight arriving through US ports of entry, yet the national security threat containers potentially posed was not yet a major concern.

The desire to protect the flow of containerized freight has long existed. However, the government regulated the industry much more as an economic issue rather than as a national security concern. In the years before the terrorist attacks, domestic policies governing container traffic existed primarily to protect the shipment of goods. This was accomplished through a dual focus on tactics designed to prevent accidental damage as well as to prevent intentional tampering with containers. The main concern was to avoid shrinkage of cargo through theft and misrouting – the risks that containerized shipping posed were not yet at the forefront of transportation policy. Policies designed to protect against theft at various points were inherently prohibitive against interference and tampering of the sort that could end up delivering compromised or missing goods. These

24 *Protecting Our Ports*

same policies protected against other transportation risks, such as intentional or unintentional sabotage (Willis and Ortiz 2004).

A 2000 Commission report on US seaport security and crime suggests that the biggest risks regarding container freight were trade fraud, drug trafficking and smuggling of other illicit or contraband materials, unlawful exportation of controlled commodities, environmental crimes stemming from inappropriate packing and shipments, and illegal aliens hiding as stowaways (Report 2000). These issues were also the concerns of the shipping and commercial industries, which informed policies. Interestingly, the report recognized the possibility of container ports as a potential terrorist target, but did not see any substantial threat. The findings of the report state:

> Although seaports represent an important component of the nation's transportation infrastructure, there is no indication that US seaports are currently being targeted by terrorists. The FBI considers the present threat of terrorism directed at any US seaports to be low, even though their vulnerability to attack is high. The Commission believes that such an attack has the potential to cause significant damage (Ibid., 5).

So while some recognized the abstract possibility of containerized freight being a potential vehicle for large-scale acts of terrorism before 9/11, resources were allocated according to previous experiences with breaches of security, which meant identifying and implementing systems to focus on monitoring, tracking, and delivering shipments without damage or theft (Christopher 2009). Additionally, resources were directed toward identifying barriers to the smooth transport of container freight goods, such as the need to harmonize customs practices, which had economic benefits.

In truth, there was rather little attention paid to the issue area on Capitol Hill or among the general population. Legislators did pass some provisions to streamline shipping processes (see Chapter 3), but again with economic interests in mind. However, few citizens probably thought much about border security, maritime operations or the possibility that a freight container could be used as a weapon (see Chapter 1). After 9/11 many viewed this as a glaring oversight by the federal government as national security came to include heightened attention on the transportation, movement and storage of containerized freight.

9/11 Effects on Port and Container Security

The attacks on the World Trade Center and the Pentagon were what Kenneth Christopher calls a "paradigm-shift" for transportation security systems in general (Christopher 2009, 3). After all, the weapon of choice was a jet-liner full of passengers, which prior to 9/11 very few thought would be possible. President

Bush's popularity rally allowed him, policy makers, the media and some in the technology industry to advance heightened security policies.

To the general public, the most visible area of heightened security measures was airports, where new policies to reduce the probability of another major terrorist attack were immediately salient to citizens and policymakers alike. No more knitting needles in carry-on luggage, and long romantic goodbyes would have to take place before the security gates. Port security, however, and the related areas of the passage of containerized freight through all modes of travel (air, land, sea), also became prominent issues among policymakers, security officials, and private industry, if perhaps publicly less visible. The large-scale effects of 9/11 on the security of containerized freight, is apparent in three related areas: new strategies, reorganization and increased interaction.

Freight Strategy

Realizing that containerized freight could pose a potential security risk, officials developed a new strategy to combat the threat. The post-9/11 strategy for securing containerized freight involves the creation of a "layered defense." A layered defense employs multiple and interconnected security layers to most efficiently protect against risks. In the case of container security, this means that an array of procedures and techniques are involved at key transportation sites to identify "risky" cargo – cargo posing a threat either by its composition, the lack of information about its contents, or the lack of information about the shipper. A layered defense aims to increase overall accountability by enacting multiple security procedures, enhancing communication and centralizing practices. Lake and his colleagues state that in addition to the implementation of strict security measures accounting for the contents of a container and the shippers involved, "the layered approach would include observation of the following: staff authentication, passengers, conveyances, access control, cargo and baggage, ports, and security en route" (Lake et al. 2005b, 2). The primary security layers of content and ownership are thus accompanied by the surrounding layers of identification of all people involved in transporting a container and all facilities and shipping entities involved in aiding the passage. A layered defense provides more security and a wider breadth of measures while limiting over-expenditures, over-reliance or over-financing of any one measure that could end up being prohibitive (Ibid.). Simply put, multiple levels of defense (domestic and international) offer multiple levels of challenge and frustration for terrorists (GAO 2008; Greenberg et al. 2006).

The international layer of defense serves to strengthen security policies along the entire supply chain by "pushing borders out" to create a sort of virtual border distant from US national shores (Lake et al. 2005a). The basic premise of extending the US sphere of security involves checks on containerized freight before it reaches a US point of entry (see Chapter 4). In order to implement the layered defense, agency reorganization was necessary.

Agency Reorganization

The new scrutiny of the post-9/11 environment revealed large amounts of pre-existing security lapses in the shipping of containers through ports. Therefore, almost immediately after 9/11, President Bush, with the support of the US Congress, began a large scale agency reorganization and centralization process. This reorganization aimed to streamline national security procedures, and specifically lay the groundwork for the monitoring of containerized freight since 9/11.

In his famous speech of September 20, 2001, President Bush explained that he was establishing an Office of Homeland Security to be run by former Pennsylvania Governor, Tom Ridge. In 2002, the office became an official Department.[6] The purpose of the new Department was to bring a number of agencies responsible for domestic security into one overarching organization. The result was the biggest government reorganization in US history – DHS eventually incorporated 22 government agencies or agency sections (Perl 2004).

There are four major agencies involved in container freight security that fall under the DHS umbrella. These are Customs and Border Protection (CBP), the Transportation Security Administration (TSA), the United States Coast Guard (USCG), and the Immigration and Customs Enforcement (ICE) (Haddal 2009). These sub-agencies work together to ensure the most secure and efficient means to importing goods into the United States (also see Chapter 3 on interagency cooperation). Most relevant for containerized freight security is CBP – an amalgamation of the previous US Customs Service, US Immigration and Naturalization Service, and a section of the Department of Agriculture. CBP's primary mission is to oversee trade, drug, and immigration issues and to prevent terrorists and terrorist weapons from entering the United States. It does this by monitoring, scanning and screening goods and people as they pass through US ports of entry and exit.

The USCG is another important DHS agency involved in securing containerized freight, in this case along US waterways. The Coast Guard's mission includes maritime homeland security, law enforcement, search and rescue, maritime environmental protection, offshore aids to navigation, and during wartime the Coast Guard can operate as a component of the United States Navy. With regard to containerized freight security, the USCG is responsible for transit on all US waterways, signified in the position of "Captain of the Port" granted to the top Coast Guard official at a seaport (Agency Interviews 2006).

---

6 The official mission of DHS is to: "...develop and coordinate the implementation of a comprehensive national strategy to secure the United States from terrorist threats or attacks. The Office will coordinate the executive branch's efforts to detect, prepare for, prevent, protect against, respond to, and recover from terrorist attacks within the United States" (DHS website. "Brief Documentary History of the Department of Homeland Security: 2001-2008."

More familiar to the average citizen is probably TSA, which is responsible for all transportation security systems (relating to both people and commerce) within the United States. In terms of containerized freight, TSA's jurisdiction is highly relevant for air travel as TSA policies apply uniformly to all aircraft entering the country, and TSA alone accounts for all screening of passengers and baggage. All air traffic, including air cargo, must comply with TSA regulations. While cargo planes do carry containerized freight, the weight and size restrictions limit the number of cargo containers on jets, thus making it more straightforward to pre-screen the contents. TSA works in tandem with CBP at land borders, where CBP has lead authority in policing the entry of people and goods into the United States (Agency Interviews 2007).

The final relevant agency under the DHS umbrella concerning freight security is ICE. The agency is the investigative arm of DHS responsible for securing US borders and ports, particularly with regard to criminal smuggling and illegal immigration. ICE officials are responsible for investigating security breaches at US borders and ports of entry, and at times interact with foreign governments to ensure proper enforcement mechanisms (ICE website 2009).

DHS development and the massive post-9/11 reorganization have been additional means by which to enhance domestic security layers. It is an attempt to streamline policies and procedures in the hopes of augmenting domestic defense response and efficiency. These agencies also contribute to the related strategy of pushing borders out by cooperating with international agents (see Chapter 4).

Increased Oversight

With a new strategy of layering domestic defense, and the creation and reorganization of federal agencies to centralize policies, there was also a need for increased interaction and oversight. Therefore, via the legislation creating DHS, Congress mandated interagency and interdepartmental communication and cooperation on freight security issues. For example, Section 202 of the Homeland Security Act (Pub, L. 2002, 107-296) specifically states that all US Departments must provide information and assistance pertinent to national defense to DHS. Congress has also attempted to more diligently oversee agency interactions and programs. In order to monitor developments, Congress has required and sought extensive oversight of DHS. In fact, today there are 79 Congressional Committees and Subcommittees that monitor the workings of the young Department. From 2001-2007, DHS testified before Congress 761 times, 224 of those in 2007 alone (National Defense Industrial Association 2008). For DHS agencies focusing on port and freight security, this means regular testimony before the House Subcommittee on Border, Maritime and

Global Counterterrorism, and the Subcommittee on Transportation Security and Infrastructure Protection among others.[7]

The enhanced attention to domestic security resulting from the events of 9/11 and the corresponding rally of support dramatically affected how the US addresses containerized freight. Though policies pertaining particularly to container tampering or product theft had existed previously, the new focus on inter-modal container transport shifted toward national security. The result was a new strategy of creating a layered defense, which included an international component where the United States seeks to create a virtual security border. A significant component of this layering required the development of new agencies and altered missions of existing agencies to include containerized freight security as a central focus. Finally, to be effective, agency and department cooperation was mandated and monitored as a part of defensive security layers. Having examined overarching components of post-9/11 freight security, we now delve deeper to discuss some of the important actors, policies and procedures that govern day to day container operations at US ports.

Additional Agencies, Actors, Policies and Programs Involved in Domestic Freight Security

Part of the challenge of enhancing the security of containerized freight through the domestic (and international) supply chain is grasping the large number of agencies and actors involved. There are also a variety of policies and programs with which shippers, port operators, security personnel and truck drivers must comply. In order to understand the post-9/11 politicization of freight security it is necessary that we introduce the most important parties involved, as well as some of the more significant programs and policies that have developed to address security of goods and freight infrastructure.

The passage of containerized freight in and out of US ports of entry is a large, multi-modal operation. The actors involved are both public and private, including seaport owners and managers, shippers, transporters, freight forwarders, airlines, trucking companies, and railroad companies, all of whom interact regularly with private commercial entities. Federal agencies include the previously discussed DHS, as well as DOC, DOD, DOS, and DOT, who must work together to ensure that security measures are streamlined and efficient. Other important actors are port authorities, which often monitor general port activities such as the financing, construction, and operation of facilities. Additionally, unions, such as the Seafarers' International Union of North America, the International Longshore and Warehouse

---

7 The number of committees now involved with DHS operations indicates the desire by many members of Congress to associate themselves with homeland security issues so that they can report back to their constituencies that they are actively engaged in securing the nation.

Union and the International Transport Workers Federation, often represent the various personnel that work at ship yards. There are also shipping companies, freight forwarders, truckers, mariners and airlines, as well as the interests and associations that have developed in support of the actors and/or issues at hand, such as the American Association of Port Authorities. With this number and variation of actors, accounting for the security of each part of a freight shipment – either domestic or arriving from abroad – is an exercise in logistical calisthenics.

From a security perspective, the most important actor is the previously introduced Department of Homeland Security. The other federal Departments involved in container security issues work together on policy design and formulation where each jurisdiction is relevant: the DOC is involved with trade and import/export issues; the DOT is involved in transportation policies of the inter-modal trade system; and the DOD and DOS are involved with homeland security and security-related initiatives with foreign governments, respectively.

It is also necessary to point out the important role that labor unions play. While some unions are more politically motivated than others,[8] most are primarily concerned with safe working environments, appropriate wages, and high training standards. The International Longshore and Warehouse Union (ILWU) union represents over 40,000 employees, primarily dock workers, on the West Coast of the United States and Canada. In 2002 tense negotiations led to the shutdown of 29 Pacific ports for ten days. The economic losses suffered are estimated at as much as $15.6 billion (Farris 2008). The incident proved that the Unions were a considerable force that must be acknowledged. The unions spend significant time lobbying on Capitol Hill. It is perhaps no coincidence that a large ILWU contingency travelled to Washington in the spring of 2006 – a time when important port legislation was being advanced and when issues involving operating rights at ports were being debated. Unions are also important disseminators of information and education for training related to security provisions, such as the implementation of a Transportation Worker Identification Credential (TWIC).[9]

The final actors to be addressed here are businesses and companies whose very existence depends on the transport of their goods in a timely and effective manner. These entities are important actors in both the formulation of policies and the ground-level implementation of new security procedures. During discussions of new policies, business associations and relevant stakeholders can, and often do, inform and protest the development of new legislation and stipulations. Legislators are just as likely to develop regulations from pre-existing practices that have served the private industry well. An example is the development of more advanced (or "smart") container seals. Container seals are intended to prevent tampering and to provide a unique identification code for each individual container. When

---

8 In May 2008, a number of ILWU employees voluntarily walked off the job to protest the war in Iraq. Though officially this was a war protest, it also occurred during a time of wage negotiations, and speculations about additional motives abound.

9 See Chapter 3 for more on TWIC.

the suggestion of embedding Radio Frequency Identification Devices (RFID) into container seals was raised so as to make seals more difficult to falsify and easier to monitor, technology companies jumped at the potential opportunity to advance the new smart seal, while shipping companies protested the cost of such new seals and the usefulness of the application (Industry Interviews 2007).

Freight Security Procedures

Procedures for incoming container sea vessels include a thorough review by CBP officials of ship manifests provided by the shipper and a calculation of risk using the Automated Targeting System (ATS). The ATS database allows officials to identify high risk containers that might be barred entry or more likely will undergo additional scrutiny upon arrival. ATS scores are based on a number of factors, including a vessel's owner, place of origin, manifest, shipping history and experience. CBP accesses over 25 years of shipping information to make these determinations. Upon entering a US port, high risk containers are off loaded and subjected to additional scanning procedures, such as x-ray using VACIS or Smith Hyman machines. X-ray images are compared to a container's manifest. If concerns remain after an x-ray image is examined, containers will be opened and stripped of their contents for a physical search. Officials estimate that 6-7% of all containers that arrive in US ports undergo an intensive x-ray process, with about 2% undergoing a physical search (Agency Interviews 2006-2007; Port Interviews 2006-2007).

Upon leaving a US seaport terminal, nearly all cargo containers roll through a radiation portal. If the portal sounds an alarm, the driver must provide his identification card and driver's license for a background check. CBP officials then use handheld isotope monitors to determine the type of radiation that is being emitted from the container. They then compare isotope readings to the container manifest to determine consistency. Certain pottery, ceramics, and other items emit particular isotopes that are consistent with radio-active materials, which accounts for the vast majority of these portal alarms. If the driver's record is clear and the isotopes are consistent with the container's manifest, the shipment is sent on its way (Ibid.).

While seaports handle a large majority of import cargo, the amount of goods crossing land borders via trucks from Canada or Mexico is also significant. Efforts toward enhanced information sharing at borders are encompassed in multiple programs, agencies and frameworks. The goal behind information sharing programs is to allow these three countries (the United States, Mexico and Canada) to address and resolve gaps in cross-border information sharing, and to ensure a comparable level of screening of all travelers and cargo (Agency Interviews 2007).

Information in advance manifests includes the forwarding of cargo information to CBP officials prior to the arrival of the truck at the US border. This began under the CBP's Trade Act of 2002, which instituted rules requiring advance electronic notice of arriving and departing cargo for all modes of transportation. This includes manifest information from the carrier or designated agent, and shipment information from the broker.[10] The number of CBP agents at borders has doubled since 9/11, with the bulk of these along the Rio Grande. Additionally, in recent years there has been an increase in the amount of new technology, staff and tactical infrastructure at both the Canadian and Mexican land borders (Agency Interviews 2006-2007).

Similar to seaports, the ATS can provide manifest and transport history data on trucks and trains crossing land borders. Since April of 2007, CBP began requiring the advance electronic filing of truck manifests at all southern land border points through the Automated Commercial Environment (ACE) e-manifest program. Advance manifests are assumed to greatly reduce the potential for error and increase the validity of security measures, resulting in improved efficiency and faster border crossings for legitimate carriers. Failing to provide an advance manifest necessitates secondary inspection by CBP at the border. Several points across the northern border also use the ACE program for truck shipments. At present, use of the e-manifest by trucking companies and other shippers at the northern border is considered voluntary. CBP is currently performing outreach to encourage the use of ACE manifests, while simultaneously working to make the use of the e-manifest mandatory at all land border points under the Trade Act of 2002 (CBP Interview 2007).

Relying on pre-arrival data, any cargo or container deemed high-risk is screened in a process similar to seaport procedures: physical checks, canine detection, and, at most southern crossings and at certain key northern crossings, radiation detection using portable machines. As of 2008 there were 241 radiation portal monitors (RPMs) at the northern border, which provides CBP with the capability to scan 90% of truck cargo and 81% of other vehicles. DHS had invested in a plan to complete the deployment of RPMs to all northern land border crossings by the end of 2008 so that CBP capabilities would increase to 100%. The southern border, which has long had substantial concerns with the smuggling of people and goods, is equipped with enough RPMs to scan 100% of all truck cargo and 95% of other vehicles. DHS had planned to increase capabilities to scan 100% of all vehicles by the end of 2009 (CBP website 2009a).

Canada and Mexico each have signed Smart Border Accords under DHS guidelines that provide a framework for sharing and monitoring the background information and credential checks of people driving trucks into the United States. The Smart Border Accord with Canada includes fingerprints and bio-data within advance manifests. The accord with Mexico is currently implementing such bio-data requirements (CBP website 2009b).

---

10   Under CBP's Trade Act, sea vessels have to provide automated manifests 24 hours in advance of incoming cargo. Air traffic has to provide manifests four hours in advance of arriving from overseas, and at "wheels up" time if arriving from NAFTA countries or Central and South American countries from above the equator. Rail has two hours, and trucks are given one hour if non-Free and Secure Trade (FAST) members, or 30 minutes if a FAST member (for more on FAST see Chapter 4).

The final means by which container cargo enters the United States is via air transport. When examining containerized freight security issues, it appears that air cargo poses the least relative concern when compared with land travel and seaports. There are three reasons for this. First, 9/11 had the biggest impact on air travel, and thus received the most immediate and noteworthy attention with regards to security. Second, the size of typical cargo containers limits the amount of cargo that can be shipped by air.[11] Only packages under 150 pounds can travel on a passenger jet. Anything heavier must travel by a freight forwarder or cargo plane (such as what is used by companies like UPS, FedEx, etc.), but even these jets are limited by space and weight considerations that are significantly more restrictive than those for sea travel or land travel. As a result, the amount of containerized freight entering the US by air is minimal. Third, as all air traffic must comply with TSA regulations, security monitoring and enforcement is managed through one centralized authority for all types of cargo planes (Industry Interviews 2007).

Cargo planes that do carry containers are also subject to high levels of screening, but not necessarily scanning. Packages over 150 pounds that are transported via cargo plane must follow a different set of regulations. These jets have a flight deck instead of passenger seating – both the pilot and jump-seating are all TSA-approved, authorized, and pre-cleared. All cargo on these jets is subject to non-intrusive scanning measures, such as x-rays, canine detection, visual examination, manifest scrutiny, and established programs of known shippers. Intrusive scanning is only done when a container is leaking, wet, exposed, has visible wiring, or some other manner of obvious threat or disrepair. Currently, RFID scanning of all air freight is voluntary. However, DHS and TSA have indicated that this measure may become a requirement in the near future (Industry Interviews 2007).

Finally, the ATS database is also in place for air traffic. Aircraft arriving from North American Free Trade Agreement (NAFTA) countries and Central and South American countries above the equator are required to submit their automated manifest systems by "wheels up." Aircraft arriving from all other places must submit their manifests four hours in advance of departure (CBP website 2009b).

The various agencies, actors, policies and programs involved in containerized freight security are numerous. New policies that sought to streamline freight security and highlight past deficiencies have been positive developments. However, 9/11 also created opportunities for political and personal advantage, and containerized freight security has not escaped such politicization.

---

11 Less than 1% of cargo tonnage enters the United States by air – however, various sources state that while the percentage of freight traveling by air is small, the value is relatively high, and so air cargo represents a disproportionate amount of freight value. Because of this, these shipments tend to be highly insured and monitored through transport, and thus have much more transparent records of their contents, origins, delivery, etc. (Industry Interviews 2006-2007).

Politicization of Port Security

The absence of opposition characterized the early weeks and months of the 9/11 "Rally 'Round the Flag" phenomenon. This was followed by an era where politicians, the media and other interested parties attempted to use fear, or to capitalize upon it, for their own benefit. Nearly ten years later insecurity issues still made headlines, still invoked memories of 9/11 and still led to political infighting. Earlier we discussed the large scale changes in how the United States manages containerized freight security. Undoubtedly, a number of positive changes have been made, and the nation's ports of entry are more secure today than they were in the summer of 2001. However, throughout the last decade there have been a number of instances where doomsday scenarios were relayed, credit was sought and freight security became political fodder.

The Creation of the Department of Homeland Security

As discussed, the Office of Homeland Security was established in the weeks following the 9/11 attacks. Not long after, in mid-2002, the US House of Representatives established a Select Committee on Homeland Security, which vested Congress in the issue. Both provide evidence of the realization that homeland defense was an enhanced focus. One of the new committee's responsibilities was to develop recommendations on the development of a Department of Homeland Security, which it did by late 2002. As with most decisions throughout the first year of President Bush's 9/11 rally, his desire to have such a Department met with little opposition. Criticism that did arise at the time of the reorganization came from those who felt the inception of DHS was done hastily and without consideration of long-term consequences (Broder 2002), though even these concerns were seldom voiced. What politician, at any time though especially during the initial 9/11 rally, would openly oppose an effort labeled "homeland security?"

Nuclear Focus

Since nuclear weapons were used to end World War II, much of the world and certainly the United States, has feared the possibility of a nuclear attack. Though the events of 9/11 had nothing to do with nuclear weapons, the security changes, particularly with regard to containerized freight, are often focused on mediating the potential risks these weapons could pose. The technology used at US ports specifically checks containers for radioactive material. Some officials suggest that this focus seems somewhat misguided. After all, the chances that someone would use a freight container, that would have to traverse stormy seas to reach a US port and then somehow be detonated is highly unlikely (Agency Interviews 2006-2007; Port Interviews 2006-2007). Many port officials indicated to us that focusing on nuclear material was politically expedient. The technology exists to detect nuclear weapons in containers. However, it is not as advanced for detecting biological, chemical or other potentially dangerous substances. However, the word "nuclear" raises particular concerns. By highlighting the threat, officials and especially politicians can justify and claim credit for the response – and they can show evidence of progress.

Dubai Ports World

By 2006, Bush's popularity rally had ended, but politicking over transportation security issues was in full force. This is exemplified by the Dubai Ports controversy. During the spring and summer of 2006 in the run-up to the November Congressional elections, some Republican members of Congress, and a number of Democrats as well, were outraged over the attempted sale of property at six large US seaports. The property, previously held by a British company, was to be sold to Dubai Ports World (DPW).[12] DPW is headquartered in the United Arab Emirates (UAE), a Muslim country with which the United States has enjoyed friendly relations for many years ("US Lawmakers Criticise..." 2006). The Bush White House brokered the deal, but it very quickly drew criticism from both sides of the aisle. Once the issue became public, many politicians were quick to criticize foreign ownership of ports for fear of not being seen as "serious" on national security. A number of Republicans questioned the wisdom in selling such a lease encompassing a significant amount of economically important land to an Arab country, which had been home to two of the 9/11 terrorists. Democrats used the event to show how "out of touch" President Bush was on the issue. They added an amendment to the original legislation to prohibit port sales to any country that had recognized the legality of the Taliban government in Afghanistan – UAE was one of only three such countries. The incident showed how both parties were attempting to utilize fear – one could even argue racism – for gain and political advantage. The media also published dozens of stories highlighting the potential risks to the country should an Arab company control the ports in question ("After Dubai Ports World" 2007).

The fact is, most US seaports, 75% in 2006, are operated by foreign entities, including a large percentage of Chinese investments along the Pacific coast (Agency Interviews 2006-2007; Port Interviews 2006-2007; Walsh 2006). In practice, the outsourcing of management contracts to international companies is illustrative of the interconnectedness of the global economy in many ways, and may indirectly offer heightened security through a wider shared interest in secure and efficient operations (see Chapter 6). It is also important to remember that DHS and its various organizations (CBP, TSA, USCG and ICE) are responsible for security implementation at all US ports of entry, regardless of who owns the operating lease. This is a fact, however, that New York Senator Charles Schumer had forgotten when he responded to the sale by publically asking, "Should we be outsourcing our own security?" ("US Lawmakers Criticise" 2006).

---

12   The Dubai Ports World controversy was about the sale of management contracts at the ports of New York, New Jersey, Philadelphia, Baltimore, New Orleans, and Miami by the British Peninsular and Oriental Steam Navigation Company.

The outcry in Washington, which roused a rather uneasy nation through excessive media coverage, seemed rather odd to many of the men and women who conducted security operations at US and international seaports. Officials both domestically and abroad suggested that there was nothing unique or improper with the DPW deal and described the situation as being overblown and fraught with political calculations (Agency Interviews 2007-2008, Domestic Port Representative Interviews 2006-2007). Due to pressure, the deal died. Prior to 9/11 the DPW sale might have remained a mostly financial venture, but in the post-9/11 atmosphere these issues have important political value and significance. The DPW controversy highlighted just how political seaport and freight security had become.

SAFE Port Act of 2006

Around the same time as the Dubai Ports incident, and likely a compounding factor, legislation was making its way through Congress that specifically outlined the country's transportation security goals and solutions. The Security and Accountability For Every (SAFE) Port Act of 2006 (Pub. L. 109-347) codified into law a number of programs designed to heighten port security practices so as to extend and centralize security operations. In addition, SAFE assigned the newly created (as of 2005) Domestic Nuclear Detection Office (DNDO) to DHS. SAFE requires that 100% of all containers at US seaports be screened and scanned. It also raised the idea of 100% scanning of all US-bound containers in Section 232 with the introduction of the Secure Freight Initiative (SFI) provision (see below). The differentiation between "screening" and "scanning" is critical, but undefined in the legislation.[13]

For many port officials and business representatives, the SAFE legislation codified into law practices that were already in place, with members of Congress taking credit. A related criticism was that the codification of existing practices did little to address the gaps in security that still exist. Other officials argued that the legislation did much to benefit prominent technology companies through the emphasis on scanning and screening as detection methods, but not enough to boost the training and education capacity of security officers working at ground-level in a manner that did not leave them too reliant on technology (Industry Interviews 2007; Agency Interviews 2007).

In sum, the legislation was lauded as a step in the right direction. However, it was fraught with political gaming. The passage of the bill came just before the 2006 elections, and Republicans hoped it would once again prove that they were the party of national security. Some Democrats opposed the bill, yet once in the majority their party would pass something relatively similar in nature. The bill

---

13 Screening involves a pre-clearance procedure to identify which containers are high-risk and which are not, while scanning involves the actual passage of containers through electronic scanning machines.

also revealed a cognitive disconnect between what was happening in Washington DC and the practicalities of actual port operation.

9/11 Commission Act and SFI

Despite passage of the SAFE Port Act, other issues superseded. The 2006 Congressional elections ousted the Republicans and installed a Democratic majority for the first time since 1994. As the Democratic Congress came to power in the beginning of 2007, it extended the SAFE Port Act and specifically SFI with the passage of what has come to be known as the 9/11 Commission Act because it was based on the recommendations of the 9/11 Commission (Pub. L. 110-53). In many ways this was a step to claim the security issue, which in recent times had arguably been a Republican stronghold. As stated in the official record, the 9/11 Act "Modifies the SAFE Port Act to prohibit a container that was loaded on a vessel in a foreign port to enter the United States unless the container was scanned by nonintrusive imaging and radiation detection equipment at a foreign port before it was loaded" – a rather explicit requirement (Ibid.). The 100% scanning obligation is to go into effect at foreign ports by 2012 with some provisions for deadline extensions to give foreign ports more time to meet the requirements if they experience unacceptable false alarm rates, significant impact to the flow of trade, and essential infrastructural problems (Ibid.). Despite the possibility of extensions, there has been considerable protest.[14]

The requirement for 100% scanning at foreign ports is opposed by virtually all major cargo shipper organizations and ocean carriers, international trading partners, and domestic transportation agencies – including DHS and CBP. The unanimous rationale behind the opposition is that 100% scanning of all inbound cargo is simply an unreasonable and unworkable goal that could cripple the intermodal supply chain – what Lloyd's List called "a slogan not a solution" (Lloyd's List 2008). The World Shipping Council (WSC) identified the following problems with the legislation:

- the lessons from pilot programs developed to test the concept of scanning inbound containers had still not been tested;
- the legislation did not specify who would be required to perform the scanning;
- the legislation failed to address health and safety issues relating to the use of this equipment, and did not take into account labor or workforce agreements;

---

14   The initial pilot program to test 100% scanning, which took place in the relatively small ports of Southampton, England, Puerto Cortes, Honduras and Port Qasim, Pakistan, resulted in a July 2008 report to Congress. The Report indicated some success, but relayed international concerns and the perceived difficulties of implementation at larger, heavier flow seaports (CBP 2008).

- the legislation did not attempt to obtain the necessary cooperation of other governments;
- there was no provision for reciprocal 100% scanning of all containers *leaving* the United States;
- there was no clarification of what would be done with the scanning data generated and if/how it would be analyzed; and
- the law failed to address scanning analysis responsibility, including the investment in labor, training, maintenance, and operating costs, as well as what to do in the situation of a container requiring secondary inspection (WSC statement 2007).

What a number of foreign officials describe as partisan efforts to compete on homeland security in the US Congress has proven to be quite contentious, both domestically and internationally (International Port Interviews 2008).

Despite objections, the Democratic Congress passed the legislation. It was deemed such an important issue that the 9/11 Commission Act was the very first piece of legislation proposed in the 110th Congressional session. Oddly enough, the actual 9/11 Commission Report did not advance the notion of 100% scanning, but Congressional leadership indicated that it was an important inclusion ("All Scan is Back" 2007). Democrats who had previously opposed the SAFE Port Act of 2006 rallied behind their party when similar legislation was advanced in 2007. The central question then becomes: why did members of Congress continue with the legislation, knowing all of the reasonable barriers to implementation? The fact is domestic politicking affected this decision more so than the practicalities of the supply chain. Republicans claimed for years after 9/11 that the Democrats were weak on security, but with the Democratic passage of the 9/11 Commission Act, the Party's security credibility was immediately bolstered. For their part, Republicans too played the game – a majority of them voted against the legislation despite arguing for similar measures only months before (Ibid.).

These examples of political gaming in the realm of containerized freight security may seem rather benign. However, the result appears to be that Congress supports security measures that some see as excessive. These measures are potentially preventing viable economic transactions based on an exaggerated threat and, as will be discussed in Chapter 4, are alienating international partners by imposing unrealistic trade requirements and time limits on them. In addition, the US is focusing resources on nuclear protection, when research and development could possibly be extended to other more plausible threats. In containerized freight security, a pattern of reaction to 9/11 is evident. Initially, during the strength of President Bush's rally, few opposed any security measures. As time advanced, it became clear that security matters garnered significant public attention and that focusing on risks could be beneficial.

Conclusion

One obvious flaw resulting from the post-9/11 politics was a tendency for public officials and private individuals to self-censor their questions and criticism of the administration for fear of perceptions that they were not supportive of homeland security measures. The proposal to scan 100% of all US bound containers is one such example, as is the amount of press and lack of analysis on the DPW sale. While the intention behind this proposal was a reaction to the problems perceived in existing container security practices, in some instances – such as the perceived need to push US borders out as much as possible – policy proposals have not always been tailored to the realities of seaport or transportation management, or to political considerations involving foreign seaports and/or governments.

To be fair, the slant is not all negative. Container security, particularly at seaports, has indeed benefited in many ways from the recent attention towards securing the supply chain (Flynn 2008). One of the primary benefits of the post-9/11 emphasis on container security policy has been the realization that the mismanagement of seaports and lack of attention to cargo containers as they flow through the global supply chain pose significant risks to the United States. Moreover, a positive outcome has been the definition of various threat scenarios concerning all three modes of container transport (land, sea and air) into the United States. The development of different layers of defense prevents vulnerabilities at each level of freight movement, thereby strengthening US national security. Finally, the increase in President Bush's popularity after 9/11 allowed for swift creation and implementation of new programs, which under different circumstances would have been much more difficult to accomplish.

Throughout this chapter we addressed the "Rally 'Round the Flag" phenomenon and examined it in relation to the post-9/11 politicization of domestic containerized freight security. It is clear that freight security was both positively and negatively affected by the events of 9/11 and the corresponding Presidential rally of support. It is also clear that the issue became a political tool for use by politicians and the media. While many new policies and programs have been beneficial, the political nature and use of fear to bolster the issue of containerized freight is somewhat concerning. Politicians and the media should concentrate less on the *possible* threats that exist (these are innumerable) and instead be more pragmatic and examine the *probable* risks that can be addressed. A means of doing this is to listen to and heed the advice of the agents and officials who stand on the front line of port security on a daily basis. Therefore, it is important that policy makers understand how the integrated agencies and departments who govern containerized freight transport communicate, cooperate and collaborate with one another.

Bibliography

Altheide, David. 2006. "Terrorism and the Politics of Fear," *Cultural Studies: Critical Methodologies*, Vol. 6, No. 4, 415-439.

"Amerithrax Investigation." 2001. *Federal Bureau of Investigation*, available at http://www.fbi.gov/anthrax/amerithraxlinks.htm.

Balz, Dan. 2002. "Democrats Speak Up On Foreign Policy: Reluctance to Criticize Bush Fades," *The Washington Post*, July 15, 2002.

"Brief Documentary History of the Department of Homeland Security: 2001-2008," available at http://www.dhs.gov/xlibrary/assets/brief_documentary_history_of_dhs_2001_2008.pdf, (7).

Broder, David S. 2002. "The Good and the Silly," *The Washington Post*, June 12, 2002.

Brody, Richard A. and Catherine R. Shapiro. 1991. "The Rally Phenomenon in Public Opinion," in Richard A. Brody (ed.), *Assessing the President*, 45-78. (Stanford, CA: Stanford University Press).

Bush, George W. 2001. "Text of President Bush's Address Tuesday Night, After Terrorist Attacks on New York City and Washington," CNN, available at http://archives.cnn.com/2001/US/09/11/bush. speech.text/.

CBP 2008. "Report to Congress on Integrated Scanning System Pilots (Security and Accountability for Every Port Act of 2006, Section 231)," available at http://commerce.senate.gov/public/_files/SFIReport_PublicRelease_FINAL_Consolidated.pdf. Retrieved October 25, 2009.

CBP 2009a. "Radiation Portal Monitors Safeguard America from Nuclear Devices and Radiological Materials," available at http://www.cbp.gov/xp/cgov/border_security/port_activities/cargo_exam/rad_portal1.xml. Retrieved October 25, 2009.

CBP 2009b. "Securing America's Borders at Ports of Entry." Office of Field Operations Strategic Plan FY 2007-2011, available at http://www.cbp.gov/linkhandler/cgov/border_security/port_activities/securing_ports/entry_points.ctt/entry_points.pdf. Retrieved October 25, 2009.

Chanley, Virginia. 2002. "Trust in Government in the Aftermath of 9/11: Determinants and Consequences," *Political Psychology*, Vol. 23, No.3, 469-483.

Christopher, Kenneth. 2009. *Port Security Management*. (Boca Raton, FL: Auerbach).

Farris, M. Theodore. 2008. "Are You Prepared for a Devastating Port Strike in 2008? Notes and Comments," *Transportation Journal*, available at http://www.entrepreneur.com/tradejournals/article/176689816.html.

Feldman, Elliot. 2007. "A Short History of Presidential Approval Ratings," *Associated Content*, available at http://www.associatedcontent.com/article/281161/a_short_history_of_presidential_approval_pg2_pg2.html?cat=75.

Flynn, Stephen E. 2008. "Overcoming the Flaws in the US Government Efforts to Improve Container, Cargo, and Supply Chain Security." Written testimony before a hearing of the Homeland Security Appropriations Subcommittee, Committee on Appropriations, United States House of Representatives on *Container, Cargo, and Supply Chain Security – Challenges and Opportunities*. April 2, 2008.

Government Accountability Office (GAO). 2008. "Border Security, Despite Progress, Weaknesses in Traveler Inspections Exist at Our Nations Ports of Entry," *Statement of Richard M. Stana: Testimony Before the Committee on Homeland Security, House of Representatives*, available at http://www.gao.gov/new.items/d08329t.pdf.

Greenberg, Michael D., Peter Chalk, Henry H. Willis, Ivan Khilco and David S. Ortiz. 2006. "Maritime Terrorism: Risk and Liability," RAND Corporation, available at http://rand.org /pubs/monographs/2006/RAND_MG520.pdf.

Greenhouse, Steven. 2002. "Labor Lockout at West's Ports Roils Business," *The New York Times*, October 1, 2002.

Haarmeyer, David and Peter Yorke. 1993. "Port Privatization: An International Perspective," *Reason Foundation*, Policy Study No.156, available at http://reason.org/files/6a983123788632131171e022e6466a7a.pdf.

Haddal, Chad C. 2009. "Border Security: Key Agencies and Their Missions," Congressional Research Service: CRS Report for Congress, available at http://www.fas.org/sgp/crs/homesec/RS21899.pdf.

Hetherington, Marc J. and Michael Nelson. January 2003. "Anatomy of a Rally Effect: George W. Bush and the War on Terrorism," *PS: Political Science and Politics*, Vol. 36, No.1, 37-42.

Huddy, Leonie. Stanley Feldman, Charles Taber and Gallya Lahav. 2005. "Threat, Anxiety, and Support of Antiterrorism Policies," *American Journal of Political Science*, Vol. 49, No.3, 593-608.

Immigration and Customs Enforcement. 2009. Available at http://www.ice.gov. Retrieved October 25, 2009.

Keefer, Wendy J. 2007. "Container Port Security: A Layered Defense Strategy to Protect the Homeland and the International Supply Chain," *Campbell Law Review*, Vol. 30, No. 1, 139-174.

Lake, Jennifer E., William H. Robinson and Lisa M. Seghetti. 2005a. "Border and Transportation Security: The Complexity of the Challenge," Congressional Research Service: CRS Report for Congress, available at http://www.fas.org/sgp/crs/homesec/RL32839.pdf.

Lake, Jennifer E., William H. Robinson and Lisa M. Seghetti. 2005b. "Border and Transportation Security: Possible New Directions and Policy Options," Congressional Research Service: CRS Report for Congress, available at http://www.fas.org/sgp/crs/homesec/RL32841.pdf.

Lemann, Nicholas. 2002. "The Next World Order: The Bush Administration May Have a Brand-new Doctrine of Power," *The New Yorker*, April 1, 2002.

McLaughlin, Lindsey. 2006. "The ILWU Goes to Washington," *International Longshore and Warehouse Union*, available at http://www.ilwu.org/dispatcher/2006/01/2006-01-washrpt.cfm.

Mueller, John. 1973. *War, Presidents and Public Opinion* (New York: Wiley).

Mueller, John. 2006. *Overblown: How Politicians and the Terrorism Industry Inflate National Security Threats and Why We Believe Them* (New York: Free Press).

National Defense Industrial Association. 2008. "Chertoff Complains of Heavy Congressional Oversight," available at http://www.thefreelibrary.com/Cherto ff+complains+of+heavy+congressional+oversight.-a0174816909.

Perl, Raphael. 2004. "The Department of Homeland Security: Background and Challenges," *Terrorism-reducing Vulnerabilities and Improving Responses*, Committee on Counterterrorism Challenges for Russia and the United States, Office for Central Europe and Eurasia Development, Security, and Cooperation Policy and Global Affairs, in Cooperation with the Russian Academy of Sciences, 176 (Washington, DC: National Academies Press).

Public Law 107-296. Department of Homeland Security Act, available at http:// www.dhs.gov/xlibrar y/assets/hr_5005_enr.pdf.

Public Law 109-347. SAFE Port Act. *The Library of Congress*, available at http://www.thomas.gov/cgi-bin/bdquery/D?d109:2:./temp/~bdQmg2::/bss/ d109query.html.

Public Law 110-53. 9/11 Commission Act. *The Library of Congress*, available at http:// www.thomas.gov/cgi-bin/bdquery/z?d110:HR00001:@@@L&summ2=m&.

Regens, James, Ronald Keith Gaddie and Brad Lockerbie. 1995. "The Electoral Consequences of Voting to Declare War," *Journal of Conflict Resolution*, Vol. 39, No.1, 168-182.

Report on the Interagency Commission on Crime and Security in US Seaports. 2000. Interagency Commission on Crime and Security in US Seaports. (Washington, DC).

Ridge, Tom. 2009. *The Test of Our Times: America Under Siege...and How We Can Be Safe Again* (New York: Thomas Dunne Books).

"Scan All is Back." January 15, 2007. *The Journal of Commerce*, available at http://www.joc-digital.com/joc/20070115/?pg=24.

Schubert, James N. and Patrick A. Stewart. September 2002. "A Defining Presidential Moment: 9/11 and the Rally Effect," *Political Psychology*, Vol. 23, No. 3. Special Issue: 9/11 and Its Aftermath: Perspectives from Political Psychology, 559-583.

Secure Freight Initiative (SFI) Fact Sheet. 2009. *US Customs and Border Patrol (CBP)*, available at http://www.cbp.gov/linkhandler/cgov/newsroom/fact_ sheets/trade_security/sfi/sfi_scanning.ctt/sfi_scanning.pdf. Retrieved October 25, 2009.

Siegelman, Lee, and Patricia Conover. 1981. "The Dynamics of Presidential Support During International Conflict Situations," *Political Behavior*, Vol. 3, No. 4, 303-318.

Stoll, Richard J. 1987. "The Sound of Guns: Is There a Congressional Rally Effect After US Military Action?," *American Politics Quarterly*, Vol. 15, No. 2, 223-237.

"Transcript of President Bush's Address to a Joint Session of Congress on Thursday Night, September 20, 2001," CNN, available at http://archives.cnn.com/2001/US/09/20/gen.bush.transcript/.

"UCLA Address – John Kerry in UCLA Address, Promises More Effective War on Terror," February 27, 2004. *UCLA International Institute*, available at http://www.international.ucla.edu/article.asp?parentid=8320#.

"US Lawmakers Criticise Ports Deal," February 21, 2006. BBC News, available at http://news. bbc.co.uk/2/hi/americas/4734728.stm.

Walsh, Deidra. March 28, 2006. "Congress Declares War on Ports Deal," CNN, available at http://www.cnn.com/2006/POLITICS/03/08/port.security/index.html.

Willis, Henry H. and David S. Ortiz. 2004. "Evaluating the Security of the Global Containerized Supply Chain," *RAND Corporation*, July 16, 2009, availalbe at http://www.rand.org/pubs/technical_reports/2004/RAND_TR214.pdf.

World Shipping Council. 2007. "Statement Regarding Legislation to Require 100% Container Scanning," available at http://www.worldshipping.org/wsc_legislation_statement.pdf. Retrieved October 25, 2009.

Chapter 3

Building on the Past: From National Security and Nonproliferation Policy to Containerized Freight Security

On September 11, 2009, the US national media reported that an incident was occurring on the Potomac river not too far from the US Pentagon where President Obama and families of the September 11, 2001 attacks were gathered to remember the tragic events of that day eight years earlier. Live images of Coast Guard boats speeding across the river were quickly beamed around the county alerting the public to the activity. Reporters explained that a water vessel had apparently entered restricted space on the river, causing the Coast Guard to fire shots – no one being sure at the time whether the shots were fired in warning or were targeted at a suspicious boat. This reporting continued for nearly 30 minutes before it became clear that the Coast Guard was conducting a training exercise in which a security breach on the Potomac was being simulated, including all the relevant radio traffic being overheard on scanners. While the incident quickly turned into a discussion about whether the media had appropriately checked its facts, what did emerge was the issue of agency communication regarding its training activities. Although the Coast Guard was engaged in a normal exercise that prepares its personnel to respond to such an incident, the agency failed to communicate, coordinate, cooperate and collaborate with others to enhance awareness about its activities, unintentionally causing significant concern, fear and potential panic. Moreover, the Coast Guard failed to recognize the significant emotion underlying the September 11 anniversary. Both the Coast Guard and the news media defended their positions in the hours and days after the non-incident, but it is clear that with enhanced communication, coordination, cooperation and collaboration, misunderstandings of this sort may be prevented and agencies may ultimately be more effective in their work.

This particular event, of course, is not an isolated one in terms of examples of missed opportunities for interaction among relevant actors. Within the US government, interagency actions have been a significant issue for quite some time – particularly in the field of national security. Port and container security is no exception. As demonstrated in Chapter 2, there are numerous US agencies and organizations that are involved in port and container security policy, procedure and practice. Although DHS agencies, such as CBP, TSA, the United States Coast Guard (USCG), the Domestic Nuclear Detection Office (DNDO) and the Immigration Customs Enforcement (ICE), primarily take the lead in port and container security efforts, the Departments of State, Commerce, Energy, Transportation and Defense, as well as the National Security Council and the intelligence community, are also involved. This "dizzying variety" of actors, as one US official describes, are attempting to work together to best secure US ports and containerized freight. How and why does such interagency interaction matter? How and why does such interagency interaction contribute to enhanced national and international security?

This chapter discusses the development of the interagency process related to port and container security. First, the chapter defines what is meant by interagency interaction and some of the theoretical understandings of interagency communication, coordination, cooperation and collaboration. Second, the chapter traces the national security interagency process that emerged after World War II and particularly after the Cold War and September 11, 2001. Although port security is not a new concern, port security from a terrorism perspective certainly is a result of the terrorist attacks of September 11. Ultimately, this chapter demonstrates that interagency interaction, collaboration and communication has grown and developed significantly over the past several years, but also outlines where such interaction, collaboration and communication is lacking and requires more attention.

The Significance of Interagency Action: General Prescriptions for Specific Issues

Interagency procedures and bureaucratic politics have been the subject of much discussion for decades. Policy makers and policy analysts alike have recognized for some time that many problems with which government agencies must grapple regularly require such agencies to work together. It is rarely the case, that public problems can be addressed by only one agency. Instead, problems require skills and capabilities that numerous agencies can provide. The recent global H1N1 flu epidemic, for example, requires the activity of numerous actors and agencies involved in public health. The US Department of Health and Human Services' Centers for Disease Control, works with other agencies such as the Department of Homeland Security and Federal Emergency Management Agency (FEMA) to prevent, manage, prepare and respond to this viral outbreak, as well as numerous other potential epidemics and disasters.[1] Similarly, environmental issues cut across a number of agency activities to bring together the US Environmental Protection Agency and other units, such as Departments of Health and Human Services, Homeland Security, Transportation, Agriculture and others to protect

---

1 For details about the organization of the Department of Health and Human Services' Center for Disease Control, see http://www.cdc.gov/about/organization/cio.htm; and about FEMA, see http://www.fema.gov/about/index.shtm#0. For more on the organization of and interagency activity on public health, see Novick, Morrow and Mays 2007.

our natural environment, ensure sustainability, and address significant threats to environmental security.[2]

Given its importance in tackling problems, it is necessary to know what is meant by interagency action. In general, interagency processes range from communication to coordination to cooperation to collaboration. These four "Cs" are often used interchangeably, but actually refer to different degrees of interagency action. Moreover, existing definitions of these four "Cs" vary in the literature. Communication, for example, has been defined in many different ways from verbal to non-verbal sharing of meanings and symbols. Most commonly, however, communication means regular interaction to exchange and share information. When interagency partners communicate, they pass information from one to another, increasing awareness and understanding of each other while decreasing uncertainty. Communication in this regard is viewed as both a process and a transaction (Miller 2005). Problems may occur, nonetheless, with *accurately* sharing information, leading to incorrect awareness and understanding and contributing to uncertainty among interagency partners (Drucker 1993).

Coordination is the next step in interagency action, which involves streamlining individual agency activities. This type of interaction is about enhancing efficiency, so that agency partners who have overlapping interests do not duplicate their efforts. When government agencies coordinate their work, they pool scarce resources, thereby decreasing cost and duplication while increasing overall efficiency and effectiveness. A primary task when coordinating agency activities is informing "each part of the whole as to how and when it must act" (Denise, no date). Moreover, partners should be aware of what they do individually and how their individual actions relate to the coordinated actions of the whole interagency effort (Ibid.).

Interagency cooperation moves individual activities toward collective actions. Specifically, cooperation, as opposed to competition, "means that a group works toward a goal in such a way that each individual's success facilitates the other's – or…that each person can attain the goal only if the others do so as well" (Kohn 1992, 4). Cooperation, however, does not mean that there is not a divergence of opinion about how to achieve common goals, but that there are attempts to work through them together – working collectively rather than at cross purposes (Denise, no date).

Finally, collaboration is typically the highest level of interagency action. Leo Denise argues that collaboration differs from communication because it is "not about exchanging information, but about using information to create something new." Collaboration differs from coordination because it "seeks divergent insight and spontaneity, not structural harmony." And collaboration is unlike cooperation because collaboration "thrives on differences and requires the sparks of dissent" (Denise, no date). Collaboration, in fact, is not necessarily process oriented, as communication, collaboration and cooperation may be, but is more strictly focused

---

2 See details of environmental partnerships at http://www.epa.gov/partners/.

on outcomes. At the end of the day, "collaborations end in some common ground, but they do not begin there" (Ibid.). An additional view suggests that collaboration among multiple agencies and organizations results when they "join together in creative ways to tackle issues that lie beyond the scope of any single organization" (Mattessich, Murray-Close and Monsey 2001, 2). Ultimately, agencies recognize that they are dependent on others to address important issues and, despite their different views, mandates or positions they avoid and defy a single-agency focus to achieve a greater good.

Nonetheless, interagency communication, coordination, cooperation and collaboration are often difficult to achieve. Some analysts suggest that because individual agencies and actors are self-interested and motivated to achieve their individual goals, they are similarly motivated to work collectively and achieve common goals. However, others argue that individual self-interest does not necessarily translate into an interest in collective goals, even when those goals significantly overlap. Mancur Olson, for example, states:

> it is *not* in fact true that the idea that groups will act in their self-interest follows logically from the premise of rational and self-interested behavior. It does *not* follow, because all of the individuals in a group would gain if they achieved their group objectives, that they would act to achieve that objective, even if they were all rational and self-interested (Olson 1971, 2, emphasis in original).

Olson suggests that the size of the group matters – smaller groups being more likely to achieve common goals than larger ones – as does the role of incentives and coercive forces. He argues that "unless there is coercion…to make individuals act in their common interest, *rational, self-interested individuals will not act to achieve their common or group interests*" (Ibid., emphasis in original). In addition, collective action raises a concern about free-riding among some members of the group whereby there is "exploitation of the great by the small" (Ibid., 3).

Different agency approaches and cultures may also prevent successful interagency interaction. The Federal Bureau of Investigation (FBI) and Central Intelligence Agency (CIA), for example, have struggled through decades of "hostile and sporadic" interactions (Gorman 2003). Since 9/11, however, both agencies share a mandate to identify, target and prevent another terrorist attack on the United States. This common mandate has forced the agencies to work together in ways they have never been able to prior to 2001. It has been well documented that throughout the Cold War the FBI and the CIA exhibited nothing but a bitter rivalry (Riebling 1994). One author explains the rivalry by suggesting that the FBI is from Mars and the CIA is from Venus:

> FBI agents speak and think about very concrete, quantifiable things, such as arrests and suspects, and they value individual achievement. CIA officers… often operate in less-regimented, less-hierarchical ways and put a high value on sharing information and developing longtime relationships (Gorman 2003).

Such different organizational cultures make it very difficult to communicate, much less coordinate, cooperate or collaborate. It is possible to solve such cultural problems, however, by developing a "single-minded mission" that will shape and develop a new culture. "That culture, ideally, would recruit and reward the intellectual, analytic, linguistic, and international curiosity of a CIA officer as well as the discipline and focus of an FBI agent" (Ibid.).

Competing organizational mandates and missions as well as different agency interests and asymmetries in agency power may also affect the ways in which they interact with each other. Differing priorities often bring agencies into conflict with one another, which ultimately influences the outcome of interagency interaction, the articulation of policy, and the eventual outcomes of policy implementation (Clapp, Halperin and Kanter 2007). A dilemma, therefore, emerges considering the extent to which interagency interaction is required for problem solving, and yet considering the challenges agencies face in actually achieving their common goals. The result is a process of interagency bargaining and the give and take of game playing whereby relevant actors, their positions and interests are identified and hopefully structured in a way to achieve optimal outcomes.

Unfortunately, like with any type of interaction, the maneuvering of players, differences in bargaining tactics and skills, problems with collective action, and differences in agency cultures may lead to a suboptimal outcome for all (Allison and Halperin 1972). Hurricane Katrina, and the resulting New Orleans levy breach, in 2005 is a prime example of suboptimal outcomes as a result of interagency failure. After the devastation of the hurricane, multiple government agencies were unable to respond due to a significant break down in communication, coordination, cooperation and collaboration (Greene 2009; Cooper and Block 2007). Not only did agencies at all levels – local, state and federal – fail to respond in an appropriate and timely manner in the wake of the hurricane to provide aid and relief and save lives, they failed in the years before the hurricane to communicate, coordinate, cooperate and collaborate on the development of disaster plans. To be fair, agencies did actually develop disaster plans prior to 2005, but there were numerous plans in place – and some suggest agencies did not even consult them when the hurricane struck (Cooper and Block 2007, 5). Moreover, hurricane planning took a backseat to terrorism issues after 2001 as US officials became preoccupied with what they considered to be a more imminent threat (Ibid., 8-9). Ultimately, chaos ensued on the ground in the wake of Hurricane Katrina – a certain suboptimal outcome due to a lack of effective interagency interaction.

Despite the numerous interagency challenges, it is clear that the national and international security environment is dependent on and tremendously affected by the interactions of bureaucratic agencies. Whether the particular subject is human health and wellbeing or war and conflict, nearly all issues require the work and attention of multiple agencies and actors. Port and container security is no exception. Port and container security is also not new to the interagency process. In fact, it is apparent that a number of interagency activities focused on

48 *Protecting Our Ports*

national and international security issues more generally contribute to a historical interagency foundation upon which port and container security interactions were built.

Interagency Action on National Security: From World War II to the End of the Cold War

Beginning in the early 20th century, the US government grew significantly with a need to address a number of issues and concerns relevant to the country. With this growth came increased government programs, regulations and expenditures and an expanded role in the life of US citizens. Government began to take on enhanced roles concerning law enforcement, commercial relations, agricultural development, public education, postal operations and various other local, state and federal activities. Much of this growth in government came during the New Deal era of President Franklin Roosevelt, which was largely a response to the Great Depression and resulting economic crisis (North 1985; Borcherding 1977). However, some have argued that the growth in government began even earlier, in the 1920s Progressive era (Beck 1932; Wooddy 1934; Holcombe 1996). These authors, for example, demonstrate that US public expenditures directly after World War I were approximately 12% of Gross Domestic Product (GDP), increasing to nearly twice that by 1930 with expenditures having grown to about 23% of GDP (Holcombe 1996). Regardless of when the US government grew, what we do know is that the 1920s and particularly the 1930s are characterized by a significant expansion of government agencies and activities. Although not a part of the initial growth in the US government, national security agencies did eventually develop as US government responsibilities continued to grow – particularly immediately before, during and then directly after World War II.

Regarding national security issues, there has been a 60-year history of interagency interaction mandated by the federal government to achieve unity of purpose and effort for the protection and defense of the United States. Beginning with the National Security Act of 1947, the US government has outlined and identified the various domestic agencies that should be involved in discussions and decisions on national security matters.[3] Specifically, the Act reorganized the primary players responsible for US foreign policy and military action. Moreover, the Act established the National Security Council as the primary agency to coordinate the interagency activities of agencies involved in foreign and security policy.[4] Also relevant are the 1948 US Information and Educational Exchange Act, which created the US Information Agency, and the 1949 Amendment to the

---

3   See the National Security Act of 1947, available at http://www.intelligence.gov/0-natsecact_1947.shtml.

4   See the US Department of State Timeline of US Diplomatic History, available at http://www.state.gov/r/pa/ho/time/cwr/17603.htm.

National Security Act, which created the Central Intelligence Agency. The primary purpose for the reorganization of existing agencies and the creation of new ones was to avoid independent agency actions that are ad hoc, sporadic and isolated from one another. US government officials acknowledged that the "nation's foreign policy interests could not be pursued exclusively through the efforts of executive departments acting separately" (Deutch, Kanter and Scowcroft with Hornbarger 2000, 265). Officials recognized then and continue to recognize today that if agencies fail to achieve unity of effort and action, the development of US policy and the achievement of optimal outcomes are limited (Gibler 2008).

Since 1947, there have been a number of US national security concerns that have required interagency activity. Clearly, throughout the Cold War era a number of agencies were involved in important national security decisions. The Cuban missile crisis is one example where the roles of multiple agencies were documented in terms of influencing decision-making and the relevant tug and pull that occurs between bureaucratic missions in the interagency process. Graham Allison demonstrated in his book *The Essence of Decision* how representatives from various governmental agencies involved in the Cuban missile crisis discussion each represented their own agency's mission and protocols regarding possible courses of action (Allison and Zelikow 1999). The President's Executive Committee (EXCOMM), assembled to discuss and consider the missile crisis and potential solutions included representatives from the Departments of Defense, State and Treasury, Attorney General's office, Joint Chiefs of Staff, National Security Council, and Central Intelligence Agency. Bringing with them their respective agency mandates and missions, the group debated the various responses to Soviet nuclear weapons in Cuba. Undoubtedly, similar interagency dynamics are evident regarding a multitude of other national security issues such as the Vietnam War, the Gulf War, and the arms race between the United States and the Soviet Union (Thomson 2003; Holland 1999; Marullo 1992; Njolstad and Gleditsch 1990).

Once the Cold War ended, officials recognized the need to shift and adjust the interagency process to address a changing national security environment. With the fall of the Soviet Union and end of the relatively stable Cold War period, a large number of national security threats and concerns became apparent – some immediately and some throughout the post-Cold War period. The list includes, but is not limited to, resource shortages and competition, environmental degradation, global economic crises, immigration, illicit trafficking of drugs, weapons and humans, transnational organized crime, human rights abuses, genocide, civil war and conflict, worries about Russia, China, India, Iraq, North Korea, Iran and other developing, changing and potentially unstable countries, terrorism, and the spread of weapons of mass destruction (Brown 2003; Litwak 2000).

With this tremendous growth in national security concerns came changes in US perspectives on national security procedures and policies. First, this new environment blurred the lines between peace and war in that it became necessary to perhaps "invade" another country's information and communications systems to access intelligence that is important for identifying and disrupting potential attacks on the United States. Second, in the post-Cold War era there are no longer clear lines of delineation between domestic and foreign issues, particularly as transnational and non-state actors, such as terrorists operating both in the United States and abroad, have increased in relevance and importance. Similarly, it is not as possible in the post-Cold War period to separate national security issues from domestic law enforcement practices. It is often the case in this new environment that domestic law enforcement officers and agencies must work to enforce laws, catch criminals and prosecute cases that are relevant to national security concerns (Deutch, Kanter and Scowcroft with Hornbarger 2000, 268).

Finally, given this changed setting, it has become more important to develop coalitions to address the various national security issues of the day – both among agencies in the United States and with foreign countries and counterparts. Moreover, solutions to national security problems in the post-Cold War era cannot be addressed with military might alone. A range of solutions, involving military, economic, social and diplomatic actions, is far more necessary in this new climate than ever before (Ibid., 268-269). Making necessary changes to the national security interagency process, however, has not been easy. Nonetheless, US officials have had no choice but to recreate and reorganize the ways in which agencies interact, and particularly the numbers and types of agencies that must be involved.

Nuclear Nonproliferation Policy of the 1990s: An Interagency Foundation for Port and Container Security

Two significant events in the late 1980s and early 1990s led to a major shift in American foreign policy – the fall of the Soviet Union and the Persian Gulf War. Both events heightened awareness of the potential spread of weapons of mass destruction. First, the collapse of the Soviet government raised concern about the security of thousands of nuclear warheads deployed across the very large region, as well as the dozens of nuclear power facilities and military installations. Soon after the Soviet Union disintegrated, reports emerged of poorly protected and controlled nuclear weapons and material residing in former Soviet states. In response, the United States signed several bilateral agreements with Russia, Ukraine, Kazakhstan and Belarus (the four successor states that inherited Soviet nuclear weapons and facilities) to shore up the protection, control and accounting of nuclear weapons and materials. Moreover, the US Congress passed the Nuclear Threat Reduction Act of 1991, otherwise known as the Nunn-Lugar program, to assist Russia and the other former Soviet states in preventing the spread of nuclear weapons, technology, equipment and materials to other states or non-state actors. Nearly $1 billion was committed to provide for enhanced security measures and training activities to protect nuclear weapons and fissile material.

In addition to US bilateral activities, a number of international organizations stepped up their efforts to address nuclear proliferation in the wake of the Soviet collapse. The Coordinating Committee for Multilateral Export Controls (COCOM), which worked to prevent the spread of sensitive technology to the Soviet bloc throughout the Cold War quickly, reorganized to incorporate its former targets in an effort to stem the flow of weapons and critical materials from the former Soviet region to other undesirable end-users. The Nuclear Suppliers Group, which was created after India's nuclear explosion in 1974, also worked to include the nuclear inheritors of the former Soviet Union. Ultimately, a large part of the international community, with the United States as the leader, championed nuclear nonproliferation in the wake of the Soviet collapse and end of the Cold War.

Second, the Persian Gulf War also raised concerns about nuclear weapons proliferation. After Iraq invaded Kuwait and the United States and its coalition allies responded to repel Iraq out of the small country, the international community became aware of the significant amount of nuclear capability that Iraq had achieved by acquiring and developing nuclear technology and materials. Before coalition forces bombed Iraq in 1991, experts believed that Iraq possessed approximately 36 kilograms of nuclear weapons grade uranium – an amount that would be appropriate for one to two small nuclear weapons (Nuclear Control Institute 1995). Iraq reportedly planned to produce highly enriched uranium (HEU) at two of its nuclear facilities, but the country failed to make progress with this effort. The Iraqis successfully hid most of their enrichment equipment from the International Atomic Energy Agency (IAEA) when the organization conducted its initial inspections. However, IAEA inspectors eventually discovered the uranium enrichment process and placed all of the fissile material under its control and observation (Federation of American Scientists 1998). The international community's concerns and fascination with Iraqi nuclear weapons continued throughout the 1990s and into the 21st century, but only after the Persian Gulf War was there an ultimate realization that nuclear weapons were indeed likely to spread. This awareness, along with the collapse of the Soviet Union motivated the United States and much of the international community to further develop and strengthen nuclear nonproliferation policies, procedures and programs.

As with other international problems, however, officials realized that attacking the spread of nuclear and other weapons of mass destruction would require interagency as well as international cooperation. In the United States, a number of agencies were tasked with the development and implementation of nuclear nonproliferation policy beginning in the early 1990s. The US Departments of Defense, State, Commerce and Energy, as well as the US Customs Service, Coast Guard and Federal Bureau of Investigation have all been intimately involved in nuclear nonproliferation issues and programs. Nongovernmental research and advocacy organizations, such as the National Research Council and National Academy of Sciences, were also focused on nonproliferation problems.

The DOD began to incorporate nuclear nonproliferation and technology export control into its defense planning after receiving a mandate from President Bill

Clinton to do so in 1993 (Gebhard 1995, 199). The Nunn-Lugar, Cooperative Threat Reduction program was the primary tool the DOD used to provide assistance and security equipment to more than two-dozen countries (General Accounting Office 2002a, 6). The Department of Energy operated two programs – Second Line of Defense Program and the International Export Control Program – in its efforts to combat the spread of nuclear weapons and material. The Second Line of Defense provided radiation detection equipment, and the International Export Control Program helped to establish legal export control measures, both in several former Soviet countries (Ibid., 5-6). The US Department of State also worked to provide radiation detection equipment from its Nonproliferation Disarmament Program Fund and Export Control and Border Security Assistance Program (Ibid., 6). In addition, the US Customs Service,[5] Federal Bureau of Investigation and Coast Guard implemented programs to detect and combat nuclear smuggling, primarily with funds provided by the Departments of Defense, State, Energy and Customs (Ibid., 6-7).

In general, experts agree that these agencies developed a positive working relationship to collaborate and cooperate on nuclear nonproliferation activities, particularly in the former Soviet region. These agencies capitalized on their various strengths and skills to provide information, assistance, equipment and training to officials abroad in an effort to manage, minimize and prevent the spread of nuclear weapons and materials (General Accounting Office 2002a). However, the GAO did suggest that coordination among these agencies is not sufficient and requires additional attention. A GAO report found, for example, that many of these agencies – the Departments of Energy, State and Defense in particular – have employed "separate approaches to installing radiation detection equipment at countries' border crossings" (Ibid., 2). With one agency focusing on one country's borders and another agency focusing on another country's borders, the result is that equipment at one location may detect certain types of radioactive material while equipment at another location might detect a different type of material. While both agencies are working together to provide important nuclear nonproliferation equipment, the agencies did not collaborate down to the fine details that would be required to work together most efficiently and effectively (Ibid.).

Although coordination could have been better, cooperative interagency interactions were a regular part of nonproliferation policy development and implementation throughout the 1990s. This did not come easy, however. US government officials have commented that agency missions, mandates and priorities often conflicted and got in the way of more effective policy coordination and practical application – particularly in the early 1990s when a significant amount of transition was underway in the wake of the Cold War and the Persian Gulf War (Agency Interviews 2006-2007). Agencies were concentrating on finding their own way, as well as focusing on how best to work together to address the

---

5 Now Customs and Border Protection.

many new concerns that were emerging – of which nuclear nonproliferation was only one (although a primary one). Civil conflict in the former Yugoslavia and a number of African countries, genocide in Rwanda, environmental degradation, and continuing problems with drug smuggling and weapons trafficking in general were also emerging as destabilizing concerns.

Unlike during the Cold War, therefore, US government agencies in the post-Cold War period were struggling to manage a larger number of issues and establish ways to effectively address them.[6] Although interagency action was a must to address nuclear weapons proliferation, agencies regularly found it difficult to manage this multitude of concerns without engaging in interagency turf battles. Nonetheless, US officials credit the nuclear nonproliferation policy process and interagency interaction of the 1990s with establishing a domestic basis for port and container security policy and procedure after September 11, 2001, allowing US agencies to more quickly, easily and successfully work together to strengthen security at US ports of entry and exit and prevent the use of freight containers to deliver dangerous weapons (Interviews with US Government Officials). Moreover, a number of specific programs in place prior to the terrorist attacks of September 11 provided a foundation upon which to build port and container security activities. It is the case, however, that port and container security required a much higher level of interaction among agencies after September 11, much of which was mandated by Congress or the White House in an effort to incentivize and even coerce interagency communication, coordination, communication and collaboration (see Chapter 2).

Interagency Action on Port Security Prior to September 11, 2001

Nearly all port and container security activities prior to the terrorist attacks of September 11, 2001 were focused on drug trafficking, commodity smuggling, theft, crime and corruption (Report of the Interagency Commission on Crime and Security in US Seaports 2000). The most significant illegal activities involving ports and freight containers concerned general criminal activities and not terrorism. There was, in fact, a lack of awareness among port officials regarding terrorist activity involving ports and absolutely no training on the issue (Ibid., 134). A number of government programs, agreements and strategies, however, comprised the overall government effort to secure the nations ports and prevent smuggling, crime and theft of goods around the world. It is upon these programs that officials were able to develop post-9/11 port and container security measures.

6　James Jay Carafano and Richard Weitz document the ways in which the US government has mismanaged a number of crisis issues throughout its history, demonstrating how US agencies struggle to work together. See James Jay Carafano and Richard Weitz (2008) *Mismanaging Mayhem: How Washington Responds to Crisis*.

Throughout the 20th century there were numerous agency efforts in the United States to secure waterways and port areas. In 1950, the Magnuson Act outlined permanent regulations regarding security at US ports and allowed for relatively wide latitude for US authorities to investigate and monitor foreign vessels in US waters and manage foreign ships in US ports. This Act was largely a result of the Cold War rivalry between the United States and the Soviet Union as it targeted ships from the Soviet region as well as Soviet allies. Based on this Act, a number of Port Security Committees and Harbor Safety Committees were created around the country to bring together and coordinate government agencies, commercial enterprises, industry representatives and interested individuals to enhance coast and port security efforts.

Port Security Committees were established with a purpose "to provide a framework to communicate, identify risks, and coordinate resources to mitigate threats and consequences" (United States Coast Guard, Port Security Committee). The committee tasked the Coast Guard to work with the Department of Defense and other relevant government agencies at all levels, as well as those who own and operate seafaring vessels and port facilities, those who provide service to and within ports, and those who work in port operations "to detect, deter, prevent, and respond to attacks against US territory, population, and Marine Transportation System (MTS) components by those intent on causing mass destruction or disruption" (Ibid.). The types of disruptions with which this committee was concerned included any involving "economic, public safety, environmental or defense operations impacts" (Ibid.). Harbor Security Committees are more focused on coordinating local government officials, unions, business representatives and port authorities. Most US seaports operate a Harbor Security Committee to address issues regarding security, safety and environmental concerns at local ports.

Also in 1950, the Department of Transportation created the Maritime Administration (MA) to focus on US waterways. The MA is actually involved in numerous areas involving water vessels, shipping, shipbuilding, port and water vessel operations, and the security, safety and environmental aspects of marine areas. The Maritime Administration's Port and Cargo Security Program operates under the MA's Office of Security with a mission to coordinate and manage agency activities related to the security of marine transportation, including security policy, plans, procedures, operations, exercises, and research and development (Maritime Administration Port and Cargo Security). The MA, working with the Department of Transportation and the Federal Ad Hoc Working group on Maritime Security Awareness, also publishes a quarterly journal entitled *Maritime Security Report*. The *Report* informs maritime industry officials and relevant members of the government of criminal activities – particularly economic crimes – that pose a threat to commercial maritime operations (Office of Ports and Domestic Shipping 1996).

US interagency interaction has also involved a number of industry representatives and private enterprise actors. In 1991, the Department of Commerce Bureau of Export Administration developed a Business Executives

Enforcement Team (BEET) to help companies increase their knowledge of export control procedures and develop their own policies and practices for detecting and preventing suspicious trade activities. This public-private cooperative program involves Commerce officials, private industry representatives, and US law enforcement personnel to prevent unlawful exports of sensitive equipment and materials and "identify projects of proliferation concern" (Reinsch 1999).

The US Customs agency also developed three industry partnership programs prior to 9/11 to enhance anti-smuggling activities. The Carrier Initiative Program was established in 1984 to bring together air, sea, land and rail carriers to work collaboratively and address the problems of smuggling and terrorism on throughout the commercial transport system. The program allowed Customs officials and private carriers to collaboratively identify and report smuggling and other criminal activity (US Customs and Border Protection 2008). The Business Anti-Smuggling Coalition, created in March 1996, works specifically to combat narcotics smuggling by examining "the entire supply chain process, from point of manufacture, through the shipping process, from foreign docks, to final destinations in the United States" ("Building Partnerships" 2003). And the US Customs program America's Counter Smuggling Initiative has since 1998 built upon the Carrier Initiative Program and Business Anti-Smuggling Coalition with a focus on Mexico, Central and South America and the Caribbean. Through this program, US Customs officials work with US law enforcement agencies to help industry partners and law enforcement officials in the western hemisphere to improve anti-smuggling efforts (US Customs and Border Protection, *America's Counter Smuggling Initiative*).

In 1993, the US government established the Southwest Border Initiative to attack drug and other smuggling activities along the US-Mexico border and waterway areas. This initiative required that the Coast Guard, Customs Service and Department of Defense, as well as other federal agencies, foreign counterparts and private industries, work together to conduct land and maritime drug and human smuggling interdiction operations. The intent of the Initiative was "to provide a maximum return on resources expended" in an effort to disrupt smuggling routes and capabilities (McCaffrey 1997). In the following years, crime at San Diego border crossings dropped 30% and narcotics seizures increased approximately 24% (Ibid.).

The 1998 International Crime Control Strategy built on the Southwest Initiative to more broadly focus on smuggling and related crimes at all levels. Smuggling at the country's land, sea and air borders were all targeted for enhanced detection equipment, stronger law enforcement, stiffer penalties for smuggling crimes and more effective prosecution of accused smugglers and their criminal organizations (Ibid.). Moreover, the 1999 National Drug Control Strategy included a section on port and border security to prevent the illegal entry of drugs into the United States. This initiative covered all US ports of entry, but focused primarily on the Southwest border. The 1999 Strategy outlined an interagency process involving border patrol agents, Customs agents, immigration agents and law enforcement agents, requiring that they improve their communication and coordination to enhance anti-smuggling efforts (Executive Office of the President 1999).

In April 2000, at least 18 federal agencies that had some responsibility for marine transportation activities signed a Memorandum of Understanding to establish the Interagency Committee on Marine Transportation System (ICMTS). Representatives from the Departments of Transportation, Agriculture, Commerce, Defense, Energy, Homeland Security, Interior, Labor, State and Treasury, Attorney General's office, Joint Chiefs of Staff, Environmental Protection Agency, Federal Maritime Commission, Domestic Policy Council, Economic Policy Council, Homeland Security Council, Office of Management and Budget and Council of Environmental Quality began meeting two or three times each year to "exchange information and resolve problems that cut across their respective programs" regarding maritime transportation issues (Transportation Research Board of the National Academies 2004, 83).[7] The overall function of the ICMTS was to "identify, evaluate, develop, and promote implementation of federal policies and make recommendation concerning resource utilization to ensure effective public funding decisions, support services, and management of the marine transportation system" (General Accounting Office 2002b, 38). Eight years into their operations, in July 2008 the ICMTS published the *National Strategy for the Marine Transportation System: A Framework for Action*, which outlined the various challenges and priorities for marine transportation agencies, officials, industries and representatives (Committee on the Marine Transportation System 2008). In addition to this interagency group on marine transportation, a number of industry leaders, marine and labor organizations, trade groups, transportation enterprises and various other interested entities developed the Marine Transportation System National Advisory Council (MTSNAC) to work with the Department of Transportation and other federal agencies to keep them informed of relevant maritime issues, concerns and solutions (Marine Transportation System National Advisory Council).

The issue of port and container security, therefore, was no stranger to interagency interaction prior to the September 11, 2001 terrorist attacks when awareness of the issue was heightened significantly. In the aftermath of 9/11, the US government sought to add port and container security as a priority concerning anti-terrorism policy, procedure and practice. Officials found that building on the past interagency experiences and pre-existing programs and policies came rather naturally. However, as history teaches us, despite the existing foundation interagency action is always easier said than done. And left on their own, agencies may not always choose to work collectively to achieve common goals, as Mancur Olson suggests in *The Logic of Collective Action*. Interagency action after 9/11, therefore, had to be significantly influenced by Congressional mandates and White House requirements.

---

7   DHS was added after its creation in 2002.

Post-September 11 Port Security Interactions and Activities

Building on the number of pre-existing programs and interagency interactions concerning port security and criminal activity, US officials were able to relatively quickly establish and insert terrorism priorities after September 11, 2001. However, the development and insertion of anti-terrorism policies and procedures after 9/11 has not been entirely smooth and successful. US officials currently involved in port and container security recognize the various missions and different perspectives affecting the interagency process. Moreover, officials themselves express very different understandings of the quality of communication, coordination, cooperation, and collaboration resulting from interagency interactions. These officials know they must work together to effectively address threats to port and container security, but they have differing views on the ways, means and effectiveness of the interagency process. Ultimately, there exists some evidence of high levels of interagency communication, coordination and cooperation, as well as evidence of interagency difficulties and a lack of communication.

Based on interviews with agencies involved in port and container security, it appears that communication and cooperation among relevant port security agencies such as DHS, DOS, DOE, the Coast Guard and others has actually been quite high. Moreover, when the Department of Homeland Security was created to encompass many agencies in one department, there was some fear that this would lead to conflict over resources, expertise or prestige. While it is certainly unfair to say that conflict has not occurred, most feel confident that conflict has been minimal, in at least the port security arena. In fact, many officials highlight this cooperative environment as a point of pride. This is the case for interagency interaction among the various US Departments involved – as well as for intra-agency interaction within particular US Departments, such as DHS. The Department of Homeland Security, most particularly, has a number of offices involved in port and container security (CBP, USCG, TSA, ICE, DNDO), so in addition to managing horizontal, interagency interactions, DHS must manage vertical, intra-agency interactions.

Regarding operations at US seaports, the Coast Guard and CBP work quite closely together. The Coast Guard serves as the "Captain of the Port" and oversees all activities on the water while CBP has jurisdiction when ships dock and off-load cargo. In instances where a ship is coming into port and is carrying suspicious cargo, the Coast Guard and CBP often jointly board the in-coming vessel. In preparation for these types of events and as a cooperation building technique, the Coast Guard and CBP regularly train together. While there will always be potential personality conflicts, and a few officials interviewed for this study did confess that some small turf battles have arisen, conflict has overall been minimal. Most officials reported that the importance of the port security issue, a history of cooperative relations among agencies, and a clear delineation of tasks lead to a high level of interagency interaction.

Some American seaports, however, do struggle with interagency operations. The Port of Seattle, for example, manages a complex system of operations that includes both the Seattle seaport and the Seattle/Tacoma airport. Port officials, therefore, must organize and manage relations with multiple local, state and federal agencies, requiring them to address numerous requirements at various levels. This type of interagency interaction is meant to make the port more efficient, by pooling resources and preventing duplication of effort, but it also contributes to significant resource concerns. Seattle port officials, for example, suggest that because they must work within this interagency process, they are stretched rather thin and must rely on port grants and federal financial assistance to address all of the various regulations and requirements relevant to port and container security.

Regarding land border activities, CBP is the lead authority. CBP works with the United States Border Patrol and TSA at land crossings, and with TSA at airports. CBP also encompasses CBP Air and Marine Surveillance and the Secure Border Initiative (SBI), as well as various ports-of-entry security programs. DHS and its sub-agencies have made efforts to streamline procedures and to ensure accountability and transparency. Officials reported that interagency cooperation and conflict among these entities is less of a problem than inconsistencies and miscommunications within each entity. The most often cited example of this was TSA, which suffers from a significantly high staff turnover rate for both junior and senior personnel. Such turnover is problematic for the interagency process as partner agencies are unsure of who their counterparts currently are or will be in the future. Moreover, there is regularly a loss of institutional memory as officials frequently rotate out the door, taking with them their knowledge of port and container security and awareness of other agency activities and programs.

Ultimately, Customs and Border Protection officials acknowledge that their agency is "at the mercy of all other agencies involved at ports" (Agency Interviews 2006-2007). Many officials suggest there has been an easy transition under DHS to consolidate agencies and to develop interagency relations with others. Some state that once they all put on the "same uniform" there was "instant identification" (Ibid.). Others, however, argue that although members of CBP are aware that everyone "has to be working toward the same end," they are not sure that this actually happens (Ibid.). Without a doubt though, CBP officials report that agencies cooperate more than they compete on port and container security. The only area where competition becomes an issue, according to officials, is in drug interdiction where multiple jurisdictions among multiple agencies remain problematic.

Perhaps one of the more difficult and controversial programs that has had an effect on and has been affected by the interagency process is the Transportation Worker Identification Credential (TWIC) program. Established by the Maritime Transportation Security Act (MTSA) of 2002 and reiterated in the SAFE Port Act of 2006, the TWIC program was touted as an essential way to prevent terrorist and criminal access to our ports and waterways. To work in transportation and have unescorted access to port facilities and container cargo areas, drivers, port employees, longshoremen and anyone who works inside port areas must undergo a criminal background check and be issued a universal, biometric TWIC card. The background check allows authorities to determine and assess the threat of any particular individual who works at a port. The process is managed by DHS, TSA and the USCG, which began to issue cards in 2007 and continued throughout 2009 and beyond (Department of Homeland Security 2007).

A number of agency, port and industry representatives and officials, however, have criticized the TWIC program and process. Some have expressed concern that the relevant agencies are moving very slowly with this program and are not sufficiently testing the cards and their readers to ensure that delays and backups at ports will not result – that communication, coordination, cooperation and collaboration among the relevant players is lacking (Hawkes 2008; "If TWIC Ever Reaches US Ports" 2006). Some have also suggested that this program is too costly with a price tag of about $1 billion, about 40% of which will be paid by ports. And the costs are likely to rise. The DHS estimated that there should be about 750,000 TWIC cards issued, but it appears that the number necessary may be closer to 2 million. Perhaps more troubling, however, is the absence of common standards for the biometrics that are to be collected from transportation workers when issued a TWIC card, as well as the lack of access to a federal biometrics database in order to assess the risk of individuals who have applied for the card. FBI biometrics databases, for example, are not available to port authorities for the purpose of criminal background checks. This alone demonstrates a significant lack of communication, coordination, cooperation and collaboration between port security agencies such as DHS and TSA and relevant counterparts at the FBI. Additional concerns center on the numerous changes that have already occurred in the TWIC program and the general confusion regarding the fluidity of TWIC plans. Finally, some groups have expressed concern about universal TWIC cards and the "one-size-fits-all" approach to port security, arguing that port and container security programs should take into consideration the differences in threat, environment, infrastructure, needs, capacities and capabilities at the nation's many different ports (Terreri 2007).

Such interagency difficulties are acknowledged among other officials as well. Department of Energy officials suggest that they see evidence of turf battles among agencies involved in port and container security including arguments and disagreements over who does what, where, when and how. Officials argue, however, that such battles are often a result of particular personality conflicts among specific people involved in the process more so than an outcome of agency competition. Despite these few problems, Energy officials argue, there is a great deal of cooperation in the area for three reasons: (1) the urgency of the port and container security issue; (2) the foundation of cooperation to build on because of existing interagency programs addressing security issues; and (3) the fact that there is a "more mature process" involved in interagency activities due to years of experience. However, even these more optimistic views are expressed in conjunction with skepticism about particular programs or activities of other agencies or institutions. Energy officials, for example, are relatively pessimistic about the SAFE Port Act and rules regarding 100% cargo scanning, indicating that even though agencies must work together, they may not always agree.

Moreover, some agency officials are unsure of their role, or are concerned about the success of interagency interaction among such a large number of government agencies. Department of State officials, for example, have established a Global Supply Chain Security Working Group to coordinate efforts within the Department, but officials involved expressed some confusion about exactly what their role should be working with other agencies. These officials indicated that there is no specific mandate regarding the port and container security interagency process – that the process seems rather ad hoc and at times cobbled together. They admit that there is a habit of interagency action that has evolved over the years, particularly on weapons proliferation and terrorism issues, but that such activities are a result of routine rather than purposeful efforts to collaborate.

DNDO officials raised specific concerns about port and security interagency processes suggesting that the "coordination of this issue is very challenging because it is so big." Moreover, there appears to be a cultural difference between DNDO official perspectives and the CBP approach to port and container security. DNDO, being comprised of a number of relevant agency representatives who work primarily on one specific issue – the detection of nuclear materials and weapons – has a fundamentally smaller, more focused mission than CBP and some of the other agencies involved. Because DNDO is most focused on the science, research and development aspects of nuclear detection, they find it difficult to place their work in the larger port and container security landscape, much like Mancur Olson might expect regarding the size of group and ultimate effectiveness of collective action. Ultimately, DNDO officials admit that agencies are not coordinating well yet, but do believe they "are making progress."

Lessons Learned: Interagency Implications for the Future of Port and Container Security

Interagency communication, coordination, cooperation and collaboration are clearly important for the successful development and implementation of policy and action, but such interagency interactions are often difficult. Individual agency missions, mandates, preferences, perspectives and priorities often get in the way of effective interagency interaction. But, it has been demonstrated and argued throughout the past several decades that collective action among government agencies is the best practice for achieving national security goals – and especially for addressing contemporary national security issues that are certainly complex, complicated and transnational in nature.

Although agencies have struggled in recent years to engage in interagency action on port and container security, there are perhaps fewer obstacles and challenges today than there were years ago when agencies developed new interagency processes to tackle emerging and imminent threats (nuclear weapons proliferation, for example) without a solid foundation of previous interagency interaction in place. Agencies involved in port and container security policies, programs and procedures have seemingly accomplished a great deal of communication with officials interacting regularly to share and exchange information. Higher levels of interagency action, however, have emerged and are solidifying, but strong collaboration appears to be lagging somewhat behind. There is, therefore, room to improve interagency activities on port and container security in an effort to strengthen and enhance optimal outcomes and prevent the use of ports and cargo containers for being used to disrupt commercial relations and endanger the American population.

Interaction among domestic agencies, however, is not the only requirement for improving port and container security results in the United States. Interaction with foreign counterparts and engagement in the international community is also necessary for the US government to sufficiently address port and container, as well as other, national security issues. How the United States approaches other governments and relevant actors abroad is key to affecting our own success on port security. The US government has clearly taken the lead on this issue around the world, but to what effect? The next chapter specifically focuses on the international impact and consequences of US efforts to lead a global port security campaign.

Bibliography

Allison, Graham T. and Morton H. Halperin. Spring 1972. "Bureaucratic Politics: A Paradigm and Some Policy Implications," *World Politics*, Vol. 24, Supplement, 40-79.

Allison, Graham T. and Philip Zelikow. 1999. *Essence of Decision: Explaining the Cuban Missile Crisis*, 2nd Edition (New York: Longman).

Beck, James M. 1932. *Our Wonderland of Bureaucracy* (New York: Macmillan).

Borcherding, Thomas E. (ed.) 1977. *Budgets and Bureaucrats: The Sources of Government Growth* (Durham, NC: Duke University Press).

Brown, Michael E. (ed.) 2003. *Grave New World: Security Challenges in the Twenty-First Century* (Washington, DC: Georgetown University Press).

"Building Partnerships." 2003. *Customs and Border Protection Today*, available at http://www.cbp.gov/xp/CustomsToday/2003/september/miami_basc.xml.

Carafano, James Jay and Richard Weitz. 2008. *Mismanaging Mayhem: How Washington Responds to Crisis* (Westport, CT: Greenwood Publishing Group).

Clapp, Priscilla, Morton Halperin and Arnold Kanter. 2007. *Bureaucratic Politics and Foreign Policy* (Washington, DC: Brookings Institution Press).

Committee on the Marine Transportation System. (2008) *National Strategy for the Marine Transportation System: A Framework for Action* (Washington, DC: Department of Transportation), available at http://www.cmts.gov/nationalstrategy.pdf.

Cooper, Christopher and Robert Block. 2007. *Disaster: Hurricane Katrina and the Failure of Homeland Security* (New York: Holt Paperbacks).

Denise, Leo (no date) "Collaboration Versus C-Three (Cooperation, Coordination, and Communication)," *Innovating*, Vol. 7, No. 3, 1-6, available at http://www.ride.ri.gov/adulteducation/Documents/Tri%20part%201/Collaboration%20vs.%20the%203c's.pdf.

Deutch, John, Arnold Kanter and Brent Scowcroft with Christopher Hornbarger. 2000. "Strengthening the National Security Interagency Process," in Ashton B. Carter and John P. White, (eds), *Keeping the Edge: Managing Defense for the Future* (Cambridge, MA: Belfer Center for Science and International Affairs, Harvard Kennedy School of Government), 265-284, available at http://belfercenter.ksg.harvard.edu/files/KTE_ch10.pdf.

Drucker, Peter. 1993. *Management: Tasks, Responsibilities, Practices* (New York: Harper Books).

Executive Office of the President. 1999. *1999 National Drug Control Strategy*, available at http://www.ncjrs.gov/ondcppubs/publications/policy/99ndcs/iii-e.html.

Federation of American Scientists. November 1998. "IAEA and Iraqi Nuclear Weapons," available at http://www.fas.org/nuke/guide/iraq/nuke/iaea.htm.

General Accounting Office (GAO). May 2002a. *Nuclear Nonproliferation: US Efforts to Help Other Countries Combat Nuclear Smuggling Need Strengthened Coordination and Planning* (Washington, DC: GAO).

General Accounting Office (GAO). September 2002b. *Marine Transportation: Federal Financing and a Framework for Infrastructure Investments* (Washington, DC: GAO).

Gebhard, Paul. 1995. "Not by Diplomacy or Defense Alone: The Role of Regional Security Strategies in US Proliferation Policy," in Brad Roberts (ed.), *Weapons Proliferation in the 1990s* (Cambridge: MIT Press), 199-213.

Gibler, Lt. Col. Michael L. 2008. *Shotgun Wedding: Interagency Transformation for the 21st Century Security Environment* (US Army War College).

Gorman, Siobhan. 2003. "FBI, CIA Remain Worlds Apart," *Government Executive.com*, available at http://www.govexec.com/dailyfed/0803/080103nj1.htm.

Greene, Linda S. 2009. "Governmental Liability for the Katrina Failure," in Jeremy I. Levitt and Matthew C. Whitaker, (eds), *Hurricane Katrina: America's Unnatural Disaster* (Lincoln: University of Nebraska, Press).

Hawkes, Kenneth Gale. 2008. *TWIC 2008: Status and Issues*, available at http://www.sealawyer.net/images/TWIC_2008_paper.doc.

Holcombe, Randall G. 1996. "The Growth of the Federal Government in the 1920s," *The CATO Journal*, Vol. 16, No. 2, 175-199.

Holland, Lauren. 1999. "The US Decision to Launch Operation Desert Storm: A Bureaucratic Politics Analysis," *Armed Forces and Society*, Vol. 25, No. 2, 219-242.

"If TWIC Ever Reaches US Ports, It May Get to the Airports." 2006. *Air Safety Week*, available at http://findarticles.com/p/articles/mi_m0UBT/is_21_20/ai_n26870468/.

Kohn, Alfie. 1992. "Cooperation: What it Means and Doesn't Mean," in Allan Combs (ed.), *Cooperation: Beyond the Age of Competition* (Philadelphia, PA: Gordon and Breach Science Publishers).

Litwak, Robert S. 2000. *Rogue States and US Foreign Policy: Containment after the Cold War* (Washington, DC: Woodrow Wilson Center Press).

Maritime Administration, available at http://www.marad.dot.gov/about_us_landing_page/about_us_landing_page.htm.

Maritime Administration Port and Cargo Security, available at http://www.marad.dot.gov/ports_landing_page/port_cargo_security/port_cargo_security.htm.

Marine Transportation System National Advisory Council, available at http://www.mtsnac.org/.

Marullo, Sam. 1992. "Political, Institutional, and Bureaucratic Fuel for the Arms Race," *Sociological Forum*, Vol. 7, No. 1, March 1992, 29-54.

McCaffrey, Barry R. 1997. "Protecting US Borders," in the *International Crime Control Strategy 1998*, available at http://www.fas.org/irp/offdocs/iccs/iccsiv.html.

Miller, Katherine. 2005. *Communication Theories: Perspectives, Processes and Contexts*, 2nd Edition (New York: McGraw-Hill).

Njolstad, Olav and Nils Petter Gleditsch (eds), 1990. *Arms Races: Technological and Political Dynamics* (Thousand Oaks, CA: Sage Publishers).

North, Douglass C. 1985. "The Growth of Government in the United States: An Economic Historian's Perspective," *Journal of Public Economics*, Vol. 28, No. 3, 359-382.

Novick, Lloyd F., Cynthia B. Morrow and Glen P. Mays, (eds) 2007. *Public Health Administration: Principles for Population-based Management* (Sudbury, MA: Jones and Bartlett Publishers).

Nuclear Control Institute. August 1995. "Iraq's Crash Program to Build A-Bomb Should Come as No Surprise," available at http://www.nci.org/pr/pr82695.htm.

Office of Ports and Domestic Shipping. 1996. *Maritime Security Report*, available at http://ntl.bts.gov/lib/24000/24100/24179/msrjan96.pdf.

Olson, Mancur. 1971. *The Logic of Collective Action: Public Goods and the Theory of Groups* (Cambridge, MA: Harvard University Press).

Reinsch, William A. 1999. *Second NSG International Seminar Session 4: The Future of Export Controls in Nuclear Non-Proliferation* (Washington, DC: Bureau of Industry and Security, US Department of Commerce), available at http://www.bis.doc.gov/news/archive99/nsgint.html.

Report of the Interagency Commission on Crime and Security in US Seaports (Fall 2000).

Riebling, Mark. 1994. *Wedge: The Secret War Between the FBI and CIA* (New York: Knopf).

Terreri, April. 2007. "Questions About Reliability Persist as Transport Workers ID Card Rolls Out," *World Trade 100*, available at http://www.

worldtrademag.com/Articles/Feature_Article/BNP_GUID_9-5-2006_A_ 10000000000000031232.

Thomson, James C., Jr. 2003. "How Could Vietnam Happen? An Autopsy," in Eugene R. Wittkopf and James M. McCormick (eds), *The Domestic Sources of American Foreign Policy: Insights and Evidence* (Lanham, MD: Rowman and Littlefield Publishers, Inc.).

Transportation Research Board of the National Academies. 2004. *The Marine Transportation System and the Federal Role: Measuring Performance, Targeting Improvement* (Washington, DC: The National Academies Press), available at http://onlinepubs.trb.org/onlinepubs/sr/sr279.pdf.

United States Coast Guard, Port Security Committee, Frequently Asked Questions, available at http://www.sfmx.org/support/amscfaq.pdf.

US Customs and Border Protection. 2008. *Securing America's Borders: Carrier Initiative Program*, available at http://www.cbp.gov/xp/cgov/border_security/international_operations/partnerships/cip.xml.

US Customs and Border Protection. *America's Counter Smuggling Initiative*, available at http://www.cbp.gov/xp/cgov/border_security/international_operations/partnerships/acsi.xml.

Wooddy, Carroll H. 1934. *The Growth of the Federal Government: 1915-1932* (New York: McGraw-Hill).

Chapter 4

The International Politics of Container Security

Introduction

On any given day, Americans are bombarded with, and in many ways reliant upon, a massive amount of goods and products. Chances are, most of the items people rely on to get through their busy days are either partially or entirely of foreign origin. An automobile manufacturing plant in the United States might be owned by a foreign company, producing cars that include Japanese parts, German engineering, and will ultimately guzzle gas from Saudi Arabia, Venezuela or Nigeria. Likewise, most of the shoes on our feet, clothes on our backs and styling products in our hair have traveled a long way to make it into our closets and bathroom cabinets. In this era of globalization and advanced technology, we have come to expect relatively inexpensive goods, offering a plethora of choices, available for purchase at almost any hour. These products and millions of others, arrive every day in large containers from foreign destinations via the country's busy seaports, land borders and even airports.

In previous chapters we addressed the various domestic actors and agencies involved in transportation security. However, the security of containerized freight is not simply a domestic issue, but it is also a significant international one. Therefore, we now move from the domestic politics and policies surrounding container security to the international context of ports, port security, and container shipping. In this chapter we paint a picture of the international port and container security landscape, outline the relevant international actors and programs, and highlight the US role in terms of the quality of interaction, the amount of imposition, and the ultimate impact it has on international trade security. What follows is an examination of the theoretical issues of sovereignty and anarchy in relation to the post-9/11 efforts to work with international partners in securing the world's seaports. Initially, we explore sovereignty as it relates to state interaction, and present the relevant agents and programs involved in the international politics of containerized freight. From there we address some of the concerns of international partners with regard to new US mandated requirements and the politics surrounding US leadership on this issue. Finally, we suggest areas where the United States could act to strengthen not just cooperation, but true collaboration with the international community. In the end it should be clear that the lack of a central authority in the international system in general, and in container security issues specifically, makes cooperation on security issues all the more important and all the more problematic.

The International System

Scholars of international relations agree that the global arena is characterized by anarchy. Recognizing the reality that there is no overarching force that can ensure justice, equality or fairness, states must act to advance their own interests. The lack of a central authority in an anarchical system requires states to provide for their own security and survival. This is not to say that state interests are fixed, or that cooperation does not exist, but rather that these things are conditioned by the anarchic structure. Various schools of thought emphasize differing interests, motivations or analytical levels of analysis, but for most anarchy is viewed as a constant (Waltz 1994; Keohane 1984; Wendt 1992).[1] Though international organizations attempt to provide some order, they are only able to moderate the effects of anarchy. They do not have the force of law, or true enforcement capabilities (Keohane 1984). In the current international system the sovereignty of the individual state – in particular that of the most powerful states – always prevails (Reinike 1997).

Scholars define the term *sovereignty* in diverse ways. Essentially, there are two basic forms: internal and external. External sovereignty refers to the ability of states to sign treaties with other governments and represent themselves in the international arena (Reinike 1997, 129). Internal sovereignty is much more "messy" than the external form. The recognition of internal sovereignty means that states have a preponderance of power to control internal activities within their geographic area. Or, to use Weber's terms, states possess a legitimate monopoly on force in a given territory (Weber 1919). Hence, states will determine ways and means for ruling and policing their territory, as well as the functioning of their economies among other things. In dealing with issues of human rights violations, ethnic disputes and environmental issues, internal sovereignty often comes into conflict with what other states deem appropriate. If states choose to get involved in the activities and internal operations of other states uninvited they are violating the long standing dictates of internal sovereignty and must consider the costs and benefits of such action. Because few states kindly accept incursions into their domestic affairs, it is only in unique situations that a state might act to challenge the internal sovereignty of another. However, the "Great Powers" – the biggest, most powerful states – have more flexibility in their options. In anarchy, it is especially difficult to counter a powerful state's activities, even if the powerful state is imposing its own preferences on another state's sovereignty (Mearsheimer 2003).

While states do enjoy a degree of autonomy in the international system, it is not absolute, nor has it ever been. In an anarchic system there is no guarantee of

---

1   The one exception might be Constructivist theorists who believe that anarchy exists, but that it is socially constructed. Realists and Neoliberals might debate the ways in which states function in an anarchic system or the means by which they can mediate the effects of anarchy, though both do acknowledge the importance of anarchy as a constraint on state action. For more on the schools of International Relations, see Chapter 5.

state sovereignty, though it is a recognized norm (Ibid.). Krasner explains that states compromise their own sovereignty through conventions, contracts, coercion or imposition. These instances might be strategic decisions to partner with other states for joint gain, or they might be situations where states believe they have no choice but to follow and yield to the influence of external actors. In the international system states do not live in a vacuum and frequently base decisions in part on relations with their neighbors, including considerations of perceptions of power, economic interests, military capabilities, and levels of amicability (Krasner 1995). In the new era of globalization, where the economic interdependence of countries around the world has increased exponentially, these influences are even stronger (Guiraudon and Lahav 2000).

Clashes over the limits of individual sovereignty can lead to conflict, even among friendly states. It is easy to see where conflict and violence might result from one state attempting to take land or resources from another.[2] We might also expect to see conflict in situations where states or international organizations feel compelled to interfere in the internal politics of other states (e.g. the Iraq war). The aforementioned issues of human rights (e.g. the US invasion of Haiti) and ethnic violence (e.g. US actions in Mogadishu) are often instances used to justify purposeful breaches of internal state sovereignty.[3]

Military actions and economic sanctions are the most visible ways to exert one state's influence over another. However, sovereignty might also be diminished when states are compelled to conform to the dictates of an external force on less important issues, without input or reciprocity. Krasner explains that this can occur when "...more powerful actors impose institutions, policies or personnel on weaker states" (Krasner 1995, 116). The conflict that arises from these situations seldom leads to violence, but if a state or groups of states percieve that an actor is exerting too much control in the relationship, negative perceptions will inevitably lead to slowed progress and tense relations (Barnett and Duvall 2005). It is in these seemingly minor challenges to the recognition of state sovereignty and the excessive exertion of one state's influence over another that the politics of international freight security sits. As it currently stands, the United States is dictating international policy in this issue area – US influence is being used to impose programs and polices – and more and more of the country's international partners are beginning to feel that there is a disregard for their national sovereignty and they feel they are being increasingly imposed upon (International Interviews 2007-2008). Keeping

---

2   In fact, some argue that the anarchical system *forces* states to act to increase their own power, territory, and resources when possible (Mearsheimer 2003).

3   For every example of intervention (Haiti, Mogadishu), there are numerous examples of places where little or no action is taken (Rwanda, Darfur, Tibet etc.). The inconsistent nature of external actions leads to questions of why one place but not another – naturally leading to motivations based on the acquisition of power or resources. Additionally, the internal actions of Great Powers, no matter how egregious, are often ignored due to concerns of a military conflict or of economic ramifications.

68   *Protecting Our Ports*

the concept of anarchy in mind, we now turn to a discussion of US foreign policy in the area of container security, and explore how the execution of policies and programs aimed to protect US ports of entry has shaped international politics.

US International Strategy to Enhance Domestic Security

Since 2001 there has been an effort to "push borders out" as part of the country's post-9/11 strategy of layering US homeland defense. This means that officials must take measures to secure containers traveling toward the country long before they reach the United States. The farther away from the United States others build compatible security infrastructure, the better. Therefore, the policy is no longer to think of national borders as the key to domestic security, but to think about security borders as being much farther away – a sort of virtual border (Agency Interviews 2006-2008; Forrest 2006). In an anarchic world with no central authority, the United States has the ability to either physically force other countries into compliance with violence, or the country can seek cooperative partnerships to reach its goals – partnerships in which it can wield significant influence because it is a great power. The United States has chosen the latter.

The strategy to extend its virtual borders requires that the United States work with international organizations, foreign governments, and foreign enterprises to ensure the security of containers originating from foreign ports. When one considers that in 2007, 12 million containers entered the United States from foreign ports and that "today, one container in every ten that is engaged in global trade is either bound for or originates in the United States, accounting for 10% of worldwide container traffic," the wisdom in this policy becomes apparent (America's Container Ports 2009, 1).

The bulk of containers entering the United States do so through one of the country's 361 domestic seaports ("LA/Long Beach February" 2009). Over 40% of ocean fairing containers enter through the neighboring seaports of Long Beach and Los Angeles. The ports of New York/New Jersey, Miami, Seattle and Houston are also sizable domestic seaports. The United States is an importer state, bringing in almost twice the value of goods as it exports. While we have historically traded with Europe, today most US imports come from Asia. In fact, over 72% of the goods imported to and 55% of exports from the United States originate from ten countries, though the country trades with more than 175 foreign countries in total. The top five countries trading with the United States, as measured by numbers of container units, are China, Japan, Hong Kong, South Korea and Taiwan (America's Container Ports 2009, 19). The strategy of pushing US borders out means working especially with these five countries to develop measures for the enhancement of security.[4]

---

4   For centuries, scholars have noted how great power countries have maximized their position and power in the international system by focusing their interactions, policies and activities with others located in prime geographic locations or possessing important

The International Politics of Container Security   69

While much of the attention in this book is on seaports, a sizable amount of containers enter the United States via truck or rail across its land borders. With this in mind, it should be no surprise that there has been a renewed focus on US land borders and the movement of containerized freight (see Chapter 2).[5]

Attempting to improve security procedures at foreign ports undoubtedly diminishes the threat posed to the United States. However, in many ways this puts the impetus for our defense squarely on foreign governments to see that they implement sufficient security measures at their ports. To ensure that this occurs, the United States has advanced a number of programs and policies to encourage cooperation with international partners. In the next section we introduce (or reintroduce in some cases) the partners and international agents involved in the international politics of port security.

Agencies Involved in International Container Security

Previous chapters address a number of domestic agencies responsible for securing the country's ports of entry. Briefly, the greatest burden naturally falls to the Department of Homeland Security. Under the DHS umbrella is CBP, USCG, ICE, TSA and DNDO.[6] These DHS bodies collaborate internally and with other domestic government agencies to secure US ports of entry (see Chapter 3). At the international level, these domestic entities work regularly with foreign governments, companies and agencies. ICE works with investigatory units in countries of freight origin to properly determine those responsible for illegal behavior. The USCG and CBP are even more heavily involved abroad, specifically dealing with implementation and oversight of the Container Security Initiative (CSI) and the Customs-Trade Partnership Against Terrorism program (see next section). In both cases, US officials travel oversees to monitor activities at program ports and to assess their level of compliance guidelines established by the United States. In the case of C-TPAT, officials parlay with business entities (both domestic and international) to evaluate program compliance (CBP web page).

---

geological resources. US efforts to enhance its security by extending its borders to foreign lands and protecting the viability and security of sea channels and supply lanes is perhaps one way of geopolitically enhancing the country's general national security. For more on geopolitics and the geostrategies of great power countries, see Grygiel 2006, O'Sullivan 1986, and Spykman 1942.

5   Obviously, much of the security attention after 9/11 focused on securing airports and air transport. While there have been some measures in this regard, little containerized freight enters the US via airports. Usually goods imported by air are of much different packaging and are in smaller containers. Therefore, most of this discussion focuses on seaports, which affect almost all of our trading partners, and land entry ports, which affects mostly Canada and Mexico (see Chapter 2).

6   TSA is also heavily involved with international partners, though again this is primarily with regard to air transport security.

The Department of Homeland Security, however, is not alone in dealing with global supply chain operations. The Department of Energy is also involved, specifically with regards to nuclear nonproliferation where it works in close partnership with the recently created Domestic Nuclear Detection Office and with international partners. One of the gravest concerns regarding containerized freight is the potential for using a cargo container to ship nuclear materials from a foreign port to the United States, or even worse to deliver some sort of nuclear device to detonate at one of the nation's major seaports or border crossings.[7] Both the DOE and DNDO work with international partners to stem the flow of nuclear materials (GAO: DNDO 2009).

Finally, the Department of State also plays an important role. The policy of pushing US borders out and engaging foreign governments has increased the involvement of DOS in the area of port security. While much DOS attention with regard to port and supply chain security focuses heavily on anti-terrorism and nonproliferation, the department is involved in general security issues as well. In fact, DOS is the country's main negotiator and serves as the face of international port security. DOS employs diplomatic tactics to partner with international governments and encourages them to implement comprehensive and compatible security measures. For example, CSI is a bi-lateral agreement (a Declaration of Principles) negotiated between DOS and foreign customs agencies. DOS also advances the Proliferation Security Initiative (PSI), which began in 2003. The aim of PSI is to involve international governments in creating a multinational voluntary legal framework that allows for the interdiction of third party ships. To date, more than 90 countries are involved in PSI (DOS web page, 2009).

All of these domestic actors have experienced a dramatic shift in responsibilities surrounding their involvement in efforts to secure domestic ports of entry and to partner with foreign entities. Ultimately, these multiple agencies and departments work together in securing the nation's ports of entry and in helping to ensure that international ports are taking appropriate security measures as well.

International Organizations Working with the US to Monitor Container Traffic

The most relevant international actors involved with the United States on container security issues are foreign governments, foreign customs agencies, and business entities. Beyond these, there are two international organizations (IOs) that aim to streamline global maritime practices and general customs issues. US participation in each of these IOs is substantial, illustrating the relevance of the importance of power and influence in the international system. By becoming a significant player in IOs relevant to container security issues, the United States is in a better position to set agendas, advance strategies, and influence other members, thus

---

7 Many of the country's major seaports lie in close proximity to large cities. Los Angeles and New York are just two examples of cities where major population areas are in and around seaport infrastructure.

The International Politics of Container Security   71

building capital and exercising expertise in policies that will be eventually adopted by member states.

The International Maritime Organization (IMO), a United Nations entity, was created after World War II. Its mission is to maintain clean and safe waterways and foster international shipping. Currently, there are 168 members of the organization, which is headquartered in London.[8] Membership in and acceptance of the IMO's various protocols signals a country's dedication to fostering a level of acceptable governance in maritime travel and transport. Initially focused on safety and the environment, in recent years the IMO has expanded its role in regards to security of vessels and seaports. Most significantly is the 2002 passage of the International Ship and Port Security (ISPS) code for port vessels and facilities (see next section). Currently, the IMO also advances dockworker and ship worker training exercises and is in the process of creating an automated tracking system that would allow officials to monitor each container as it traverses the world's oceans (IMO web page). The IMO is not a supervisory body, and there is no mechanism for assured compliance with agreements other than potential ostracism of the noncompliant state. Maritime trade is a multi-billion dollar enterprise, so such ostracism could mean hefty economic consequences for violators (America's Container Ports 2009; International Interviews 2007-2008).

Focusing more on the economic side of international freight transport, the other IO of significance is the World Customs Organization (WCO), which is headquartered in Brussels. The WCO's mission is to harmonize and streamline the customs procedures of its 174 members. It collectively helps organize customs standards for its members, now covering "98% of global trade" (WCO web page). The organization's primary goal is to track and monitor goods as they are traded across international borders and to see that global customs agencies follow universal guidelines. Such guidelines include tracking procedures, manifests requirements and means of revenue collection. Like the IMO, the WCO paid only secondary attention to security issues prior to 9/11. With the increased attention of freight security, the WCO too has enhanced its attention to security areas (WCO web page 2009; International Interviews 2007-2008).

The United States has fostered relations with both the IMO and the WCO. For example, CBP is active in drafting and writing best practice recommendations for the security of the international supply chain that inform the guidelines and standards the WCO eventually considers and even adopts (CBP web page 2009). US influence with the IMO is also significant. As will be demonstrated, it was due to US insistence that a set of facility and vessel guidelines were created (see ISPS in next section), and the IMO was the means by which the United States achieved a degree of international adherence.

---

8   The United States is represented by the Coast Guard at IMO meetings. Aside from its official members, the IMO also has three associate members.

Joint Cooperative Programs

The United States, in conjunction with other governments, organizations and agencies has sought to advance security of the international supply chain. Regional partnerships are also in a unique position to encourage their members to heighten port security, which the United States has actively supported. Regional unions and trading blocs are an additional means by which states attempt to mediate anarchy, by giving up a degree of autonomy to make independent decisions.

The European Union, in particular, has taken on the container security issue. Another partnership worth highlighting briefly is the North America Free Trade Agreement (NAFTA), which has also put greater emphasis on security than might have been expected when it became law in the early 1990s. Other, less familiar trading blocks and regional agreements dealing with trade, (APEC and ASEAN in Asia, UNASUR and MERCOSUR in South America, CARICOM in the Caribbean, the Union of African States and OPEC) have taken steps toward enhanced trade security to keep up with the changing environment of containerized freight movement. Although pressure from the United States, the IMO and the WCO occurs, most of these regional organizations have made only minor advancements on port and container security.

The European Union

The European Union (EU) is a supranational organization[9] originally designed as an economic partnership. Since the 9/11 attacks the EU has taken strides to facilitate cooperation and compliance with international port security mandates. Simultaneously, it has passed legislation to further tighten security at ports within the Union's 27 member states. This is extensive, as the EU has 1,200 seaports within its jurisdiction.

The United States has certainly led efforts to advance freight and port security measures, but the EU has not been far behind. Initially, the EU agreed to various international and US agreements, and in recent years has advanced its own security requirements for member states (see Chapter 5). In 2005 the EU passed Directive 2005/65, which required all member states to enhance security at ports of entry beyond the IMO recommendations, instituting one of the world's most stringent security programs. The binding directive states that great attention should be given to the security of "people, infrastructure and equipment" at seaports and has a number of security related provisions. The EU has taken an active part in ensuring compliance with the Directive by way of routine and random port inspections

---

9 Though there is some discussion over the proper classification of the European Union, here it is described as a supranational organization because its legislative and executive bodies create rules and regulations that significantly affect the national policies of its diverse member states in numerous areas. Additionally, the EU has some enforcement capabilities through its judicial branch (Guérot 2008).

The security of containerized freight through European land and sea borders is of special significance due to the Schengen Agreement. Schengen is a program among many (22) EU members and some additional European countries (Iceland, Norway and Lichtenstein), which essentially eliminates national borders of participants.[10] Once inside the external Schengen border, the program ensures the free transfer of people and goods. Schengen borders are thought to be highly secure and countries wishing to join the agreement, especially those that might someday make up the periphery border, must meet stringent requirements. However, what Schengen means is that once a container has entered a European port or crossed a Schengen border, it can travel among the other partnership members – to The Netherlands, Italy, the Czech Republic, Portugal and elsewhere without undergoing further customs inspections ("Schengen Enlargement" 2009). So while the US has sought to harden its borders in recent years, Europe has worked toward opening at least its internal state borders.

The North American Free Trade Agreement

Though very different from the EU, the United States belongs to the North American Free Trade Agreement. NAFTA originated to advance trilateral trade with no intention of becoming a security bloc. However, as trade between Canada, the United States and Mexico has increased exponentially since implementation in 1994, the three countries have strong economic motivations to enforce consistent security regulations for incoming cargo at both US borders, and at all points of the North American periphery. Various agencies and programs within the NAFTA framework are attempting to heighten security measures and initiatives in a manner that furthers trilateral trade. For example, Canada and Mexico each have signed Smart Border Accords with the United States under DHS guidelines that provide a framework for sharing and monitoring the background information and credential checks of people driving cargo trucks into the United States (Treat 2002).

Asian Unions (ASEAN and APEC)

Two significant regional partnerships exist in Asia – the Association of Southeast Asian Nations (ASEAN) and the Asia Pacific Economic Cooperation (APEC). ASEAN was created in 1967 and is currently comprised of ten members. The current mission of the group is to develop along the lines of the EU to form a border free economic community. APEC, on the other hand was created in 1989 and includes 21 member states located in the Asian and Pacific regions (this

---

10   Simply being an EU member does not make a country part of the Schengen Agreement. Additional requirements and criteria must be met.

74   *Protecting Our Ports*

includes countries as diverse as Japan, the United States, China, South Korea, New Zealand, and Mexico).

Both organizations have been compelled, by US and international persuasion, to take action to encourage stronger maritime security measures among its members. In this regard APEC has been much more proactive than ASEAN (Bradford 2005). APEC organized meetings to examine maritime security as early as 2003 and has continued to advance the issue. They have begun to have joint drills and exercises among some members. In 2007, APEC drew upon the WCO's SAFE Framework of Standards (see next section) and developed a similar guideline known as the APEC Framework to which member countries are encouraged to adhere. ASEAN, though smaller in membership, has had more difficulty pushing for changes in maritime security. There is some hope that the cooperation of ASEAN states regarding land border issues will eventually lead to greater cooperation on seaport security. However, given the geographical and historical situation of some of its members, this has been short in coming. Territorial issues surrounding the South China Sea and the Celebes Sea have made and likely will continue to make this difficult. Should the organization truly aspire to become an EU of Southeast Asia, the organization will eventually have to begin to address some of its maritime issues (Mak 2008; Bradford 2005).

Latin American Groups (MERCOSUR, UNASUR and CARICOM)

While much of US attention regarding port security has focused on Europe and Asia, it is important to remember the geographical proximity of the United States to Central and South America. These are countries that export a number of goods to the United States on a yearly basis. They are also regions where drug trafficking, organized violence and even acts of terrorism occur. Beyond NAFTA, there are a number of other agreements between states in Latin America aimed at trade cooperation.

The most well known of these partnerships is MERCOSUR (the Southern Common Market), which began in 1991 as an economic union between Brazil, Uruguay, Argentina and Paraguay (Esteradeordal et al. 2001). The economic power of this organization is significant as most consider it to be the third largest global trading block after the European Union and NAFTA. Though incorporating free-trade zones among its members, there appears to be only minimal attention paid to seaport security. While the Port of Buenos Aries in Argentina and the Port of Santos in Brazil participate in the CSI program, they are among only a small group of ports in all of South America to do so (CBP web page). MERCOSUR, as an organization, has accomplished what is necessary to keep its ports functioning, but has not taken important steps toward enhanced container security (Oelsner 2009).

UNASUR, the Union of South American Nations, is a newly created partnership among 12 South American states. Created in 2008, UNASUR also molds itself on the European Union. Although it is not possible to assess its record regarding freight security given its recent creation, one of the stated goals of the union is to develop a Common Customs Union, which could potentially lead to greater attention to maritime security. However, it is unlikely that there will be much input from the United States, as Venezuela's President, Hugo Chavez has been vocal at union meetings about his unwillingness to work with the country (Pearson 2009).

Finally, some of the closest neighbors of the United States belong to the CARICOM, or Caribbean Community. While Caribbean countries have experienced significant lapses in freight protection, as security technologies and infrastructures lag far behind more affluent areas of the world, CARICOM has started to dedicate itself to improving the security of its exports. CARICOM created the Implementation Agency for Crime and Security (IMPACS) in July 2006, and it is currently attempting to draft regional implementation standards for ISPS certification that mirror US and EU models (Edmunds 2009).

The Union of African States and OPEC

The Union of African States is a declaration on the part of various member states to jointly accelerate the process of integration into the global economy while enhancing joint efforts to address shared economic, political, and social problems (African Union web page 2009). In October 2009, a summit of African states met to examine the issue of maritime security from a regional perspective. The summit was a realization that African states have significant maritime security needs that are not being met. Hijacking of vessels, theft of goods and delayed transport are notorious problems for much of African trade. Recognizing the benefits that could be derived from cooperation among members of the Union of African States (and presumably non-members), the pamphlet for the 2009 summit explained "Despite the continent's waters including some of the world's busiest waterways and at least four chokepoints, Africa has little in the way of an integrated capability or capacity to survey, police or secure its own waters of ports…" This realization is perhaps delayed, but it is a positive step for the continent, which has in general fallen behind on this issue (Engelbreacht 2009).

Finally, the Organization of the Petroleum Exporting Countries, which was established in 1960, has only implemented minimal requirements regarding international port security measures. OPEC members are primarily in Africa and the Middle East, though there are members in Asia as well as Venezuela and Ecuador in South America. The goal of the organization is to monitor and synchronize petroleum costs and supplies among member states. They also work to ensure a constant supply of petroleum to importing countries. Given this latter mission, it is surprising that OPEC has paid relatively little attention to secure seaports among member states. Perhaps this is a result of their monopoly on petroleum exports and their confidence that their products will be in demand regardless. Or they might simply expect shippers to take on the responsibility of safe loading and transport. Even when the IMO pushed OPEC ports to become ISPS compliant, most members were slow to respond and did so only at the last moment with little political will (Ambrogi 2004). OPEC does not appear to have addressed the issue of maritime security as an organization in any large or meaningful way. Evidence of this comes from Nigeria, an OPEC member, which only in early October of 2009 began exploring the possibility of creating a federal Maritime Security Agency to protect its petroleum exports, which are regularly stolen or obstructed by insurgents ("Nigeria Considers" 2009). The current absence of such an agency highlights the lack of attention paid to the issue among some OPEC states.

International Policies and Programs

Over the last decade, the United States has encouraged, promoted and negotiated a number of significant programs and policies that rely on international cooperation. US efforts to heighten domestic security in general and international seaport security in particular, have been extensive and in many ways have brought port security into greater focus. In an attempt to address some of the most important policies, it is helpful to categorize them into policies that seek to secure the supply chain via en route containers, and those that attempt to secure ports of origin (America's Container Ports 2009) (see Table 4.1). In the first case the goal is to increase security past the port, be it along road or water routes. In the second instance, the aim is to further enhance security at international ports so as to strengthen US security at home. Both types of policies are manifestations of the desire to push US borders out and increase the layers of defense.

Table 4.1   Secure Freight Policies and Programs

Port of Origin	Supply Chain
24-Hour Manifest Rule	96-Hour Rule
ISPS	C-TPAT
CSI	PIP/AEO
Megaports	SAFE Standards
SFI	FAST
	MTSA

US Influenced Policies and Programs Aimed at Securing the International Supply Chain

Adhering to the plan to extend borders out, there are a number of US and international programs that seek to enhance security along the global supply chain. These include domestic policies such as the USCG 96-Hour Rule, MTSA and others. They also include policies advanced by international actors: SAFE Framework of Standards and the Authorized Economic Operator (AEO).

US officials want to know the shipping plans of vessels preparing to enter US waters long before those vessels are in close proximity to the country. Therefore, shortly after 2001, the USCG established a four day pre-arrival requirement.[11] The 96-Hour Rule or Advance Notice of Arrival (ANOA) requires that all large trading vessels submit an itinerary and manifest to the Coast Guard 96 hours before reaching US waters. The information required provides an initial indication of vessel plans and cargo. The document submitted to the Coast Guard must provide sufficient evidence to demonstrate that a standard of safety has been met (Mayer 2004). Failure to submit the necessary documents can lead to transport delay. In the worst case it can result in the US Coast Guard boarding noncompliant vessels that enter US waterways (Agency Interviews 2006-2008).

Just over a year after the events of September 11, the US President signed the Maritime Transportation Security Act. The purpose of MTSA was to create a tracking system for trading vessels. Therefore, MTSA requires that all ships entering US waterways be outfitted with an Automatic Identification System (AIS), which sends readings to US port officials indicating the positioning and identity of ships. The policy also requires shippers to provide a security plan to DHS before they can off load at US seaports. MTSA also recognized the importance of international ports establishing a mechanism (a check list) for US review of port security procedures abroad (Establishment of US 2004).

The Customs-Trade Partnership Against Terrorism program, which partners government agencies and private companies (domestic and international) to enhance international supply chain security, is another attempt to secure freight beyond ports of entry. C-TPAT is particularly important because it involves private (business) entities in the security process. In fact, Secretary Bonner recognized it as the "largest federal government public/private partnership in US history" (CBP website 2009). In many regards, it is business that has the greatest investment, certainly financially, in maintaining a reliable balance between security and economy (see Chapter 6). C-TPAT recognizes this (Szyiowicz 2004). There are a set of safe and secure transport guidelines that C-TPAT participants must observe and implement. Once a shipper or company attains certification, these partners can enjoy less obstructed access to US shipping ways and trading ports. CBP oversees C-TPAT companies who show that they not only meet the initial program criteria, but that they continue to do so at various intervals after official certification.

The C-TPAT concept has been rather successful and emulated around the world. New Zealand and Japan have implemented similar programs and have signed mutual recognition agreements with the United States. The US has also developed C-TPAT style programs with its NAFTA partners. In Canada, Partners in Protection (PIP) allows private organizations to sign an agreement with the Canadian Border Services Agency (CBSA) as a goodwill commitment to enhance security, exchange information, and increase employee awareness of security issues. In return, these organizations gain an enhanced reputation with the trading community and can participate in the Free and Secure Trade program. FAST is a joint US-Canada and US-Mexico venture involving CBP and CBSA. It is designed

---

11   Previously, there was a 24-hour request which officials extended after 9/11.

as a commercial process to offer pre-approval clearances to importers, carriers and registered drivers to expedite trade after companies have demonstrated the implementation of security procedures compatible with C-TPAT and PIP. At the Mexican border, voluntary partnerships to expedite trade and enhance security exist through FAST and remain under CBP jurisdiction. FAST requires detailed personal information from all applicants. Key benefits of being a FAST (commercial) member includes having access to dedicated FAST custom lanes at certain border crossings and having a shorter advance time-frame for truckers to provide their advance manifests (30 minutes as opposed to 60 for non-FAST members) (Treat 2002).

Recently, the EU too took a similar approach with the Authorized Economic Operator program. However, while programs elsewhere are almost identical to C-TPAT and have resulted in mutual recognition agreements, the EU's AEO structure is quite different. Though based on the same premise that shippers can help create security past the port, AEO is much more specific in its requirements than C-TPAT and it focuses both on import and export activities. To date, the US and EU have been unable to agree upon a mutual recognition of both programs (McDermott 2007). This means that companies trading in both the US and the EU, for now, must be certified by both programs to reap the benefits of expedited travel (see Chapter 5 on AEO).

Finally, another significant policy to enhance overall security of containerized shipments is the WCO's SAFE Framework of Standards. The SAFE Framework is a list of minimum standards that members should follow to keep trade moving in a secure manner. These standards deal with harmonization of procedures, consistent risk management protocols, outbound inspection and business incentives. The SAFE Framework also seeks to increase the number of containers screened and places heightened emphasis on detection technology (WCO website).

Policies and Programs Aimed at Securing International Ports of Origin

While it is important to protect containers as they are en route, the major concern of the United States has been to enhance security infrastructures at foreign ports. The policies and programs in this group include the 24-hour rule, the Container Security Initiative, the Megaports initiative and the International Ship and Port Security code. These are all either US led programs or policies in which the United States has been heavily involved and for which the country has advocated.

In 2003, CBP instituted the 24-hour manifest rule. This requires that all trading vessels sailing to a US port must report the contents of their cargo 24 hours before not just leaving, but before lading (loading) at a foreign port. Information required is rather specific. CBP officials need to know the designated number for the importer of record, consignee number, seller address and container loading location among other data points. The 2006 passage of the SAFE Port Act included provisions for an Importer Security Filing (ISF) program. The ISF, or more commonly, 10+2, requires that shippers, carriers and owners include two additional pieces of information – vessel stowage plans and container status messages – in their CBP filing ("10+2 Program" 2009). The 24-hour manifest rule gives CBP the opportunity to scrutinize records of container contents, origination, and shipper history to assess the degree of threat. This information is cross referenced against shipper histories and vessel routes and origins among other data points found within the Automated Targeted System (ATS) to determine anomalies. The data is also used to double-check container contents when they are off loaded at a US seaport. This triangulation of data is important for utilization at both foreign and domestic ports to find suspicious containers that warrant additional inspection (CBP web page, Agency Interviews 2006-2008).

Along with the 24-hour rule, CBP began laying the groundwork for the Container Security Initiative. The CSI program is a series of bi-lateral agreements between the US Department of State and foreign government customs agencies. There are a number of security guidelines to which partners agree, and with the help of CBP and Coast Guard officials, they work to enhance the development and implementation of advanced screening techniques. The program requires members to agree to oversight from CBP agents and requires foreign custom agents to share information with US officials (GAO 2005). The benefits for CSI ports include enhanced security clearance and a quicker process once ships reach US ports.

Though former CBP Commissioner Robert Bonner often gets credit for the creation of the CSI program, he is quick to point out the immensely important role played by the government of The Netherlands, and specifically their Ambassador to the United States. Seaports in Canada were the first to reach agreements as CSI ports. However, it was The Netherlands that really made the difference. Once The Netherlands (home to Europe's largest seaport in Rotterdam) signed their CSI agreement in September of 2002, a domino effect resulted. Dutch participation gave legitimacy to the program (Agency Interviews 2008). As of 2009, there are 58 international ports in the program which covers about 85% of US bound container traffic (DHS website).

All foreign ports are eligible for eventual CSI membership, yet another strategy has been to focus on some of the largest ports and specifically to help those ports build infrastructure specifically aimed at nonproliferation of nuclear materials. The Megaports initiative, directed by the Department of Energy, encourages large ports, which "serve as regional hubs for containerized cargo," to improve their radiation detection technology with guidance and assistance from US officials (Lewis et al. 2002, 1). At these large ports, which are potentially viable options for terrorists and smugglers to ship dangerous cargo to the United States, officials have deployed monitoring systems to detect nuclear and radioactive materials in shipping containers (Lewis et al. 2002).

Finally, one of the earliest and most widely hailed steps to enhance international port security was the IMO's ISPS code. While implemented through the IMO, significant US influence and lobbying assisted in the quick passage of the ISPS program. In fact, in an unusual twist, rather than introduce ISPS as an independent directive, the code was an amendment added to the Safety of Life At Sea update of 2002 (see Chapter 5). Packaging ISPS with SOLAS assisted in and streamlined the code's passage (Homeport 2009).

ISPS guidelines address seagoing vessels upwards of 500 gross tonnage and the port facilities that handle such vessels. The program institutes three levels of security preparedness based on perceived threat. At the initial level fencing, lighting, cameras and the securing of personnel entering and leaving ISPS areas of a seaport are required. As security threats heighten, so do restrictions on the port. Ships are likewise required to have a high level of security, which is the responsibility of the flagship country or a third party agent hired for such purposes. ISPS passed the IMO in 2002, and went into effect in 2004 with individual ports working to earn certification. Of the seaports we visited, more than half had been ISPS certified and others were working toward that goal (Homeport 2009; International Interviews 2007-2008).

Since IMO policies are not binding, there is some flexibility in how individual countries interpret ISPS requirements. This allows individual ports and governments to address their concerns and capacities. ISPS certification comes from the member government, not the IMO, leading to some criticism regarding enforcement. In an effort to help with ISPS compliance, the US Coast Guard works closely with other members of the IMO to help officials at international ports meet acceptable standards. These Coast Guard personnel are International Port Security Liaison Officers (IPSLO). If an IPSLO determines that an international port does not comply with the ISPS code, the result could be the delay of goods going to the United States and other foreign ports (Homeport 2009; Agency Interviews 2006-2007; International Interviews 2007-2008).

The above policies are illustrative of the United States exerting its influence abroad in the realm of containerized freight security issues. This process, easily encapsulated by the phrase "pushing borders out," involves the country persuading other governments to cooperate and participate in US designed programs. The weight of US power is evident in this process. The impetus for heightened security is placed on foreign governments even though the motivation stems from US defense interests. Such imposition of US interest on foreign counterparts has not always been well received, and certainly has implications for state sovereignty.

European and Asian Perceptions About US Leadership

International partners have made and are continuously asked to make a number of expensive and timely alterations to their port policies and infrastructures. US economic and political influence and the apparent unidirectional focus of many policies have not gone unnoticed abroad. The more requirements, the louder are the questions regarding state sovereignty. The United States has for almost a decade been dictating how other states secure and operate their seaports (and in the case of Mexico and Canada, their land borders as well). There are a number of concerns international partners voice about US led policies and programs. As time goes by, it has become apparent that international port security and overarching supply chain security has its own set of politics relating to perceptions of, and relations with, the United States.

The United States initially had a great deal of political capital in this area following the events of 9/11, when the country was able to advance a number of programs and policies. Less than a decade later, this has changed, resulting in a more skeptical international perception of the US role. The interrelated concerns with US led policies discussed below revolve around issues of reciprocity, a perceived lack of US knowledge of international procedures, concerns about external and internal politicking, conflated threat perception and specific program requirements.

Port and Country Variation

Many concerns of foreign actors emanate from a perceived lack of US knowledge about international port activities. Numerous port officials, especially in Europe, expressed concern that the United States creates and implements programs and policies under the assumption that all ports are similar in structure and operation to US seaports. Europeans see this as at best an oversight by US officials, and at worst as arrogance and ignorance. Though not as vocal, representatives at Asian ports had similar complaints (International Interviews 2007-2008).

It is important to remember that there are multiple models of port operations around the world. Ports have unique concerns pertinent to their own domestic situations and constraints. For example, in Europe much movement of containerized freight travels via train or river barge (to a much greater extent than in the United States). Scanning from barges requires a completely different infrastructure than scanning containers that enter a port via truck or even rail. This could slow the movement of goods substantially. Also, roll-on-roll-off ships transport a number of goods between states. These vessels are more like ferries and at times they may also include passengers. This is especially the case with goods going across the English Channel between France and England. Another example is that of the Port of Singapore, which relies a great deal on off shore container loading and unloading, which also requires unique security measures (International Interviews 2007-2008).

Additionally, there is the issue of identification cards and background checks, which are procedures the United States is promoting. In the United States all people who work at port facilities as well as truck drivers are issued identification cards and routinely undergo background checks, the information from which shows up when their ID cards are checked.[12] However, some countries, for example Belgium and Japan, will never be able to implement universal background checks due to ridged

---

12   For increased uniformity and centralization, the US now uses the Transportation Worker Identification Credential (TWIC) card (see Chapter 3).

82   *Protecting Our Ports*

privacy laws. In other places, like The Netherlands, officials can conduct such in-depth checks only if there is information to arouse suspicion (see Chapter 7).

Reciprocity

Another issue of concern is that of reciprocity. The United States places unapologetic attention on imports over exports and while there is *de jure* reciprocity, few interviewed felt that reciprocity was a serious offer. The CSI program, while regarded as successful, provides evidence of the perceived lack of reciprocity of the United States. The program requires that CBP and Coast Guard officials oversee and monitor CSI port security activities. IPSLO representatives go to the port as a means of oversight to ensure that the partner ports are operating under CSI compliance. To the best of our knowledge, there are only a few foreign officials – Japanese and Canadian – that station their customs officials at US ports (Implementation of CSI 2009). This lack (or perceived lack) of reciprocity gives some international officials the impression that the United States is arrogantly dictating procedure with little willingness to engage in true "give and take."

Domestic Politicking

A number of international port officials also suggest that their countries and ports often find themselves caught in the middle of US domestic politicking (International Interviews 2007-2008). The best example of this is the situation with Dubai Ports World where both Democrats and Republicans attempted to stand strong on security and to distance themselves, before the 2006 midterm elections, from a President whose popularity was waning. After the elections, the two parties fought to be the party of national security with the Democrats seeking to further enhance port security with the passage of the 100% international scanning requirement (see Chapter 2).

In Chapter 2 we argue that the freight security issue has been heavily politicized by politicians, the media and others with an interest in using fear of a new attack to their advantage. These actions certainly have domestic effects, but they also have international ramifications. US foreign partners observe this politicking and view themselves as being caught in the middle or possibly even used to the advantage of certain interests in the United States. Officials at foreign ports are left questioning the true value and intent behind US policies – do such policies and programs actually enhance security, or are they simply a means to a political end?

Conflated Threat

Linked to the politicization of the issue domestically is the growing feeling among international officials that the United States is conflating the threat of terrorism. Theft, smuggling, human trafficking and safety are the concerns that international port officials described as their top security related priorities. With the exception of officials at the Port of London[13] few seaport representatives we interviewed felt that terrorism was a major threat to their port (Interviews 2007-2008).

Many officials we interviewed claimed to be sufficiently confident that the initial post-9/11 port security measures (MTSA, ISPS and even CSI) had created a secure environment at their seaports – going beyond these programs, some argued, is creating a situation of diminishing returns. In large part, those interviewed claimed that the early programs were successful because they did not simply limit the potential for terrorist activity, but simultaneously addressed concerns with theft and smuggling. Adding subsequent measures simply to strengthen security against terrorism, a concern of the US government not necessarily of their own governments, appears superfluous to many (International Interviews 2007-2008).

The Costs Associated with US Mandates

Each new program put into place requires technological and infrastructural advances at the world's seaports. Additional policies create significant barriers for international partners due to the financial costs of such upgrades. While some ports may have the resources to implement all the latest technologies and meet new detection requirements, others simply do not have the funding at their disposal. There is a great deal of concern that smaller ports will be forced to limit traffic or close down and that the expenses (financial and infrastructural) of bigger ports could over burden even the most solvent seaports.

In terms of infrastructure, some ports can simply expand no further. For example, the extremely large Port of Antwerp in Belgium is along a river and already backs up to its national border with The Netherlands. There is simply no room to expand, which added security lanes would likely require (International Interviews 2008). Other ports sit in densely populated urban areas where land for development is also limited. These are situations that a number of domestic ports face as well (America's Container Ports 2009). One option for ports with enough water clearance might be to take Singapore's lead and operate more off-shore loading and unloading, though as already mentioned, this creates its own set of security obstacles.

The Secure Freight Initiative[14]

By far, the largest point of global contention revolves around the passage of the Secure Freight Initiative in 2007. Many international officials are particularly

---

13   The Port of London is in an area that runs near the House of Parliament and is within a country that has a history of terrorist attacks – various IRA bombings, Lockerbie and July 7, 2005 bombings.

14   In the fall of 2006, the US Congress passed the Security and Accountability For Every (SAFE) Port Act which authorized the Secure Freight Initiative (SFI). By 2007 the program was passed as part of the 9/11 Commission Act. SFI calls for 100% radiation

84 *Protecting Our Ports*

concerned with SFI, based on the mandated 100% scanning of all goods coming from foreign ports destined for the United States. While there are a number of loopholes and extensions, many in the international community remain displeased. Ports around the world are unsure how they can even begin to find the money, the infrastructure, the technology or the political will to make the changes that SFI requires – again, particularly at the smaller ports. Moreover, many foreign port authorities are particularly concerned about the impact on their port's efficiency if they are to implement a 100% scanning program. Even the US led pilot program operators testified before Congress that there were inherent problems with SFI and that in any case it would not likely be ready for a 2012 implementation date (Congressional Testimony 2008).

Additionally, some officials expressed concern that US motives are malicious in this instance and that the United States may be using SFI as a means to limit imports in order to increase the sale of domestic goods (Interviews 2006-2008). The size of European states also means that competition can be quite high among ports. Officials in Athens expressed concerns that their potential inability to immediately meet the SFI standards would result in shippers going to Italian ports for more direct shipment to the United States.

There is growing restlessness among the international partners – the same international partners upon which the US relies to provide security to protect our national ports of entry. The issues highlighted here – domestic politicking, reciprocity, lack of international port knowledge – have led to heightened concerns over US programs and mandates. The requirements of SFI in particular have port officials around the world frustrated and in some instances angry. In the concluding section, we discuss ways in which the US can reorient its approach to international port security so as to ameliorate some of the aforementioned concerns.

Conclusion

Politics surrounding the international components of container security have grown in parallel to security policy developments in the international supply chain. US policies in this area rely heavily on international actors to implement programs designed to enhance domestic defense. The ramifications of these policies are widespread and not always positive.

At the international level, containerized freight security is quite complex. Numerous agents are involved (individual states, customs agencies, IOs and regional trading blocs) and a myriad of programs have been put in place (ISPS, CSI, C-TPAT) – all of which are laden with US preferences. Yet, today there are more and more officials abroad questioning US actions than in the months and years immediately following September 11, 2001. US strategy and the implementation of the programs

---

scanning at foreign ports of all US bound containers. The 9/11 Act update requires that SFI go into effect at foreign ports by 2012 (see Chapter 2).

it advances have implications for the country's relations with international partners and the progress that should and could be taken to continually work together to enhance freight security. As we have shown, the international political environment is shifting and the United States must take steps to retain its influence and achieve its port security objectives. To do this, the US should focus on how it frames the issue of port security. It should also recognize how unilateral actions are sometimes perceived abroad.

Framing

A significant problem has been the inability of the United States to more effectively frame international freight security as an issue that affects all countries. As discussed, few of US partners see terrorism as a direct threat to their seaports. They are much more concerned with issues of theft and smuggling. Yet, as more and more requirements are put in place for trade with the United States, the message its international partners are receiving is that they must secure their (and consequently US) ports of entry from terrorism. This framing may be effective in places like Great Britain or Israel, countries which have witnessed their own terrorist events, but at ports like Athens and Taicang it does not resonate.

The most successful tactic that the US has used to encourage participation in its freight security programs is through the use of economic incentives. C-TPAT for example allows for participants to move more quickly through security steps both abroad and in the United States, creating a functional green lane. CSI also uses economic incentives as a means for partnership inducement. Ships leaving CSI ports face slightly less scrutiny, and therefore fewer time delays, when they reach US ports because their ports of origin are known to have achieved an accepted level of security, whereas non-CSI ports cannot provide a recognized guarantee (CBP website 2009).

Rather than simply looking at economic advantages as a means for incentivizing port programs and rules, it would behoove US officials to more effectively use economics as a framing tool. By focusing more on the economic benefits that cooperation can generate and less on the security (terrorist) related aspects, the US can more effectively frame port security. This new focus might also help dispel the feeling among many of our international partners that port security developments aim solely at securing the United States.

Message

US policies and actions on port security send messages to foreign counterparts. Political maneuvering, the national focus and the tenants of US strategy to push borders out, whether perceived correctly or incorrectly, cues foreign officials how to respond to US port security policies and programs. US representatives and indeed the US Congress should recognize that they are asking other countries to make and support significant changes, and should constantly work to ensure that those countries understand what is asked of them and that they understand the shared benefits that can be reaped. It is important that US policies and programs make an effort to appeal to international concerns so that the sovereignty compromise that they have made to participate in US programs is not viewed as an unfair exchange. The United States can better accomplish this by making greater efforts to consider the perceptions of international actors. It should also be cognizant of the differences in global port facility operations (infrastructural, geographical and political) and the financial and practical viability of its programs in given ports.

One of the most obvious ways to do this is to enhance reciprocity. This means not only allowing (and indeed encouraging) foreign officials to provide oversight to policy implementation at US ports, but it also means an effort to extend US focus to it own exports. Enhanced reciprocity means that the United States should be willing to scan the millions of full and empty containers that it ships abroad. This would indicate that the United States is committed to not just securing its own ports of entry, but that it is genuinely concerned with the security of the entire containerized freight system. US officials are quick to point out that most of their programs do ensure reciprocity. The CSI program does allow for foreign officials to visit US ports. However, most port officials we spoke with did not feel that this was a genuine offer. A little more effort to reiterate the desire for international officials to not just visit US ports, but to participate and collaborate to some degree, would likely incur greater willingness to cooperate with US designed policies.

It is important to keep in mind that there are a number of conferences and working groups of US and international partners. Despite this, many international officials continue to complain about a lack of give and take regarding US port of entry mandates. The complaint is that the US plays by its own rules and does not always undergo the same procedures that it is asking international ports to undergo.

In a world characterized by anarchy, lacking a central authority, states often agree to give up a degree of their sovereignty for the benefits of joint activity. However, partners to the bargain need to feel that the arrangement is mutually beneficial and that they have not compromised too much sovereignty. When one partner uses too much influence to push policies that the other must abide by without collaboration, reciprocity or input, progress is prevented. After examining this issue of cooperation and balancing state sovereignty in relation to containerized freight security, evidence suggests that dissent among some partners is growing. In the next chapter, we continue our examination of the relationship between the United States and its international partners by exploring the development of an International Maritime Security Regime.

Bibliography

"10+2 Program: Importer Presentation," February 12, 2009. *Customs and Border Protection*, available at http://www.cbp.gov/linkhandler/cgov/trade/cargo_ security/carriers/security_filing/10_plus_prgm.ctt/10_plus_prgm.ppt.

African Union web page, available at www.africa-union.org. Retrieved October 2009.

Ambrogi, Stephano. 2004. "New Anti-Terrorism Law May Deliver Whammy to OPEC Exports," *Indian Express Limited*, available at http://www.indianexpress.com/oldStory/43219/#.

"America's Container Ports: Fright Hubs that Connect Our Nation to Global Markets." 2009. *US Department of Transportation Research and Innovative Technology Administration* (Washington, DC).

"Border Barriers Come Down for New Schengen Members," December 21, 2007. *Sofia News Agency*, available at http://www.novinite.com/view_news.php?id=88748.

Bradford, John. Summer 2005. "The Growing Prospects for Maritime Security Cooperation in Southeast Asia," *Naval War College Review*, Vol. 58, No.3, 63-86.

Congressional Testimony of CBP Deputy Commissioner Jayson Ahern. June 12, 2008. Available at http://www.cbp.gov/xp/cgov/newsroom/congressional_test/pilot_ports.xml.

Customs and Border Protection. 2008. "Commissioner Testifies on Land Border Enforcement Plans," *CBP.com*, available at http://www.cbp.gov/xp/cgov/newsroom/congressional_test/land_border_prog.xml.

Department of Homeland Security web page, available at http://www.dhs.gov/index.shtm.

Department of State web page, available at http://www.state.gov/t/isn/c10390.htm.

"Directive 2005/65of the European Parliament and of the Council: On Enhancing Port Security," October 26, 2005. *Official Journal of the European Union*, available at http://eur-lex.europa.e/LexUriServ/LexUriServ.do?uri=OJ:L:2005:310:0028:0039:EN:PDF.

Edmunds, Anton. 2009. "Caribbean Maritime Economic Security Program," *Caribbean Central American Action*, available at http://www.c-caa.org/pdf/CARICOMMaritimeEconomicSecurityPresentation.pdf.

Engelbrecht, Leon. 2009. "Defense Web Maritime Security Conference Successful," *Maritime Security Africa*, October 19, 2009, available at http://www.defenceweb.co.za/index.php?option=com_eventreg&task=show_event&eventname=Maritime&eventid=3&Itemid=406.

Esteradeordal, Antoni, Junichi Goto and Raul Saez. 2001. "The New Regionalism in the Americas: The Case of Mercosur," *Journal of Economic Integration,* Vol. 16, No.2, 180-202.

"GAO (Government Accountability Office): DNDO Should Improve Planning to Better Address Gaps, Vulnerabilities in Nuclear Detection." March 12, 2009, available at http://aero-defense.ihs.com/news/2009/gao-dndo-nuclear-detection-031209.htm.

Gross, Leo. 1948. "The Peace of Westphalia: 1648-1948," *The American Journal of International Law*, Vol. 42, No.1, 20-41.

Grygiel, Jakub J. 2006. *Great Powers and Geopolitical Change* (Baltimore: Johns Hopkins University Press).

Guérot, Ulrike. 2008. "State Building and the EU's Supra National Momentum," *Global Policy Forum*, available at http://www.globalpolicy.org/component/content/article/173/30543.html.

Guiraudon, Virginie and Gallya Lahav. 2000. "A Reappraisal of the State Soverighty Debate: The Case of Migration Control," *Comparative Political Studies*, Vol. 33, No. 2, 163-195.

Homeport. "The ISPS Code," *US Department of Homeland Security: United States Coast Guard*, available at http://homeport.uscg.mil/mycg/portal/ep/channelView.do?channelId=-18389&channelPage=/ep/channel/default.jsp&pageTypeId=13489. Retrieved October 2009.

"Implementation of Container Security Initiative (CSI) with Canada," *Ministry of Finance Japan*, available at http://www.mof.go.jp/english/tariff/ka210121e_b.htm. Retrieved 2009.

International Maritime Organization (IMO) web page, available at http://www.imo.org/.

Krasner, Stephen. Winter 1995. "Compromising Westphalia," *International Security*, Vol. 20, No. 3, 115-151.

Lewis, Brian, Alan Erera and Chelsea C. White III. July 2002, "Port Security and Efficiency – A US Perspective," *Port of Singapore Magazine*, 6-9.

"LA/Long Beach February Port Cargo Down 36.6 pct yr/yr," March 18, 2009. *Hellenic Shipping News Worldwide*, available from http://www.hellenicshippingnews. com/index.php?option=com_ content&task=view&id=40430&Itemid=79.

Mak, J.N. April 2008. *Sovereignty in ASEAN and the Problem of Maritime Cooperation in the South China Sea*, Working Paper No. 156. (Singapore: S. Rajaratnam School of International Studies). Available at http://www.gees.org/documentos/Documen-02975.pdf.

"Maritime Security Africa 2009," October 2009. Conference Pamphlet, available at http://www.defenceweb.co.za/index.php?option=com_eventreg&task=show_event&eventname=Maritime&eventid=3&Itemid=406.

McDermott, Will and Emery. 2007. "New EU Customs Programme: Authorised Economic Operator." *Newsletter.* Available at http://www.mwe.com/index.cfm/fuseaction/publications.nldetail/object_id/61581f82-7f64-4c88-b797-c2e63964ed1a.cfm.

Mearsheimer, John J. 2003. *The Tragedy of Great Power Politics* (New York: W.W. Norton & Co.).

"Nigeria Considers Maritime Security Agency in Delta Region," October 7, 2009. *Reuters*, available at http://www.defenceweb.co.za/index.php?option=com_co ntent&task=view&id=4458&Itemid=363.

Oelsner, Andrea. 2009. "Consensus and Governance in Mercosur: The Evolution of the South American Security Agenda," *Security Dialogue,* Vol. 40, No. 2, 191-212.

O'Sullivan, Patrick. 1986. *Geopolitics* (New York: St. Martin's Press).

Pearson, Tamara. 2009. "Venezuela Tells UNASUR Meeting, US 'Talking About War,'" *Venezuela Analysis*, August 31, 2009, available at http://www.venezuelanalysis.com/news/4755.

Public Law 110-53. 9/11 Commission Act. *The Library of Congress*, available at http://www.thomas.gov/cgi-bin/bdquery/z?d110:HR00001:@@@L& summ2=m&.

Public Law 109-347. SAFE Port Act. *The Library of Congress*, available at http://www.thomas.gov/cgi-bin/bdquery/D?d109:2:./temp/~bdQmg2::|/bss/ d109query.html|.

Reinicke, Wolfgang. 1997. "Global Public Policy," *Foreign Affairs.* Vol. 76, No.6, 127-138.

"Schengen Enlargement," March 2009. *Europa: Justice and Home Affairs-Freedom, Security and Justice*, available at http://ec.europa.eu/justice_home/ fsj/freetravel/schenge n/fsj_freetrave l_schengen_en.htm.

Spykman, John Nicholas. 1942. *America's Strategy in World Politics: The United States and the Balance of Power* (New York: Harcourt, Brace and Company).

"Study: Economic Impact of 9/11 Was Short Lived," July 9, 2009. *NBC Los Angeles. Lived*, available at http://www.nbclosangeles.com/news/business/ Study-bin-Ladens-Strategy-Was-Short-Lived.html.

Szyliowicz, Joseph. 2004. "International Transportation Security," *Review of Policy Research*, Vol. 21, No. 3, 351-368.

Treat, Jonathan. 2002. "A New, Improved US-Mexican Border? Smart Border to Weed Out Terrorists, Offer Frequent Crosser Plan," *America's Program*, available at http://americas.irc-online.org/commentary/2002/0203immig. html.

Waltz, Kenneth. 1979. *Theory of International Politics* (Boston, MA: McGraw-Hill)

Weber, Max. 1919. "Politik als Beruf: Politics as a Profession," in H.H. Gerth and C.W. Mills (ed.), *From Max Weber* (New York: Oxford University Press, 1946), 77-128.

Wendt, Alexander. Spring 1992. "Anarchy is What States Make of It: The Social Construction of Power Politics," *International Organization*, Vol. 46, No.2, 391-425.

World Customs Organization (WCO) web page, available at http://www.wcoomd. org/home.htm.

Chapter 5

Global Governance and an International Maritime Security Regime

In August 2003, Fiji police found a stowaway in a shipping container originating from New Zealand. The man had been in the container for eight days ("Fiji Police" 2003). Two years earlier a man made himself a comfortable living area in a freight container travelling from Egypt to Canada. Authorities discovered and apprehended the stowaway during a scheduled offloading stop in Italy ("Egyptian Stowaway" 2001). Other container related events have had even great consequences. The 1998 bombings of the US Embassies in Kenya and Tanzania, which killed over 200 people, were the work of Al Qaida linked operatives. The weapons and materials used in the attack were smuggled using cargo containers ("Troubled Waters" 2004). In another example, in 2004 a container became a weapon against Israel's Ashdod Port facilities. Two suicide bombers from the Gaza Strip used a container with a fake wall to travel to Ashdod, enter the port and detonate a built-in bomb ("Suicide Bombing" 2004). These events make it apparent that containers can pose a potential security threat. But, the incidents also illustrate the very international nature of that threat. Maritime security, in this era of globalization, is indeed an international concern requiring joint action.

As discussed in Chapter 4, the United States has taken the lead in calling for more international cooperation and convergence of policies and procedures for the review of containerized shipments and the maintenance of security at the world's seaports. Examining the post-9/11 political environment, it is clear that the focus of the United States is on national security concerns, viewing additional international security as a positive externality. At the same time, the United States relies on international cooperation for implementation of policies and procedures that strengthen the security and safety of imports to the United States. In this chapter, we examine the ramifications of US actions related to maritime security and to the creation of what has become an International Maritime Security Regime (IMSR). Drawing from international relations and international regime theory, we also examine the motivations of the United States and the international partners who accept US leadership and choose to cooperate in this regime. Therefore, this chapter addresses the following questions:

- What is an international regime?
- How has the International Maritime Security Regime developed?
- What is the current and future role of the United States in this regime?

In this chapter we push beyond the international politics of container security and explore the development of an International Maritime Security Regime. First, there is an introduction of international relations theory and an exploration of the *regime* concept in the IMSR context. Next, we address the questions of state interest and motivations as well as international concerns based on the tenants of regime theory. Finally, we discuss the future of the regime and the challenges it will face in the coming years. Ultimately, we determine that a US-led IMSR has developed, though the leadership position of the United States in the regime is not as absolute as it once was.

International Relations Theory and State Behavior

International relations (IR) scholars have long believed that we can best explain state behavior by examining how states react to and perceive the international environment. Do states feel the need to balance other states, do they seek partnerships for absolute gains or do they coalesce with other states they view as having similar values? Do they mainly seek security, stability or similarity? Though there exist numerous variations within each worldview, most scholars are adherents to some form of realism, neoliberalism or constructivism. Briefly explaining these views of the international environment will help us understand the situations in which international regimes can form.

Realism has been a dominant approach in the international relations literature for about 60 years. Realists[1] believe that the international environment is characterized by anarchy[2] and self-help (see Chapter 4) where states, because they are rational actors, must take steps to protect themselves and their interests. Often they must do this by force or coercion. Because power is a central theme and conflict is always possible and probable, states must balance, attain or store power to ensure future security. Therefore, states are motivated to operate in terms of relative gains where states view their capabilities and international position in relation to other states in the international system.

---

1 To learn more about realism, see these classics: Morgenthau, Hans J. 1985, 6th Edition (1st Edition 1948). *Politics Among Nations: The Struggle for Peace and Power.* Waltz, Kenneth. 1979. *Theory of International Politics* and Mearsheimer, John J. 2003. *The Tragedy of Great Power Politics.*

2 Anarchy in this sense refers to the lack of a central authority in the international arena.

Neoliberals[3] are slightly more optimistic in their view of the international anarchical environment and specific state interests. These scholars agree with realists that the structure of the global system is anarchic and that states are rational actors. However, they argue that states pursue a multitude of interests, not just power and relative position. Additionally, they argue that there is not a finite amount of influence or prosperity in the system so states can focus on absolute rather than relative gains. Moving slightly beyond the state focus, neoliberalism acknowledges the role of international institutions, such as formal international organizations or informal cooperative arrangements such as regimes. Participation in institutions enhances transparency and diminishes international transaction costs, thereby helping to mediate the effects of anarchy (Keohane 1984).

Finally, the field of social constructivism also enlightens us about international relations and state behavior. This approach focuses primarily on the concept of identity and interest formation among states. While realists and neoliberals argue that anarchy externally constrains and influences state choices and behavior, constructivists[4] contend that internal ideas and identities effect how states respond to the external world. States view the international environment based on their knowledge of and interaction with other states – those that are like them and those that are not – and they create social constructs to make sense of this world. Wendt famously stated that "Anarchy is What States Make of It" arguing that anarchy itself is a socially derived idea. State interests are, therefore, endogenously created rather than universal and exogenously given. States will determine their interests based on their interactions with others and their own identities. Interaction with other states is of utmost importance (Wendt 1992).

These three approaches present quite different views of the world. Yet, they also indicate where to look in determining the source of state actions. In examining why states cooperate in this international environment, we can use regime theory to winnow the three large scale concepts of international relations (realism, neoliberalism, constructivism) down to their core components: power, interests and ideas. In the next section we explore the concept of international regimes and become familiar with the tenants of basic regime theory.

---

3 See: Keohane, Robert and Joseph Nye. 1977. *Power and Interdependence: World Politics in Transition.* Keohane, Robert. 1984. *After Hegemony: Cooperation and Discord in the World Political Economy.* Moravcsik, Andrew. 1997. "Taking Preferences Seriously: A Liberal Theory of International Politics," *International Organization,* Vol. 51, No. 4, 513-553.

4 References include: Ruggie, John. 1998. *Constructing the World Polity: Essays on International Institutionalization (The New International Relations).* Wendt, Alexander. 1999. *Social Theory of International Politics.* Wendt, Alexander. Spring 1992. "Anarchy is What States Make of It: The Social Construction of Power Politics," *International Organization,* Vol. 46, No. 2, 391-425.

International Regime Theory

Despite, or perhaps because of, the anarchic global environment, states might decide it is necessary or beneficial to work in cooperation with other states toward common goals. Multi-state cooperation at this level generally occurs through some sort of international organization (IO), or a rather fluid and often informal endeavor known in the literature as an international regime (Milner 1997).

Because the international environment is generally uncertain, states may choose to decrease uncertainty and enhance predictability by forming an international regime and establishing accepted patterns of behavior. Specifically, an international regime can be defined as:

> Implicit or explicit principles, norms, rules, and decision-making procedures around which actors' expectations converge in a given area of international relations. Principles are beliefs of fact, causation, and rectitude. Norms are standards of behavior defined in terms of rights and obligations. Rules are specific prescriptions or proscriptions for action. Decision-making procedures are prevailing practices for making and implementing collective choice (Krasner 1983, 3).

Keohane's focus on the function of regimes is also helpful. He explains that regimes facilitate international cooperation and agreements between countries on specific issue areas. He further articulates that, "Regimes are institutions with explicit rules, agreed upon by governments that pertain to particular sets of issues in international relations (Keohane 1989, 4). Therefore, when we want to determine the existence of a regime, we should look to see if there are expectations of behavior, if regulations are in place and if there is a focus on a specific issue area. It is important to remember that regimes need not codify norms and rules; in some cases norms and rules exist but are rather implicit (Keohane 1984).

Though sometimes confused, regimes and international organizations are not the same, though they are both international institutions and they often work in tandem. Moreover, an international regime may lead to the formation of an IO, or an IO may take up the purpose of a regime. It is useful to differentiate the terms based on the level of formality. An international organization generally has a headquarters, a large staff and a formalized[5] structure (Barnett and Finnemore 2004). At the other end of the spectrum, regimes are rather informal arrangements, often simply comprised of a series of agreements and conventions. Regimes have

---

5   In an IO there is a structure, formality and history as well as a hierarchy. If we think of NATO as an international organization we can quite easily see how the partnership operates and who is responsible should an immediate problem arise. On the other hand, a regime is an institution in that it has members and operates to affect change, but it is not formally structured to the extent that an IO is. For example, there is a nonproliferation regime, but there is no specific place, person or process to address grievances.

no headquarters or staff, the way we would think of an IO having employees and offices (Keohane 1984). Hasenclever and his colleagues (2004) argue that the more formal nature of IOs enhances their ability for quick response to changing situations. Regimes cannot react to events in the same manner or at the same speed as an IO. Also, regimes, as Keohane described them, are issue specific, and IOs likely encompass a much wider breadth in the issues that they address (Hasenclever et al. 2005, 10-11).

It is helpful to assess regimes by exploring their levels of effectiveness and robustness. We can judge a regime's effectiveness by assessing the extent to which adherents follow the norms and rules of the regime. Additionally, one can measure effectiveness by determining to what extent the regime has fulfilled its mission or stated cause. On the other hand, robustness refers to the persistence of the regime. If a regime is in place for a number of years and continues despite changes and challenges, we would consider the regime robust. Though we would hope to see both effectiveness and robustness in regimes, it is possible for a regime to be effective yet lack robustness, or vice versa (Hasenclever et al. 2005).

Regime Participation and Cooperation

The motivations for joining a regime may depend on a country's focus and whether it perceives that there are direct benefits resulting from regime participation. The three international relations theoretical approaches discussed above – realisim, neoliberalism and constructivism – provide a lens through which to understand how states behave in the international arena. In analyzing international cooperation and state participation in regimes or IOs, theorists have built on these ideas to understand why states join together and create, maintain and comply with regime or organization principles, norms and rules. Regime theory provides three explanations for understanding cooperative motivations: power, interests and ideas. These three motivations correspond to the larger theories of international relations: realism and power, neoliberalism and interests, and constructivism and ideas.

Regime theory helps us understand cooperation through motivations to participate. From the power perspective, states seek regime cooperation when they expect such collaboration to advance state power and increase relative gains over other countries. States choose to cooperate or join international regimes because of the power advantages that membership is expected to bring, recognizing that they might need cooperation to further their own goals and aspirations in an anarchic global system. For these analysts, cooperation is a power game where states aspire to wield the most influence in the system. As Hasenclever et al. suggest, therefore, "Power is no less central in cooperation than in conflict between nations" (Hasenclever et al. 2004, 3).

Those advancing an interest based perspective argue that cooperation in the form of treaties, formal IOs, or international regimes is desirable to states because of perceived joint benefits from working with other members. For these theorists, the cost/benefits analysis extends far beyond calculations of power. The advantages of such cooperation in groups can be broad, and benefits and costs can differ between members. Some members may not reap the same benefits as others, but there remains a view that the advantages of membership are greater than noninvolvement. Therefore, cooperation is not just a means to the end of state power, but a method for creating better conditions for all partners indicating a concern for absolute gains (Hasenclever et al. 2004).

Finally, there is the idea or knowledge based perspective of regime cooperation. Both power based and interest based theories consider nation-states as the most important actors in the system and they assume a degree of rationality on the part of these actors. From the ideas perspective, states do not organize and cooperate based on external interests, but because of internal notions of shared cause and identity. States cooperate because interaction has made some states or partners realize their commonalities with one another and there is a drive to work together with those of a state's "in-group." Here cooperation is a mechanism for transferring values and norms between likeminded members (Hasenclever et al. 2004, 136-211). Hasenclever and his colleagues relate these structure and motivation theories nicely:

> Neoliberals stress (self-) *interest* as a motivation for cooperation among states and likewise for the creation of, and compliance with, international regimes. Realists emphasize how *power* and considerations of relative power position affect the content, and circumscribe the effectiveness and robustness, of international regimes. Cognitivists [or constructivists] point out that both the perception of interests and the meaning of power capabilities is dependent on actors' causal and *social knowledge* (italics added. Hasenclever et al. 2005, 211).

Regime Creation

An additional consideration important for our study of port and container security is regime creation. Research suggests that regimes form following a time of conflict or when there are large scale upheavals in the international arena that lead to greater attention on specific issue areas (Milner 1998). Therefore, a number of international organizations and regimes originated after World War II, as did a number after the Cold War. For example, regarding nuclear nonproliferation, it is clear that the issue really came to the fore after 1989-1991 when the Soviet Bloc begin to break down and its nuclear arsenal became less secure (see Chapter 3). As with all international institutions or organizations, it is easier to develop regimes out of existing relationships than to create them from nothing. This means that it is often more effective to develop a regime out of existing ties, conventions or agreements (Keohane 1984).

Regime Persistence

A robust regime, as mentioned, is one that endures. Regime concepts of power, interest and ideas also address this issue of persistence. In terms of longevity, a power based theorist would suggest that as long as gains remain probable and the relationship beneficial to the individual state, the regime will continue. When power benefits cease, the state will leave the cooperative partnership. An interest based scholar would suggest that the effects of partnership lead to a greater understanding of joint interests and joint benefits beyond the initial goal of regime creation. Therefore, from this perspective a regime will continue as long as participants continue to see absolute gains. Finally, an advocate of an ideas based theory would suggest that interaction within the group lead to greater feelings of "we-ness" and feelings of partners belonging to the same "in-group." Members of a regime, through continued interaction, see themselves as having joint concerns and similar identities. From this point of view the regime continues not due to material or power benefits, but because of a sort of kinship and growing social knowledge of each other. It is possible that a regime could begin due to power or interest based motivations, but might endure because of idea based notions of joint identity (Keohane 1984, Hasenclever et al. 2004).

An International Maritime Security Regime

With an understanding of international regimes we can now ask: does a regime on international maritime security exist and if so how effective and robust is the regime? To answer the first part of the question we can look at the indicators that Krasner, Keohane and others identify: rules (regulations), norms (standards of appropriate behavior) and functions (activities on specific issue area). Particularly since the events 9/11, a number of new rules (the 24-Hour Rule, MTSA, ISPS to name but a few) have been created and now govern much of the global transport of containerized freight. Additionally, new norms of information sharing, agency cooperation and partnership domestically and internationally are now accepted and expected. Finally, the programs and policies enacted in recent years indeed function in a manner that seeks to enhance global cooperation and discourse related to greater security of maritime trade. Therefore, based on these indicators, the answer is yes. Yes, there is an International Maritime Security Regime.

Before 2001

Prior to 2001, there were no specific rules or norms governing international port security, indicating that there was no regime on international maritime security. However, there were some IOs in place that dealt with the international transportation of freight and maritime safety. There were also important conventions that sought to provide guidelines for maritime practices among the world's countries. Significant as these were, there was very little focus on security or the threat of terrorism. In fact, seaports were one of the most easily accessible points of entry and exit for goods or people entering and exiting the United States (see Chapter 2).

In old movies and TV shows (*On the Waterfront, The French Connection* and at least one of the *Lethal Weapon* movies come to mind) it is not unusual to see members of organized crime meeting behind a cargo ship to transfer money to their associates, or to see a police chase at a large seaport as containers are being dramatically swung from dock to ship. Seaports have provided intriguing backdrops for action shots. In these films, US (and certainly international) ports seem quite open and accessible to the public. It appears as if anyone could enter the ports to conduct whatever business or activity they wanted. Though undoubtedly exaggerated for effect, up until recently, there was some truth in these entertainment portrayals of seaports. Government officials presenting their findings in the 2000 *Report of the Interagency Commission on Crime and Security in US Seaports* discovered that to varying degrees US seaports lacked entry controls, had few physical barriers from public space and were the sites of untold amounts of unlawful activities.

Historically, port security had not been a priority for the US government or its international partners (Christopher 2009, 34). As Szyliowicz explains, "transportation security was not viewed from either an international or an intermodal framework" (Szyliowicz 2004, 357). By 2000, international intermodal trade was extensive. However, there was very little attention to the possibility that ports could be the site of terrorist activities ("Report of the Interagency" 2000, 5). Despite the bombing of the Murrah Federal Building in Oklahoma City in 1995 and the attack on the World Trade Center in New York City in 1993, there was a sense that terrorist events were tragedies that happened in other parts of the world, not in the United States (Agency Interviews 2006-2008).

Most international ports were lacking security measures before 9/11. In the 2000 interagency report there was already an acknowledgement that the policies and protocols of international ports greatly affected the United States. Due to the growing interconnectedness of global trade, the US was becoming more reliant on imports, mostly entering the country as ocean going freight, and was hence more vulnerable economically than it had been in previous decades. However, as was the case when examining domestic ports, government officials did not perceive the vulnerability due to terrorism. Again, the main concern was theft and smuggling.

At the end of the 20th century, US concern with lax international port security was focused on the exposure of the United States to the smuggling of drugs, illicit currency, alien workers, stolen goods and counterfeit products by way of powerful international organized crime networks ("Report of the Interagency" 2000).[6] In the

---

6   It is interesting that the 2000 report focused so much on this issue of organized crime, which has earned markedly little attention in the post-9/11 IMSR. However, one can assume that IMSR programs and policies do affect the ability of international organized crime syndicates to utilize ships and seaports to the extent they did previously, even if this is just an externality of the post-9/11 focus on terrorism.

1990s, there was a significant increase in the activity of such groups (particularly in the new states of the former Soviet region). Advances in transport technology and growing globalization contributed to the extensive reach of these groups. The US report called for international cooperation to deal with this concern stating that, "The United States must seek the cooperation of its trading partners in eliminating crime..." ("Report of the Interagency" 2000, 158). The report continues to outline what the international community could do to tackle international organized crime. In the report, however, there is only secondary mention of terrorist groups and little to no concern that international seaports could be the point of origin for sending bombs or other destructive materials for detonation upon reaching the United States ("Report of the Interagency" 2000).

Despite general inattention, there were developments in the international community pertaining to maritime trade before 2001, though again the focus was seldom security or even organized crime related. While there was no IMSR previously, there were agreements and IOs that operated to secure passage of vessels, people and freight.

The World Customs Organization (WCO) has been in operation since 1947 under varying configurations and names with the mission of monitoring global transactions around the world. The organization was the first international body tasked with monitoring the world's waterways. Naturally, theft and piracy were and continue to be concerns of the WCO (WCO Interviews 2008; WCO web page 2009). Likewise, the International Maritime Organization (IMO) has spent over 60 years advocating for clean and safe waterways (IMO Interviews 2007; IMO website 2009). The work of the WCO and the IMO aside, until 2001 there was little attention paid to maritime security. Officials from both organizations, readily admit that their primary focus was on trade practices, tariff policy and safety of ship crew with security as a secondary focus in so far as it affected their central missions (International Interviews 2007-2008).

In the 20th century states signed treaties and conventions that addressed various aspects of international exchange and travel. The *International Convention for the Safety of Life at Sea* (SOLAS) and the *United Nations Convention on the Law of the Sea* (UNCLOS) were the two most significant international maritime agreements of the last century. The first SOLAS agreement came about in 1914, two years after the sinking of the *Titanic*. It was an attempt to specify safety practices for ocean going vessels – the proper number of life boats and jackets for example. In the latter part of the 20th century, SOLAS came under the jurisdiction of the IMO. Through the 1960 and 1974 revisions of SOLAS partners added safety and environmental regulations to the agreement, as well as additional guidelines for shipping and cargo practices. It is fair to say that SOLAS is the most important legacy of the IMO (International Convention 2002).[7]

---

7 It is no coincidence that ISPS was a SOLAS amendment. Not only was there symbolism involved in tagging the program on to SOLAS, but there was acceptance in the basic tenants and resilience of SOLAS as an international convention.

Whereas SOLAS dealt with safety standards, UNCLOS addressed the heady issue of marine jurisdiction. UNCLOS specified control of marine resources, named international waters, acted to preserve the environmental integrity of the oceans and instituted a ban on the use of nuclear weapons on the sea floor. Essentially, the UNCLOS "defines rights and responsibilities of nations in their use of the world's oceans, establishing guidelines for business, the environment, and the management of maritime natural resources" (Christopher 2009, 32). The 1982 UNCLOS agreement established a "12 mile territorial limit" for national control over proximate coastal waters. The demarcation was set with fishing and fossil materials in mind, but it gave authority to state agents to control their waterways from a viable off-shore distance and hence the jurisdiction to provide security along those waterways. The US signed the agreement that went into effect in 1994, but has yet to ratify the convention due to sovereignty concerns. Despite this, the US recognizes and adheres to the practices put forth in UNCLOS ("Oceans and Law" 2007).

Though two IOs existed to monitor and protect the world's oceans, and at least two significant international conventions had been in place, throughout the 20th century there was no strong sense that international partners should act together to address seaport security issues, least of all that such security related to the potential for terrorism.

Post-9/11 Regime Development

September 11 changed the security focus in the United States and around the world. The events of that day were widely felt creating the sort of upheaval that leads to new regime creation. The hijacking of four airplanes by terrorists who had crossed US borders with apparent ease, and lived in the country for some time, highlighted the porous nature of the country's land borders. It was not long after that additional means of entry, air and sea became areas to further secure. Quickly, the United States and other governments as well as the IMO and the WCO, reassessed their goals and missions determining container security to be a major area of concern ("America's Container Ports" 2009).

The first couple of years after 9/11, parties signed a number of significant pieces of domestic legislation and international agreements (see Chapters 2 and 4). Between 2001 and 2006 a great deal of progress occurred. Labeling and tracing programs were instituted via the IMO's International Ship and Port Security code book and the Maritime Transportation Security Act advanced by the US Coast Guard. Additionally, the SAFE Framework of Standards was created by the WCO to institute a set of minimum standards for shippers and vessels.[8]

As a sign of consensus and international concern, in 2002 the world's most powerful nations jointly declared their dedication to enhance transportation security at the *G8 Summit* in Canada. At the first meeting of the G8 since 9/11,

---

8   For a detailed description of these programs, see Chapter 4.

international maritime security was among the most important topics addressed. Upon concluding the gathering, the G8 published a joint statement expressing their commitment to working together with international organizations, with each other and with non-G8 states to enhance transportation security, specifically at global seaports. They also declared their intent, "recognizing the urgency of securing global trade, to work expeditiously, in cooperation with relevant international organizations" to develop an international regime to address the issue. The meeting minutes further declared that "the G8 will develop, in collaboration with interested non-G8 countries pilot projects that model an integrated container security regime" ("Cooperative G8..." 2002).

There is now a clear international commitment to port security and cooperation toward that end, indicating an issue specific focus. Though some tensions have arisen, these norms remain strong. After 2001, there can be no doubt that an International Maritime Security Regime exists and that its reach and scope is extensive.

The effectiveness of the IMSR appears strong, though its robustness has perhaps waned slightly in recent years (Interviews 2006-2008). To reiterate, an effective regime is one where states adhere to norms and rules and where the regime's mission has been, or is being, addressed. In this regard the IMSR has been effective. The early programs resulted in high levels of cooperation and general consensus. The mission of this newly developed regime is to enhance security at the world's seaports. Every official we interviewed, though perhaps raising some specific policy concerns (see Chapter 4), acknowledged that port security is much stronger today than it was a decade ago (International Interviews 2007-2008, Domestic Agency Interviews 2006-2008).

The robustness or resilience of the IMSR is more questionable. In the years following 9/11, the IMSR garnered a great deal of support and attention. However, more recently, an increasing number US international partners are beginning to question the path that the IMSR is taking (International Interviews 2007-2008). Much of the concern results from the position of the United States as regime leader. It was after all, the United States that was the target of actions on September 11, 2001 and it has been the United States that has pushed for policy in this issue area. The leadership position of the United States in the regime was initially quite helpful in the formation and extension of the IMSR, but today it is also one of the main reasons why questions of robustness exist.

Piloting International Port Policy: The Role of the United States

While some port security programs and policies have emanated from international bodies, the United States has been the primary player and most active proponent in almost every case. Evidence of the US commitment to port security is in the 700 % increase in federal spending on the issue from 2001 to 2005 (America's Container Ports 2009, 26). We can delineate the role of the United States pertaining to the seaport security regime post-9/11 into two phases. The time from 2001 through

2006, when the SAFE Port Initiative was passed in the US Congress, and the period of time since 2006. The first period, especially 2002, was characterized by quick action, high levels of cooperation and relatively unquestioned US primacy on the issue area. For example, one European official explained that the swift passage of ISPS in 2002 was due to overwhelming sympathy for the United States, which resulted in little debate and few challenges to the program (International Interviews 2007-2008). This is not to say that no one questioned early programs or that concerns did not arise. However, foreign officials and representatives, for the most part, saw early steps in a relatively positive light and as mutually beneficial. The support of the US waned slightly as 9/11 became more distant. However, it was not until the 2006 SAFE Port Act and its extension through the 2007 Secure Freight Initiative (SFI) that US dominance in the regime became more heavily scrutinized (International Interviews 2007-2008). The characterization of the recent phase of the US role in the maritime security regime is more about incentives, questions of reciprocity, international frustration and in some cases resentment (see Chapter 4). Table 5.1 provides a simplified delineation of the international support US policies and programs (part of the IMSR) have garnered over the last decade.

Table 5.1   Port Security Programs/Policies and International Support Since 2001[9]

Law/Program	Year in Effect	Initial Level of International Support
MTSA	2002	High
USCG 96-Hour Rule	2003	High
CBP 24-Hour Rule	2003	High/Medium
ISPS	2004	High
CSI	2004	High
C-TPAT	2004	High
SAFE Ports	2006	Medium/Low
SFI	2007	Low

US strategy regarding the safety of the nation's seaports and the passage of containerized freight since 2001 is to employ a "layered defense" and "extend its borders out" (see Chapters 2 and 4). The latter extensively and the former to a lesser and related degree requires cooperation and communication with and reliance upon international actors. To enhance the security of ships and cargo bound for the United States, it *must* look to partners abroad.

---

9   Based on review of available literature and our extensive research in the field, Table 5.1 displays our general perceptions of how US seaport policies and programs have been perceived internationally. This is not a scientific evaluation and is only used to give the reader a general sense of how programs are perceived and of the increasing contention levels.

US leadership in the International Maritime Security Regime has both facilitated and hindered the regime's development over the past decade. The United States in many ways pushed for the creation of the regime and through its leadership brought attention to the issue area. Additionally, the US played a significant role in the conception and implementation of a number of important programs which have served to make for safer shipment of goods around the world. Despite this remarkable progress, US leadership has also, and certainly recently, led to some serious concerns regarding its role in the IMSR. It has also left other states seeking to exert some influence of their own.

US Facilitation of Port Security Around the World

Perhaps the greatest and most lasting influence of the United States has simply been to bring port security into the international consciousness. As mentioned, prior to US engagement of this topic, countries paid only secondary attention to the security of seaports and their cargo. While it is possible that some international ports and foreign governments independently would have made some of the changes of the last decade, there can be little doubt that US leadership has led to the implementation of policies that have positively affected the security of the globalized supply chain. Countries around the world have taken significant steps to increase security of their ports and to secure the international movement of freight. Additionally, the IMO and the WCO have made port security important pillars of their organizations. The United States can take a great deal of credit for these accomplishments (Interviews 2006-2008).

The earliest, and one of the most tangible successes of the US led IMSR was the implementation of the ISPS code as an extension of SOLAS in 2002. The process from introduction to passage was remarkably short, and within a couple of years, ports around the world became ISPS compliant. For the first time there was an international set of security related regulations which a number of ports agreed to adhere to. ISPS, with only minor exceptions, has been welcomed and embraced with the number of compliant seaport increasing yearly.[10] Seaport officials acknowledge increases in safety, security and even efficiency due to the implementation of ISPS requirements (International Interviews 2007-2008; Port Interviews 2006-2008).

The CSI and C-TPAT programs are also notable US and IMSR accomplishments. The CSI is a series of bilateral agreements between the United States and foreign customs agencies negotiated through diplomatic channels. This partnership indicates the willingness of governments to make port security a priority and allows for quality assurance through US oversight ("CSI in Brief" 2008). While the CSI functions to tighten security at seaports, the C-TPAT program attempts to strengthen security beyond the port of entry. C-TPAT acknowledges the important

---

10 At the time of our visits, many of the ports investigated in this research were ISPS compliant or working toward that goal.

role of business in maritime security as well as the inherent incentives for business cooperation to ensure a balance between security and economic efficiency (see Chapter 7). C-TPAT has allowed for the airing and attempted remedying of economic concerns ("Securing the Global Supply Chain" 2004). For example, the program has encouraged a great deal of security related Research and Development, which has contributed to the discussion and development of safer seals, more secure boxes and even secure parking lots for container trucks that travel long distances to or from seaports. Business is not only concerned with continued efficiency of transport, but these new developments also lead to greater security not just from terrorism or smuggling, but particularly from theft of merchandise (International and Domestic Interviews 2006-2008; Industry Interviews 2007-2008).

While most officials interviewed agree that taking steps to advance security at their seaports is positive, there remain some questions about US leadership of the IMSR. As the United States advances more and more programs and expensive requirements, many international ports are contemplating how they will be able to adjust. While some ports such as those in Great Britain and some countries of the former Communist Bloc had significant security procedures in place long before 9/11, others are playing catch up.[11] Smaller ports most acutely feel the strains of meeting the increasingly difficult and expensive changes required. Additionally, there is a growing sense, especially in Europe, that the United States pays too much attention and focus to domestic rather than international security (International Interviews 2007-2008).

The United States as IMSR Leader

As there is little doubt that an International Maritime Security Regime exists, there can also be little doubt who has been the instigator and "primary mover" of agreements and policies related to the issue of maritime security. The United States initiated and has thus far retained significant control over policies, programs and procedures. Given that the terrorist attacks of 9/11 were perpetrated against the United States and that the country is a major player on the international stage, it is perhaps not surprising that the US took on this mantel. It might even be argued that had the US not chosen to advance the issue, many of the programs and policies enacted would not exist today. However, leadership has brought challenges and

---

11   Great Britain has a long history as a terrorist target due to the situation in Northern Ireland. This history has made it especially aware of the vulnerability of its water ports. An added complication is the fact that the Port of London, a geographically extensive port, is near the British House of Parliament. Some countries of the former Communist Bloc also had a history of tight security. Mainly this was to keep citizens in and western goods out. However, that past made it relatively easy for former communist countries in Eastern and Central Europe to adjust to new requirements (International Interviews 2008).

declining international attitudes toward the United States, on this and other issues, which has at times made progress difficult.

Acceptance of US Leadership

International actors have generally accepted US leadership of the IMSR for three reasons. First, the United States is arguably the primary power in the international arena. The superpower designation of the United States enhances the ability of the country to advance self-interested issues and policy initiatives. Second, the 9/11 terrorist attacks happened on US soil giving the country the impetus, and some might say the right and duty, to push for security level changes at the international level. 9/11 also created emotional capital and sympathy around the world. With few exceptions, the countries of the world showed sympathy and support for the United States. Finally, the third reason US leadership was acceptable is that the country had "first mover" legitimacy or advantage. Most commonly used in business, the "first mover" concept denotes the advantage that a company has if it is the first to sell a specific product or to manufacture in a new way. Because the business is the first on the scene it garners a higher percentage of market share and often gets to brand the idea it is advancing (Lieberman and Montgomery 1988). Likewise, in politics, "first mover" legitimacy allows the instigator leeway in determining policy based on the notion that the country was the first to advance the idea (Keohane 2002). Because the United States was willing to push for various new programs and policies to secure seaports, and worked toward creating the IMSR, it has been difficult to challenge its leadership in the area.

US Motivations to Lead

On the surface we can clearly pinpoint reasons that explain why the United States is interested in enhancing domestic and international port security. We have already explicitly stated here and in other chapters many of these motives. Clearly, the primary motivation of the United States is based on the terrorist attacks of 2001 and the natural desire to prevent future attacks. Additionally, in looking at the country's aspiration to mold and lead a regime around this issue area we can return to the strategy of pushing the borders out or creating a virtual border that requires cooperation from international actors. These are valid explanations, yet US motivations run deeper. It is not just that the United States wants more secure seaports, it wants to direct seaport policy at the domestic and international levels. The United States wants and feels its need to lead.

To understand US motivations for advancing and leading the IMSR we can use the tenets of regime theory. To reiterate, regime theory understands state behavior through the lenses of power, interests or ideas. If power drives motivations we would expect states to join the IMSR for possible relative gains and the influence that they can yield on the issue area. If interests provide the impetus for cooperation, we might look for material gains for members, or some sort of absolute gains where all members reap benefits by participation. Finally, an idea based explanations would expect cooperation in the IMSR to occur because partners identify with one another or share a common worldview.

Based on our research and utilizing the tenants of regime theory, we argue that the US role in the IMSR is based primarily on power considerations. We see evidence of this in the overwhelming domestic and import focus of the United States. As explained elsewhere in this book, US strategy has been on securing its seaports by securing and controlling imports. There has been much less attention to the security of those containers and goods exported out of the United States. An overall reciprocity is lacking. A power perspective also explains US program mechanisms that send our officials to oversee activities at foreign ports. Finally, the fact that the US is dictating policy to international governments in its own legislation (particularly the SAFE Port Act of 2006 and the SFI program) indicates just how much dominance the United States is wielding. The lead position of the United States in the IMSR gives them a great deal of control and influence regarding not only policies and programs, but implementation of those initiatives. Working as agenda setter means the United States is able to place its concerns front and center.

The power that the United States is exercising is obviously not of physical force or military coercion.[12] There is no direct physical threat imposed by the United States. Therefore, it is helpful to broaden our understanding of the word *power*. Generally, power indicates the ability of one state to force or cause another state to act in a way in which the second state would not normally act (Barnett and Finnemore 2005). This narrow definition of power does not explain US motivation in the IMSR. Rather, the United States is attempting to create a situation in which other states feel its explicit and implicit pressure and influence and in response take action favorable to the United States.

On seaport security, the United States is exerting what Barnett and Finnemore (2005) call *institutional* power. This idea contends that an important state creates institutions (or regimes in this case) in such a way that other actors are constrained and hence must act in a way beneficial to the regime creator. Barnett and Finnemore describe this referencing hypothetical states A and B. They explain that in some instances "*A* does not 'posses' the resources of power but because *A* stands in a particular relation to the relevant institutional arrangements its actions exercise power over *B*" (Barnett and Finnemore 2005, 16).

Regarding the IMSR, the United States works through social processes and interactions with other states to set a policy agenda on port security, hence

---

12 Traditionally and historically, scholars have written about how states exert their power in a maritime setting via naval forces. In this case we argue that the United States is exerting its power in a maritime setting with the development, facilitation and implementation of maritime rules and regulations that enhance US national security and power. For more on the historical role of seapower and naval forces, see Mahan 1890, Harkavy 1982, and Kemp and Harkavy 1997.

influencing the corresponding actions of states. In creating and leading cooperative endeavors, the United States is setting the "rules of the game" and formulating policies and procedures that most clearly benefits its goals. This is somewhat similar to the "first mover" advantage mentioned earlier. The United States has important seaport security concerns, and in order to address those it has determined that by "pushing borders out" and fostering the growth of a security regime, it can best meet its domestic security aims. The United States cannot reasonably use force to achieve international cooperation, yet it can use this institutional power (the regime it created and "the game" it established) to direct international partners to act favorably. In many ways, by doing this, the United States constrains its international partners' actions. If another country wants to continue to play the game and engage in trade with the United States, it must act within the parameters created by the United States.

International Motivations for Cooperation

The US global position, the country's experience on 9/11, and its "first mover" status explain why other countries accept US leadership on the port security issue. However, these are only secondary explanations for understanding the motivations of foreign governments and actors to participate in the IMSR. It is plausible that international governments would accept US leadership on the issue, but might choose not to participate in the US led regime. Yet, despite some concerns in many countries we see both acceptance and cooperative participation (see Chapter 4).

Here we can turn once again to regime theory. As explained, the United States works with international partners from a power based perspective, through a specific form of power. On the other hand, adherence of international actors to US dictates within the IMSR cannot provide those states any real relative gains or additional power status. As will be seen, recent activities, particularly taken by the European Union, have served to challenge the US role in the IMSR and perhaps alter the balance of power (even institutional power), yet this does not appear to be the primary reason explaining why the EU and the individual member states are currently choosing to participate in the IMSR. Power helps explain US activities, but it does little to account for foreign partner motivations.

It is also difficult to see where an idea based perspective describes international incentives for cooperation in the IMSR. Ideas might describe some participation. Canada and European countries, for example, were quick to join the CSI program. Canada certainly feels an affinity with the United States and European countries have been traditional allies of the United States. Additionally, the early adherence to US programs in 2002 and 2003, as mentioned previously, resulted from international sympathy for the losses suffered on September 11, 2001. There was some sense of kinship with the United States. However, sympathy and kinship have worn off with the distance of time, and in large part cooperation persists ("What Does the World Think of US?" 2007). It is also important to remember that the world's largest ports, and those of greatest concern to the United States, are in Asia ("America's Container Ports" 2009). In China, Japan, Singapore and elsewhere, port officials and national governments have also become part of the IMSR. Based on our interviews and review of available port security literature, there is little sense of identity or shared values between the United States and its Asian partners. Therefore, while ideas might explain some instances of IMSR cooperation, it is lacking.

Borrowing a phrase from the Clinton years, in the simplest terms, "It's the economy stupid!" Economic considerations, or material interests, appear to trump all other international motivations for IMSR cooperation. In large part, cooperation with the IMSR has developed because the benefits of participation (trade with US markets) are substantial and the costs of non-participation are likewise financially high. For example, when the US implemented the 24-hour and 96-hour rules, or the MTSA guidelines, it meant that those shippers not willing to comply or governments not willing to facilitate cooperation were unable to bring their goods to the United States. As other programs like the CSI, C-TPAT and ISPS were put forward, the incentives of membership (quicker security clearance and near green light status) made participation appealing (International Interviews 2007-2008; Agency Interviews 2006-2008).

Despite what some international actors see as unreasonable requirements, the allure and money making potential of US markets serve, or have served, as sufficient motivation. Consider the fact that US imports in 2008 reached a record of $2,100.4 billion with exports only about half as much. Of imports, $242.6 billion was from OPEC countries, $378.8 billion were goods imported from the 27 countries of the European Union, and a staggering $337.8 billion was from China alone (US Census Statistics 2008). In true interest based theory, absolute gains are the result of IMSR cooperation. The United States gains security and international partners gain significant economic benefits. However, US leadership has not gone unchallenged.

Questioning the US Leadership Role

While few can doubt the positive effects of US leadership in the early days of the IMSR, voices of discontent are becoming louder. With 9/11 becoming more distant and the requirements put forward by the United States more cumbersome, there are some that are not only questioning US leadership, but taking actions to alter some of the "rule of the game." This is not to suggest that the IMSR will dismantle, rather there are simply some international partners that would like to have more input in creation of regime policies and programs.

The United States still remains a super power, though its international reputation has declined over the last few years. Additionally, sympathy arising from 9/11 has waned and the "first mover" advantage the US enjoyed during the IMSR development have also begun to run out. As countries begin to realize that the United States needs their imports as much as they need the US market, one wonders how much longer economics alone will continue to motivate international IMSR cooperation. This section explores how events beyond maritime security have affected the regime and at some of the measures taken to reign in US dominance within the IMSR.

International Reputation

Though impressions of the United States after the events of 9/11 were quite favorable, the international reputation of the United States has plummeted over the last decade. It is likely that we can attribute this decrease to the realities of a post-Cold War world. As the bi-polar structure of the Cold War era disappeared, the pedestal upon which the United States sat began to crumble and new states emerged out from under Soviet and US dominance to find their own paths. At the same time, old allies, such as Germany, sought to gain their own footing and to step out from the shadow of US leadership. September 11 put a halt to this process, but the capital gained during those trying weeks slowly diminished and throughout the last decade the reputation of the United States once again was on the decline (Wallerstein 2002; Nye 2004).[13]

In recent years, this situation has further deteriorated due to US involvement in Iraq. Though North Atlantic Treaty Organization (NATO) partners and others around the world generally supported US operations in Afghanistan, the US decision to invade Iraq and depose Saddam Hussein in 2003 received a much more skeptical and critical reception. As the war in Iraq continues, so too do the protests around the world. And now in 2009, there are serious questions about US policy in the on-going conflict in Afghanistan ("Obama's Afghan Troops" 2009; Andrews 2005). This has been most obvious in Germany and France, but other countries are also questioning the US mission in Iraq and a number of countries that sent troops in the early years of the conflict, have stopped their participation. Other events surrounding the war in Iraq and the "War on Terror" have also contributed to the troubling drop in US influence and prestige around the world ("Guantanamo Tarnishes" 2007; "What Does the World Think of US?" 2007).

Though international port security has very little, if anything, to do with the war in Iraq or the broader "War on Terror," the situation has affected US leadership in the IMSR. When the US loses influence in any aspect of foreign relations, it makes action on seemingly unrelated activities difficult. As citizens around the world begin to question US actions and leadership in some areas, there is a spillover effect to other issues (Nye 2004; Sloan 2003; International Interviews 2006-2008). Many protests to US actions in Iraq and elsewhere have occurred in Europe. Therefore, it should actually come as no surprise that the greatest challenge to US leadership in the IMSR has also originated in Europe.

---

13   Many attribute much of the more recent decline to the policies of President Bush. It is true that with the Obama administration, the US image has improved, but it is still somewhat tenuous.

110 Protecting Our Ports

A European Commission Lawsuit and Challenge to United States Supremacy in the IMSR

Questioning not policy but procedure, disagreements with some European partners in the IMSR resulted in legal action. Bilateral CSI agreements between the US and some members of the EU actually resulted in a lawsuit filed by the EU Commission. The Commission sued EU member states, which had signed the CSI agreement with the US, because members did not go through proper EU channels. The European Commission argued that all members must be given equal opportunity to make these types of agreement as they affect trade (Stivachtis 2007, 165).

It was not that the EU had problems with the tenants of the CSI. Rather it was the fact that the US DOS negotiated CSI agreements (bilateral trade agreements) with individual countries within the Union without dealing with the EU as a whole. In some regards the EU perceived the US approach as somewhat of an affront, and the court case was an effort to re-exert the Union's influence over its member states (Stivachtis 2007, 165). The European Commission dropped the suit in early 2007 ("EU Proposes" 2007).

While the lawsuit was not a large incident, it did signal that there might be more significant issues in the future. It was an indication that the EU felt challenged by the United States and that the Commission was willing to take extraordinary steps to maintain its influence over its member states. The EU was not challenging the IMSR, but rather seeking to retain its own sphere of influence.

Authorized Economic Operator Program

Previously, international officials indicated that they felt little choice but to go along with US measures, but that they often resent the apparent unidirectional focus of US efforts. European officials have attempted on a couple of occasions to alter the "rules of the regime game" to retain EU control over policies, rather than simply complying with US dictates. Again, they were not attempting to destroy the IMSR, but sought to maintain their position. This is evident in the EU's Authorized Economic Operator (AEO) program, referred to as "an EU harmonizes accreditation regime for importers and exporters" (McDermott 2007). The program is styled after the US C-TPAT program, but AEO is an attempt by the European Union to challenge US leadership and to create a very European program within the IMSR ("The AEO" 2005; International Interviews 2007-2008).

Working with the WCO's SAFE Framework for Standards, the European Union served as a testing ground and has now implemented, as of January 2008, a new program aimed at rewarding traders who have met a set of safety standards. The European Commission officially explained that "The idea was to grant AEO status to reliable operators including those that are also compliant in respect to security and safety standards and can therefore be considered as 'secure' traders" ("The AEO" 2005). For full AEO Customs and Security certification, operators must be in good standing, show evidence of strong management of records, and the applicant must prove that security measures are in place which serves to protect the entire chain of transport (McDermott 2007). The incentives for AEO status is the smooth and quick movement of cargo through the supply chain as accepted operators are required to submit fewer pre-departure and pre-arrival data points and expedited treatment (Trade Concerns 2006). Similar to the US C-TPAT program, this is an attempt to not only encourage companies to advance better safety standards, but also to encourage companies to pressure their governments to advance such policies as well.

Though the intention – enhanced policy past the port – is the same there are some significant differences between the AEO initiative and the C-TPAT program. C-TPAT is rather flexible in dealing with private entity peculiarities. On the other hand, AEO is specific about its requirements and in fact offers 36 pages of guidelines, as compared to three pages with C-TPAT, for its participating companies to follow. The certification program is also much more streamlined with C-TPAT than AEO (Woodard 2007). Another difference is the emphasis AEO places not just on imports, but on exports.

Both American and European officials indicated that the AEO is an attempt for the EU to no longer just maintain, but now to exert some influence in the maritime security area (International Interviews 2007-2008). Similarly, Woodard noted that "While there is a question as to how well this approach (AEO) will actually mitigate the risks associated with global supply chains, the European have certainly exercised their independence" (Woodard 2007). The US and EU are currently working on a system of mutual recognition for the two programs, though the process has been slow going. It is notable that due in large part to EU pressure, and in accord with the future mutual recognition declaration, the United States has promised that it will reexamine its export policies (Abridged External Partner 2009). This is a small victory for the EU.

IMSR Persistence

In Chapter 4 we suggested ways in which the US could mitigate international concerns in regards to container security policy. These recommendations – better framing and message consideration – hold true for IMSR persistence as well. If the US wants to continue to lead the regime and exert its institutional power, it will need to be more open and flexible. It will also have to take situations like the creation of the AEO and the European court case and consider those steps as not just minor incidents, but as very real efforts by Europe, in this case, to exert some influence.

It is difficult to know the future of the IMSR. There are some signs that indicate an approaching saturation point with international partners. Grumblings outlined in Chapter 4, EU attempts to restrain the United States, the waning of a positive US reputation, and a general sense among many of the world's largest seaports that the objectives have been attained – that only general maintenance is necessary – suggest that resilience may become an issue in future years.

However, the motivational basis of US international partners may maintain the IMSR even as complaints grow. When interests motivate cooperation, persistence calculations are not just about the continued benefits of participation, but also about the costs of leaving the cooperative arrangement. Even if international partners come to the conclusion that the economic advantages that they are gaining by participating in the IMSR have waned or no longer exist, they must think about the financial and temporal costs of failing to participate in the future. This may bode well for the continuation of the US led IMSR, at least for a while.

Conclusion

Using mainstream approaches of international relations regime theory, this chapter has explored the creation, development and persistence of an international regime addressing global seaport security. Initially, we address the regime concept. Analyzing US and international port security activities before and after September 11, 2001, we argue that though some attention to seaport activities existed in the form of important IOs and international conventions, it was not until after 9/11 that a maritime security regime actually existed. After 9/11 an IMSR quite quickly developed with the United States at the helm.

Regime theory perspectives on state cooperation based on power, interests or ideas allow us to assess the motivations of the United States and international actors within the post-9/11 International Maritime Security Regime. We argue that US actions to advance and lead the regime originate from power considerations. However, in this instance it is not military power the US seeks, but rather institutional power that allows the US to set the agenda, create the rules of the game and garner implicit control over international seaport security issues. On the other hand, there is a possible link between the motivations of international partners with ideas and sense of affinity. It appears that interests, primarily economic interests, predominantly drive international cooperation in the IMSR. If Europe (the EU in particular) continues attempts to enhance its influence on the issue area, it might be necessary to reassess their motivations for IMSR cooperation. However, at the moment Europe, like the rest of the world, seems propelled by interests, but power (specifically the institutional power the US is relying upon) could be a growing consideration.

Finally, this chapter explained some challenges to US dominance in the IMSR. Whereas Chapter 4 highlighted some very specific concerns regarding US port and container security policies and programs, this chapter takes a broader international view, briefly discussing the country's waning international reputation and the corresponding spillover effects. We also discussed some efforts by the EU to increase their own influence among members and within the IMSR. At present the short term prospects for the IMSR appear relatively positive. However, as concerns about US leadership increase and 9/11 becomes more distant, we should expect to see more challenges to US leadership potentially resulting in diminished robustness in the long term. Evidence suggests that the EU will continue to seek greater independence in dealing with seaport security issues.

Chapters 4 and 5 addressed the international dynamics of container security in general and seaport policies more specifically. In the next chapter we examine the difficult prospect of balancing economic interests and national security, specifically as it relates to port and container security.

Bibliography

"Abridged External Partner Version of the US-EU Joint Customs Cooperation Committee: Roadmap Toward Mutual Recognition of Trade Partnership Programs." January 2009. *Customs and Border Protection*, available at http://www.cbp.gov/linkhandler/cgov/border_security/international_operations/partnerships/recog_roadmap.ctt/recog_roadmap.pdf.

"America's Container Ports: Freight Hubs that Connect Our Nation to Global Markets." 2009. *US Department of Transportation Research and Innovative Technology Administration* (Washington, DC).

Anderson, David. 2005. *The Atlantic Alliance Under Stress: US European Relations After Iraq* (Cambridge, UK: Cambridge University Press).

"The Authorised Economic Operator" April 13, 2005. *European Commission: Directorate-General Taxation and Customs Union Customs Policy* (Brussels).

Barnett, Michael and Raymond Duvall. 2005. *Power in Global Governance* (Cambridge, UK: Cambridge University Press).

Barnett, Michael and Martha Finnemore. 2004. *Rules for the World" International Organizations in Global Politics* (Ithaca, NY: Cornell University Press).

Christopher, Kenneth. 2009. *Port Security Management* (Boca Raton, FL: Auerbach).

"Cooperative G8 Action on Transport Security" 2002. *Government of Canada*, available at http://www.g7.utoronto.ca/summit/2002kananaskis/transport.html.

"CSI in Brief" March 20, 2008. *Customs and Border Protection*, available at http://www.cbp.gov/xp/cgov/trade/cargo_security/csi/csi_in_brief.xml

"Egyptian Stowaway Had Canadian Passport." October 26, 2001. *CBC News*, available at http://www.cbc.ca/canada/story/2001/10/25/stowaway_farid011025.html.

"EU Proposes Tighter Customs Regulations," 2007. *CalTrade Report*, available at http://www.caltradereport.com/eWebPages/front-page-1059820986.html.

"Fiji Police Still Questioning Container Stowaway." August 29, 2003. *Radio New Zealand Radio*, available at http://www.rnzi.com/pages/news.php?op=read&id=6290.

"Foreign Trade Statistics" 2008. *United States Census Bureau*, available at http://www.census.gov/foreign-trade/statistics/highlights/annual.html.

"Guantanamo Tarnishes US Reputation Abroad," June 25, 2007. *Chicago Sun Times*, available at http://www.highbeam.com/doc/1P2-7484786.html.

Harkavy, Robert E. 1982. *Great Power Competition for Overseas Bases: The Geopolitics of Access Diplomacy* (New York: Pergamon Press).

Hasenclever, Andreas with Peter Mayer and Volker Ritterberger. 2008. *Theories of International Regimes* (Cambridge: Cambridge University Press).

Kemp, Geoffrey and Robert E. Harkavy. 1997. *Strategic Geography and the Changing Middle East* (New York: Carnegie Endowment for International Peace).

Keohane, Robert. 2001. "Governance in a Partially Globalized World," *American Political Science Review*, Vol. 95, No. 1, 1-13.

Keohane, Robert. 1984. *After Hegemony: Cooperation and Discord in the World Political Economy* (Princeton, NJ: Princeton University Press).

Keohane, Robert and Joseph Nye 1977. *Power and Interdependence: World Politics in Transition* (Boston, MA: Little, Brown and Company).

Lieberman, Marvin and David Montgomery. Summer 1988. "First-Mover Advantages," *Strategic Management Journal*, Vol. 9, Special Issue, 41-58.

Mahan, Alfred Thayer. 1890. *The Influence of Sea Power Upon History, 1660-1783* (Boston, MA: Little, Brown and Company).

McDermott, Will and Emery. 2007. "New EU Customs Programme: Authorised Economic Operator." *Newsletter*.

Mearsheimer, John J. 2003. *The Tragedy of Great Power Politics* (New York: W.W. Norton & Co.).

Milner, Helen V. 1997. *Interests, Institutions and Information: Domestic Politics and International Relations* (Princeton, NJ: Princeton University Press).

Moravcsik, Andrew. 1997. "Taking Preferences Seriously: A Liberal Theory of International Politics," *International Organization*, Vol. 51, No. 4, 513-553.

Morgenthau, Hans J. 1985, 6th Edition (1st Edition 1948). *Politics Among Nations: The Struggle for Peace and Power* (New York: Knopf).

Nye, Joseph. 2004. "The Decline of American Soft Power: Why Washington Should Worry," *Foreign Affairs*, Vol. 83, No. 3, 16-20.

"Obama's Afghan Troop Response is Key For Europeans," September 23, 2009. *Reuters India*, available at http://in.reuters.com/article/southAsiaNews/idINIndia-42654820090923.

Phillips, Kevin. 2003. "Political Fireworks Possible in 2004," *Los Angeles Times*, available at http://articles.latimes.com/2003/nov/30/opinion/op-phillips30.

Report of the Interagency Commission on Crime and Security in US Seaports. Fall 2000. Published by the Commission (Washington, DC).

Richardson, Michael. April 11, 2004. "Troubled Waters," *The Age*, available at http://www.theage.com.au/articles/2004/04/10/1081326976347.html.

Ruggie, John. 1998. *Constructing the World Polity: Essays on International Institutionalization (The New International Relations)* (London, UK: Routledge).

Stivachtis, Yannis. 2007. *International Order in a Globalizing World* (Aldershot, UK: Ashgate).

"Suicide Bombing at Ashdod Port," March 14, 2004. *Israeli Ministry of Foreign Affairs*, available at http://www.mfa.gov.il/MFA/MFAArchive/2000_2009/2004/3/Suicide+bombing+at+Ashdod+Port+14-Mar-2004.htm.

Securing the Global Supply Chain: Customs-Trade Partnership Against Terrorism (C-TPAT) Strategy. 2004. *US Customs and Border Protection*, available at http://www.cbp.gov/linkhandler/cgov/trade/cargo_security/ctpat/what_ctpat/ctpat_strategicplan.ctt/ctpat_strategicplan.pdf.

Sloan, Stanley R. 2003. *NATO, The European Union, and the Atlantic Community: The Transatlantic Bargain Reconsidered* (Lanham, MD: Rowman and Littlefield).

SOLAS (International Convention for the Safety of Life at Sea). 1974. Available at http://www.imo.org/Conventions/mainframe.asp?topic_id=250.

The International Maritime Organization, web page available at http://www.imo.org/. Retrieved 2009.

"The United Nations Convention on the Law of the Sea: A Historical Perspective." 2007 Oceans and Law of the Sea: Division for Ocean Affairs and the Law of the Sea. *United Nations. http://www.un.org/Depts/los/convention_agreements/convention_historical_perspective.htm)*

"Trade Concerns Over European AEO Proposal." Summer 2006. *SITPRO News*, Vol. 57, available at http://www.sitpro.org.uk/news/articles/snar200608c.html.

Wallerstein, Immanuel. July-August 2002. "The Eagle Has Crash Landed," *Foreign Policy*, 60-68.

Waltz, Kenneth. 1979. *Theory of International Politics* (Boston, MA: McGraw-Hill)

Wendt, Alexander. 1999. *Social Theory of International Politics* (Cambridge, UK: Cambridge University Press).

Wendt, Alexander. Spring 1992. "Anarchy is What States Make of It: The Social Construction of Power Politics," *International Organization*, Vol. 46, No. 2, 391-425.

"What Does the World Think of Us?," April 2007. *PBS-NOW*, available at http://www.pbs.org/now/shows/314/opinions-of-us.html.

Woodard, Kelby. 2007. "C-TPAT-AEO the Lessons of Globalization," *Trade Innovations*, available at http://www.tradeinnovations.com/NewsDetail.aspx?NewsItemID=36.

The World Trade Organization (WTO) web page, available at http://www.wto.org/. Retrieved 2009.

Chapter 6
Balancing National and Economic Security

Introduction

The events of 9/11 highlighted the economic realities of global trade and its importance to national economies. The US government immediately closed all borders, airports, and seaports in the aftermath of the terrorist attacks. By the evening of September 11, 2001 miles upon miles of trucks were backed up at the US borders with no idea how to proceed, and, in many cases, with agricultural goods that quickly spoiled. The cost of a port or border closing, even for a short amount of time, is devastating. The events of 9/11 led US border officials to shut down all incoming traffic, causing what Stephen Flynn called the equivalent of the world's most powerful country imposing a trade embargo on itself (Flynn 2002). The days following 9/11 illustrated how security measures at their extreme could become a barrier to trade. US border inspectors were put on a Level 1 alert, defined as a sustained, intensive, anti-terrorism operation, which ended up slowing down cross-border traffic significantly. Peter Andreas writes about the northern border:

> The United States and Canada conduct $1.3 billion worth of two-way trade a day, most of which is moved by truck across the border. 40,000 commercial shipments and 300,000 people cross the 4,000 mile-long US-Canada border every day. In the days after the attacks, delays for trucks hauling cargo across the border increased from one to two minutes to 10-15 hours, stranding parts shipments and perishable goods. For example, trucks were backed up for 36 kilometers [22 miles] at the Ambassador Bridge linking Windsor, Ontario and Detroit. Before 9/11, trucks with pre-clearance could often cross the border in one to two minutes (Andreas 2003, 7-8).

The economic repercussions of this slowdown hit the auto industry particularly hard. The unplanned production loss resulting from parts shortages cost manufacturing facilities millions of dollars, and Ford was forced to close an engine plant in Windsor and a vehicle plant in Michigan. The US-Mexican border was also significantly affected. High-intensity border checks severely slowed down the vast number of trade traveling by truck. Retail sales in both US and Mexican border cities immediately plummeted, leading the city of San Diego to declare a state of economic emergency. Cross-border trade fell an average of 15% in the months following the attacks, costing at least $100 million by one estimate (Andreas 2003). The auto industry was also quick to suffer the results, with the Mexican factories supplying electronics, textiles, and chemicals to US auto companies exhibiting the biggest losses (Ibid.).

One of the largest considerations in container freight security policy formulation and implementation is, necessarily, the pragmatics of global trade. The very idea of containerization as a shipping method was motivated by economic considerations, and consequently economic interests regularly inform the breadth of possibilities within the container security framework. In addition, economic and security interests intersect within the context of national security, blurring the distinction between each set of interests. Economic security is of course a crucial component of national security in both the short-term and long-term health of the US economy. Conversely, well-developed freight security policies can speed up the passage of trade and smooth the process of shipping for legitimate stakeholders, while clumsier security procedures serve as trade barriers and can end up hindering the import and export process.

This chapter tackles the messy intersection of containerized freight security and economics and offers a discussion of the major interests and stakeholders involved from a financial perspective. We begin with an overview of the major tensions between security and economic policies, as well as the areas of compatible motivations and procedures. Next is an analysis of the private business community's involvement in recent containerized freight security policy, both procedural and political, including the major concerns of important business entities. This is followed by an outline of how recent security developments affect trade and economic interests, both positively and negatively. A case study of one major shipping company is included here to illustrate the details of how container security is being framed within the business sector. We conclude with a brief discussion of the future direction of freight security and where public and private interests will continue to merge and diverge. We conclude with a brief discussion of how public and private interests will likely continue to merge and diverge regarding freight security.

Where Economy Meets Security

To better illustrate the intersection between economics and security for containerized freight issues, it is helpful to begin first with an example of one supply chain process. Every day, thousands of containers arrive at US seaports from all over the world. Each shipment represents a different supply chain, from industrial materials for a factory plant or a specific product ready-made for sale at a large US store. A supply chain example prepared by Port of Tacoma officials in Washington state demonstrates the process.

An athletic supply store in Washington State places an order for 500 new pairs of shoes, which are manufactured in Northern China. The company that makes the shoes arranges transport with a Canadian freight forwarder to bring the container-load of shoes from China to the United States. A Chinese trucking company loads the shoe order from the factory in Northern China, and packages the shoes along with orders from other retailers in a 40-foot container, which is bolted shut and fitted with a high-security seal. The seal involved is tamper resistant and contains a unique identifier that cannot easily be forged, meeting the standards of the World Customs Organization for security of containerized freight. The freight forwarder determines it is most economical to truck the container to the Port of Tianjin for trans-Pacific shipment to the United States and contracts with a shipping line to handle the land transportation. The shipping line submits manifest data, which includes information about the exact contents, the exporter, the importer, and the transportation agents involved, to US authorities at least 24 hours before the ship leaves the port. Specifically, the manifest data is sent to CBP and ICE for officials to rate and evaluate the risk level of the container, using intelligence databases. The container is then loaded onto a container ship headed for the Port of Tacoma. The trip takes 12 days. When the ship is 96 hours from Tacoma, the captain of the vessel prepares a report that includes details on each member of the crew, voyage, vessel, cargo, operational and safety information. This report is sent to the US Coast Guard which – if it believes anything to be suspicious – will board the ship at sea to investigate. Once the ship arrives, Port of Tacoma Security, Tacoma Police and other federal, state and local agencies ensure perimeter security around the Port and operate the gates that allow entry. Terminal security ensures only authorized people have access to the terminal and vessel. The USCG, meanwhile, remains responsible for waterside security. Longshore workers in the form of crane operators, lashers, clerks and cargo equipment operators, all of whom have been subjected to relevant background checks, arrive to unload the ship, directed by a terminal operator. CBP officials instruct terminal operators to pull specific containers for further inspection based on risk analyses from the advance manifest. Those that are inspected are subject to a physical inspection of the contents (a six- to 40-hour procedure) or inspection by a Vehicle and Cargo Inspection System machine (VACIS), which uses gamma-ray technology to look inside and confirm the contents of the container without opening it (within three to five minutes). Once cleared by CBP, the container is loaded on a truck chassis and is ready for departure. As the truck exits the Port of Tacoma it passes through a radiation portal monitor, which detects the presence of any radioactive material in the container. The truck and container then leave the Port and arrive at an import distribution center nearby, where the container is opened and the orders by individual stores are separated and prepared for shipment. The next day, the athletic supply store receives its 500 pairs of athletic shoes (Port of Tacoma 2006).

This example demonstrates how trade practices have been influenced by the process of containerization. The standardization of container structure and sizes has made the idea of bringing in goods from China and elsewhere a reality, if not common sense, as containers can travel as intermodal freight transport on ships, rail, trucks, and planes loaded and sealed intact (see Chapter 1). The barriers to importing and exporting at such a distance have consequently been greatly reduced. The advance of telecommunication technologies has allowed shipments to be ordered,

120 *Protecting Our Ports*

processed and transported in a just-in-time framework, and the use of containers reduces the cost of shipping to a point that allows overseas manufacturers to be highly competitive with domestic ones. The borders have been blurred – literally and figuratively – for the entire process of making and selling goods.

The Port of Tacoma case also illustrates the primary concerns for both economic and security purposes. Economically speaking, the overarching goal is for the shipment to be processed and delivered as quickly as possible and with the correct type and number of goods, avoiding loss, theft and damage along the way. In the security realm, the essential task at hand is to make sure there is nothing considered contraband, dangerous, or even plain false about the container's contents and that all personnel involved in the transportation of the shipment are identified as posing little or no risk to the United States. The two sets of goals are not necessarily contradictory. While business and trade interests undoubtedly place a value on speed and cost, and national security interests would likely assert that the safety of the United States trumps all other considerations, both realms have common ground in the constant search for efficiency and accountability. The tensions that do exist between business interests in smoother trade, on the one hand, and container security policies, on the other hand, lie in the specific areas of mandated scanning, the level of identification screening for different levels of transportation workers, issues of privacy and data outsourcing, new technologies, and contingency plans for post-recognition of threats. More generally, the main concern of business is that some new security policies and requirements are layered on top of existing layers too hastily and without enough consideration given to previous standards of practice. Conversely, those on the security side are concerned about security weaknesses in the passage of containerized freight that cannot and should not be ignored, such as the lack of strict surveillance around seaport access or seaport operations, the possibilities for subterfuge with falsified advance manifests and ship reports, and tampering with containers in transport.

Theories of Economic and National Security

Theories of international relations, more often than not, tend to isolate and separate different forms of "security" apart from each other. In an anarchical system characterized by state autonomy and without any overarching authority, states cannot escape the awareness of their own sense of security and their status in relation to other states (see Chapter 5). It is this self-help environment that leads realist scholars to suggest that economic issues are of secondary concern. Other approaches, like neoliberalism, emphasize economic issues and cooperation instead of self-interest and military capabilities (Baldwin 1993, 4-5). Neoliberalism views wealth as a main priority of states in addition to power and, therefore, concentrates on economic issues over military concerns (Gilpin 1987).

These theories illuminate how economic issues are normally considered separately from military or defense security. Economic security for a country can be loosely defined as having stable national income, resources, and production levels that translate into predictable GDP and manageable debts for the foreseeable future (Gilpin 1987). Economic wellbeing may be perceived as part of a country's national security, along with military and political power (to include diplomacy) (Morgenthau 1948). Defense security, when contrasted, can be loosely defined as a component of military power that addresses intelligence, readiness, and preventative measures along with preparedness for events requiring military intervention (Waltz 1979). In reality, however, economic security and military security are often intimately entwined and cannot be easily parsed as separate entities. Oil as an increasingly scarce natural resource is certainly evidence in support this point as it illustrates the messy intersection between a major economic resource and the military strength and capability of a state.

For the issue of containerized freight security, the intersection between economic security and defense security is occasionally at odds when considering the speed and volume of trade that is transported via containers daily. Usage of containers is now commonplace to the point of being essential for global trade, and the financial dependence on global trade for businesses, companies and investors makes the smooth passage of containerized freight a critical component of national GDP. At the same time, the volume of containerized freight that passes through US ports, borders and airports presents a series of overwhelming security risks in the form of intentional acts of aggression against the United States. The international supply chain and container shipping represent – for all countries – a true amalgamation of different forms of national security. Economic strength *is* a major defense, and military security is often employed to protect national economic interests when federal agencies such as the US Coast Guard have critical roles in smoothing and securing the passage of containerized freight. To polarize economic security and defense security is to create barriers that inhibit effective problem-solving, but to consider them as intertwined forms of national security promotes creative solutions. Reconciliation between the two areas ought to take place where economics and security share common ground – efficiency and accountability.

Brief Overview of the Economics of Container Port Shipping

According to the American Association of Port Authorities (AAPA), deep water ports accommodate ocean-going vessels, which carry more than 99% of US overseas trade – imports and exports – by weight and 64% by value. In addition, the inland and intracoastal waterways provide a low-cost means for moving domestic bulk commodities, such as grain, coal and petroleum. This port-based trade represented $3.15 trillion to the US GDP in 2007 (AAPA 2009). In 2009 the top ten trading partners with the US were (in order) Canada, China, Mexico, Japan, Germany, United Kingdom, South Korea, France, The Netherlands, and Brazil (US Census 2009). Of the top ten container shipping companies in terms of TEU

(20-foot equivalent units) capacity, four are from Western Europe, two from China, one from the United States, one from Japan, and one from South Korea (ALPHALINER 2009). Trade with Canada and Mexico occurs primarily – but not exclusively – through trucks at land borders. Trade with these countries contributed $412 billion of exports and $556 billion of imports in 2008 (US Census Bureau 2008a; US Census Bureau 2008b). Additionally, trade with other countries overseas may involve containers being shipped to a Canadian port and then put on trucks to enter into the United States, depending on the shippers, shipping companies, and freight forwarders used for transport. The northern border in particular then absorbs more US trade than is reflected in statistics dealing with Canadian imports from and exports to the United States

The US ports receiving the highest volume of global containerized freight in 2008 in terms of TEUs were (in order): Los Angeles, CA; Long Beach,[1] CA; New York/New Jersey; Savannah, GA; Oakland, CA; Hampton Roads, VA; Tacoma, WA; Houston, TX; Seattle, WA; and Charleston, SC (AAPA Survey 2008). An estimated 70% of the containers arriving at the ports of Los Angeles and Long Beach are put on trains or trucks bound for a port on the East Coast, to then be shipped to Europe. The Port of New York/New Jersey receives a great deal of containers headed in the opposite direction – towards a West Coast port to then be shipped to Asia (Port Interviews 2006-2007). The cargo that comes into all ports is then quickly dispersed by truck or train to the intended destination. Seaports receive by far the majority of containerized shipments of imports arriving from other countries. Trucks and trains bring in a large amount of goods from North American neighbors, while air traffic brings in a much smaller percentage of containerized freight imports due to size and weight restrictions on most aircraft (see Chapter 2).

The Private Sector: Issues and Concerns

This section comprises a review of the major issues private industry and businesses perceive in the implementation of existing policy and procedures. Data for this section comes from interviews conducted with private sector officials and related organizations, such as the AAPA (American Association of Port Authorities), UPS, FedEx, XLA (Express Delivery and Logistics Association), the US Chamber of Commerce, Lockheed Martin, and the ATA (American Trucking Association). The purpose of studying the goals and perceptions from the business or private enterprise side of containerized freight issues is to understand the economics behind the movement of containerized freight and to outline the economic considerations that need to be accounted for in security policy formulation. The

---

1   The neighboring Ports of Los Angeles and Long Beach are technically two separate entities. However, due to their close proximity CBP treats them as a single port with regard to security.

following provides an overview of the major issues and developments that have preoccupied the private sector with regards to container freight security – from shippers to port authorities to freight forwarders to technology companies. For recent container security policies, the main financial considerations for seaports, shippers, and business entities involved in international trade include the implementation costs of new technologies and upgrades and maintenance of existing technologies, such as container seals, personnel identification systems, and new databases.

Relationships between public entities and private industry in the field of container security have been relatively successful, by all accounts. Collaboration has taken place primarily through business organizations such as the US Chamber of Commerce and its sub-groups dealing with transportation research and security regulations, and through interest associations such as the Express Delivery and Logistics Associations. These organizations and associations have sought to establish strong and long-lasting relationships between their member businesses and the regulators and legislators that affect their bottom line. They do this by advocating the issues and interests that are important to the business community, and by informing and responding to the policy agendas of the legislative branch. As an industry, the container shipping, importing, and exporting fields and the businesses contained within them are strongly organized and represented to policymakers. This is due in large part out of necessity. All businesses involved in importation must maintain relationships and information-networking opportunities to stay apprised of laws and regulations in order to stay in business.

Container Seals

There has been a great deal of discussion among politicians and the media regarding the creation of safer, smarter seals and better containers. Both government and private companies have invested money in this direction. Most of the officials we interviewed were, however, skeptical that the answer to supply chain security could be found in "wired" seals and containers. Officials highlighted the ease with which seals could be broken in the course of sea transfer. Moreover, they demonstrated how containers might be compromised without even touching the seal. When asked about developing "smart" containers that had detectors, pessimism remained. We were reminded that these containers are handled by big machinery and placed on a ship that traverses stormy waters where containers might be knocked around. If the trip is enough to knock seals off of containers, it would surely be enough to set off motion alarms. Even a small number of false alarms, officials argue, could be debilitating to trade. Containers going by rail or truck are likely to face similar problems. While the officials we interviewed were careful not to dismiss new technological developments, they were not convinced that the safer seals or containers being proposed at the time were the answer (Industry Interviews 2007).

Transportation Worker Identification Credential

Another issue that was often raised concerned the introduction of the TWIC cards. These new, universal identification cards were required as of mid-2009 of all personnel involved in port and border operations under the MTSA of 2002 and SAFE Port Act of 2006. Officials expressed concern about replacement cards, computer failures and the significant cost of outfitting facilities for TWIC usage, either for the TWIC itself or in having the resources to hire enough officers to issue and maintain the TWIC system. While officials were careful to say that they did have enough officials on the ground, they all admitted that their further development is limited due to financial concerns. Currently, TWIC only applies to personnel involved with maritime transportation and not with personnel involved with transport across land borders or at airports. Interviewees at the AAPA Trade Partners division stated that their members had expressed frustration that the technology selected to develop TWIC was done internally by DHS, without consulting port authorities. In addition, many reported that their members were concerned about how TWIC could potentially result in the exclusion of potential workers and thus harming "laborability." The specific concerns were that workers with minor misdemeanors on their record would be identified and excluded from the workforce, making hiring a problem, and that the cost and burden of TWIC could potentially make employee recruitment and retention a problem (Industry Interviews 2007).

Data Access

Both public and private sector officials applauded efforts to increase data gathering and electronic submission of manifests as a means of tightening security procedures and expediting legitimate trade. E-freight capabilities at border crossings offer CBP advance notice with which they can conduct more thorough and rigorous evaluations of incoming cargo, vehicles and personnel, and offer the private sector a consistent means of preparing for customs clearance. In this sense, a focus on data gathering policies appears to meet the needs of both heightened security and economic mobility.

However, one area of trouble cited by businesses and organizations is the sometimes sensitive nature of revealing company data (Industry Interviews 2007). Some business interviewees stated that in the highly competitive environment of freight forwarders, express delivery and trucking companies, privacy is critical for the protection of company trade secrets from competitors. In the business world, data is leverage. Increasing amounts of proprietary information, such as the price and content of products, are being required and potentially shared as businesses interact with government agencies. Businesses worry about losing their competitive advantage when CBP begins to require more and more data at earlier advance time points. Most of this worry is centered on where this data will be stored and who will have access to it. Some officials stated that there are currently ongoing projects dealing with third party, nongovernmental data collection strategies that would address the concerns of business. The possibility of a third party, nongovernmental entity collecting data from industry for the purposes of security manifests was highly relevant for private businesses. Some private enterprises did not express support for this idea, citing concerns regarding trust and reliability of those involved in protecting trade data and its impact on competitiveness. More often, industry representatives expressed concerns with the cost of switching to a new data gathering system. New data gathering programs carry the possibility of upsetting years of IT work within private industry. Industry interviewees stated that their members were extremely comfortable with automation and data collection as risk management and assessment tools, as many members had programs that were voluntarily developed years before 9/11 in the interests of harmonizing certain automation measures and getting through customs quickly, both at home and abroad. As such, there is concern within the industry that requiring a standard set of new programs could be costly and take years to implement and streamline, when many existing programs may be just as effective (Industry Interviews 2007).

Advance Manifests

A 2004 article in *Frontline Solutions* details the costs importers and exporters were faced with after DHS and TSA implemented new cargo security requirements in 2003 – namely, the new reporting requirements for ground and air cargo, and new advance manifest requirements for human and animal food shipments. The 2003 requirements, as detailed in Chapter 4, stated that manifest reporting timelines for inbound freight to the United States should be at "wheels up" for air and courier (or four hours prior to arrival if the flight is longer than four hours), two hours prior to arrival at a US port of entry for rail, 24 hours prior to lading at a foreign port for ship vessels, and 30 minutes to an hour prior to arrival in the United States for trucks, for FAST and non-FAST members respectively. These new rules had the biggest impact on air and land freight, which were not previously subject to routine automated targeting systems. Within that, the "just-in-time" supply chain operators[2] perceived the most hassle as the new electronic advance notice requirements incurred some time delays for companies importing from Canada by truck. An interviewee from Purolator Courier Ltd. in the *Frontline Solutions* article stated that complying with the new rules – particularly the related Food and Drug Administration (FDA) rule that required food importers to provide electronic advance notice of food shipments – meant that Canadian companies had to invest in redoing its own software systems in order to communicate with CBP, adjust its operational window, and add staff to provide the advance manifests. In addition,

---

2   "Just-in-time" refers to a business inventory strategy of production on demand. This strategy relies on constant signals between the supply side (production and shipping) and the demand side (business partners and consumers) in order to reduce inventory, warehouse, and carrying costs (Schonberger 1982).

some brokerage services had increased processing costs to meet the new advance manifest requirements, and Canadian shipping companies redesigned their routes to avoid crossing the US border with food items destined for Western Canada (Albright 2004). The primary concern for the food industry is that any new regulation that was assigned extra time to the shipping process carries the risk of spoilage and waste for food shipments.

Most of our own interviewees expressed similar opinions for the "just-in-time" freight forwarding industry. While most interviewees recognized that advance manifests have been successful in streamlining trade and allowing CBP more time to analyze data and identify potentially insecure shipments, the express industry has many members that have contracted out to just-in-time freight forwarders, and consequently the industry is concerned with CBP efforts to demand more data in shorter time frames. Some interviewees worried that the "10+2" in effect at seaports – the rule that requires ten information-related elements at all seaports in conjunction with the 24-hour advance manifests, plus two additional elements (vessel stowage plans and container status) 48 hours in advance of vessel departure from a foreign port (CBP Press Release 2008) – would eventually be extended in some manner to land and air containerized freight. Express industry members suggest that extending "10+2" to land and air contradicts the rapid response nature of the immediate shipping industry. Others, however, acknowledged that money would need to be spent on understanding and communicating with the rest of the supply chain, and that this could have long-term positive impacts on efficiency (Industry Interviews 2008).

Reliance on Technology

Private industry also includes firms specializing in technology, particularly systems deemed useful for security measures. Technology represents an interesting point of commonality between economic security and defense security for the economic development it incurs in the domestic technological sector and for the security advances it potentially stands to innovate. Investments in security technology, specifically those that can be used as protective deterrent measures against terrorism, offer a source of economic advantage for domestic companies and serve the purposes of public entities concerned with tightening security measures at points of entry to the United States. At the same time, an emphasis on technology as a prime solution to container security issues can easily be "overemphasized," in the words of one official from a freight forwarding company. Many interviewees felt that there could be no substitute for human oversight – only technological tools as complements to trained and skilled workers. Another concern relevant to the above point of potential problems with data storage and access was that too much technology used in endeavors such as advance manifests and trusted-traveler programs could easily translate into a storehouse of material that could, if it falls into the wrong hands, be used as a weapon against the United States (Industry Interviews 2007).

An implicit criticism weaving through many discussions of security technologies with certain interviewees was that some of the container security measures being considered reflected the more privileged position of higher-speed technology companies with government as compared to the position of various transportation associations. Essentially, some interviewees felt that government was pushing technological developments as the primary way to enhance containerized freight security because it would boost the national economy via the technological sector – and not because it was necessarily the best way to enhance security. This frustration was usually targeted at endeavors such as CSI and measures calling for increased scanning at ports and borders. Generally speaking, businesses that have heavy investment in speedy trade prefer security developments that utilize risk assessments instead of inspection methods. Therefore, some perceived the proposal for 100% scanning as successful lobbying on the part of technological industry leaders, rather than the smartest security practice (Industry Interview 2007).

Consultation and Involvement

A recurrent frustration recognized by almost all interviewees, public and private, was that a great deal of policy formulation was being done without consultation with actual port authorities or port operation experts. For many, this was a necessary frustration as CBP could not share many protocols or logistics out of a security need for heightened confidentiality. For others, the worry was that new DHS regulations would place too heavy a burden on port facilities and shippers, and that the fallout from this would hurt industry and the general economy. The overarching concern is essentially that security protocols tend to focus on specific problems and not the entire shipping process, rather than designing policy that recognizes the integrated process of container shipping as a whole. Public officials' response to this criticism has been to encourage industry leaders and associations to come forward and remain involved in all parts of the security policy process. To this end, many successful ventures have come about as a result of joint public-private collaboration, and all interviewees were strongly supportive of such collaborations as future policy prescription (Industry Interviews 2007).

C-TPAT is an example of policy formulation that has been widely perceived as sensible. The inter-modality of express delivery operations entails that the supply chain cannot be understood in isolation. C-TPAT's mission is to heighten the security of the supply chain through voluntary government-business partnerships that strengthen joint endeavors to keep US borders safe from trafficking and terrorism. The logic of C-TPAT relies on business initiative to raise security standards in their interactions with business partners. Government then offers priority processing and other benefits, such as training, in reward for C-TPAT membership (CBP 2007). Companies such as UPS and FedEx use all modes of transportation (plane, ship, train, truck) and have been among the private business members that helped pioneer security and automation systems even prior to 9/11. Industry interviewees all emphasized that threats in the supply chain have long existed in the form of criminal activities. Accordingly, many of the security practices in place today were initiated by business as a means to track shipments and enhance performance. The private sector continues to lead the way in security research and development across the globe. For this reason, most private sector interviewees felt strongly about maintaining the voluntary principles of C-TPAT in any additional security measures. The number of companies involved in the supply chain makes the business atmosphere very competitive, and the logic of using financial motivations to get people to comply resonated with all interviewees. In addition, many parts of the supply chain are outside the jurisdiction of CBP or the United States government. Interviewees felt that allowing businesses to raise their security standards on the basis of competitive advantage and government incentives was the most appropriate manner to implement new security regimes, as a system of minimum criteria would be impossible to design (Industry Interviews 2008).

Related to this is industry's expected criticism of government actors in general. For the most part, the creation of DHS as an umbrella agency was viewed positively as a solid organizational step, but the perception of agencies and bureaucracies within DHS was that of high turnover, excessive secrecy, and a great deal of disjoint between government infrastructure and port and border practices (Industry Interviews 2007). While undoubtedly such criticisms are unsurprising and merit analytical assessment, the volume of responsibility placed on CBP and the relatively high turnover of senior TSA officials are worrisome signs for industry leaders with high stakes in container security policy. It should be noted, however, that generalized criticism against regulators is a likely feature of an environment as complex as the international supply chain, regardless of the security context.

Need for Centralized Contingency Plans

One of the main containerized freight security issues that all interviewees cited as still being very much in need of attention is that of contingency plans, or response protocols, in the event of a security breach or national emergency. Both the public and private sector are concerned with the lack of comprehensive emergency management systems at all points of freight access. However, each sector has different motivations for their concern. Government and security agencies remain primarily concerned with response times, communication infrastructure between border, airport and seaports, and effective planning. The private sector remains primarily concerned with contingency plans that do not cripple the flow of trade and do not invite an overreaction towards all cargo entry points. An area of commonality between both sectors is in the perceived need for consistency of regulations and a streamlined approach. At present, there is no platform plan among businesses or organizations as to how to conduct operations in the event of a terrorist-related security threat, outside of isolating suspicious cargo and waiting for US government authorities to deal with the said cargo. CBP, for example, cannot tell ports what to do or how to handle emergency closings. Emergency response details are left to port authorities and operators, which makes consistency among the many US ports receiving international shipments a near impossibility (Agency Interviews 2007).

In the event of another border shutdown, TSA and DHS have said that they will work first in line with C-TPAT members and recognize the strongest volunteers to the program once trade is resumed, allowing these volunteers to be among the first to move their cargo shipments across the border – in a sense, creating a "security elite," though this does not answer the question of what shippers should do before the resumption of trade. Other groups began conducting outreach programs and table top testing of contingency plans after the events of 9/11. However, all interviewees from the private sector expressed concern that issues of responsibility and reliability, along with areas for potential calamity, remain outstanding with no overarching agency, office, or set of principles to adhere to in the event of a large-scale security threat. The general consensus among private sector interviewees is that the nature and length of the border shutdowns immediately following the events of 9/11 were an "overreaction" in terms of how it affected trade, and that there ought to be some sort of overarching protocol for what shippers can do with their products to avoid millions of dollars of losses in revenue (Agency Interviews 2007).

The lack of plans for redirection in the event of a port closure was troubling for many officials we interviewed, but most were unsure about how to develop and implement such a plan. If authorities are serious about protecting ports and the system of global trade, industry officials argue that there must be a joint procedure for incident response, recovery and especially redirection. In order to minimize the interruption to trade, it seems reasonable to have rerouting plans and recovery procedures. These programs, however, are currently lacking. Contingency plans in the form of response and recovery frameworks suffer from a lack of infrastructure. Air transportation is less of a problem in this regard than land operations. Airports come under the jurisdiction of TSA and 94% of all air traffic around the world is operated by an International Air Transport Association (IATA) member. The air traffic and security operations at US airports also tend to be more streamlined and hierarchical than what might be found at a seaport or land border crossing (Industry Interview 2007). Border crossings, while subject to the same basic standards as laid out through DHS and the DOS, have more variation in their operations depending on location, amount of traffic, staffing, and capabilities. CBP officials working on the border also lack reliable communication infrastructure between different border points at both northern and southern locations. Seaport closings are highly problematic, as vessels have fewer options of where to dock if turned away from a particular port. Should it be necessary for a port to shut down, there is presently no set policy to which all US ports adhere so that not only the port equipment is protected, but so ships can be rerouted and the disruption to trade minimized. All ports have their own close down and weather policies. Even in terms of terrorist threats and what will happen if a port or terminal must close due to an attack, there is no standard procedure for assuring that goods are re-routed and the economic impact managed. This lack of a coherent and consistent policy and procedure is part of what the SAFE Port Act hopes to change. Part of the problem, however, stems from geography. If Seattle is closed down, some of its shipments can be diverted to other ports along the West Coast, but the time that it would take to traverse the Panama Canal to divert to the East Coast would be impractical and edible goods would likely spoil. As mentioned, if Los Angeles/Long Beach were to close down completely, it is unlikely that its massive load of cargo could be handled by other West Coast ports (while still accepting and facilitating their scheduled shipments). Moreover, the Panama Canal cannot be navigated by many of the large ships that off load in large West Coast ports (Agency Interviews 2007; Port Interviews 2006-2007).

Other Financial Considerations

It is important to be aware of the financials of emergency closings, or even re-routings, as terrorism is not the only situation that could cause a port or border closing. Inclement weather, traffic accidents, union strikes, and security concerns other than intentional attacks have the potential to necessitate a large-scale closing of US points of entry, and thus the potential for large-scale economic losses.

The Port of Los Angeles/Long Beach, when viewed as a singular port, is the busiest port in the country in terms of the volume of containers that come into the United States. The port handles over 40% of US imports of containerized freight. The port is also close in proximity to a major US city and not far from a porous land border with Mexico. Because of its location on the Pacific, Los Angeles/ Long Beach sees some of the world's largest ships, which are unable to traverse the Panama Canal and could not be easily redirected to smaller ports along the Western seaboard in the event of some catastrophic incident. The closing of the Los Angeles/Long Beach port due to an attack or disruption, even for a day, could have detrimental effects on the nation's economy. As was so clearly evidenced in New Orleans during Hurricane Katrina in 2005, the weather often becomes the biggest threat to US seaports in terms of a potential closedown or delay of business. Officials in both Seattle and New Orleans suggested that weather is a much more immediate issue as it has the potential to significantly affect traffic. Miami, Houston and other ports along the southeast coast have similar hurricane worries as those in New Orleans. A CBP officer in New Orleans explained that when a hurricane warning is issued, they are required to move all transferable machinery to an established location in land. The officer commented that this happens on average twice every year, closing the port to shipping traffic. Other ports vulnerable to hurricanes and bad weather have similar policies in place (Agency Interviews 2006-2007; Port Interviews 2006-2007).

Another economic factor in port closings and financial losses is the circumstance of striking by organized interests for either issues related to working conditions or those related to ideological considerations. As detailed in Chapter 2, the International Longshore and Warehouse Union endured a worker shutdown in 2002 due to stalled negotiations with employers, and voluntarily went on strike for one day in May 2008 to protest the war in Iraq (McLaughlin 2006; Yardley 2008). As with any union situation, discussions between workers' unions and employers associations have the potential to halt workforce activity and production if negotiations come to an impasse. Depending on the issue at hand and the level of organized interests, such impasses can affect either a single port or a single set of workers at a port, or can affect a larger group of multiple workers at many ports. Security policies for work halts must also be in place to account for shipments that are stalled as a result, and to account for the appropriate training and screening of temporary workers that might be brought in to maintain port activity during a strike. In 2002, a short strike by longshoremen, clerks and bosses at West Coast ports from Seattle to San Diego were locked out for ten days over a contract dispute, costing the nation's economy an estimated $1 to $2 billion a day, the lockout ended only when President George Bush invoked the Taft-Hartley Act to send the International Longshore and Warehouse Union back to work ("Longshore Stoppage Closes US Pacific Coast Ports" 2008). The closure shut down loading and unloading operations at ports, creating a ripple effect through all the industries that depend on containerized freight. Examples of such strikes on smaller scales are not uncommon, as are threatened strikes and other forms of organized action between unions and employers associations. On May 1, 2008, approximately 10,000 workers from the ILWU staged a one-day strike at West Coast ports reportedly in protest against the war in Iraq. The single day of striking did not have a severe impact economically, as labor officials had alerted shippers and carriers ahead of time, and so the slowdown was tantamount to port activity on an official holiday (Yardley 2008). The main implication from this for security policies ought to be that advance planning and a framework of contingency plans for any kind of emergency – from the extreme example of a terrorist attack to the seasonal example of severe weather – will provide at least some sort of structure of action for business actors and federal agencies alike.

Security concerns exist also for basic logjams and line-ups with heavy port traffic and the unloading of thousands of containers. In September 2004, a huge traffic jam at the Ports of Los Angeles and Long Beach held up the unloading of ships and containers to double the amount of time that it normally takes. During the height of the crisis, 83 vessels were stuck waiting to be unloaded. The traffic jam was blamed on the much higher volume of imports arriving from China and the Far East than in previous years (Bartholomew 2005). Traffic jams of this nature pose a serious risk of human error and oversight as well as enhancing the possibility of a terrorist designing an intentional attack to take advantage of the chaos. Economically, the delays in unloading and transporting incoming cargo are severely detrimental to businesses at home and abroad. While many West Coast ports have been working on increasing capacity and training workers, some manufacturers are recognizing the potential pitfalls of traffic jams and are turning their importing methods to air freight and sourcing materials from North America to reduce their dependence on ocean shipping (Ibid.).

132 *Protecting Our Ports*

Emergency closings of port and border operations and the contingency plans that ought to accompany them, are a definitive example of how security and economic goals can be one and the same – speedy, facilitated trade between trusted entities with explicit systems in place to identify anomalies and potentially high-risk people and/or shipments. Contingency plans would assist shippers and the companies that work with them to know what their priorities and options are during any kind of import blockage, and would at the same time lend additional structure and hierarchy to the public agencies involved in domestic security.

United Parcel Service (UPS): A Case Study of Supply Chain Security

UPS, as one of the world's biggest package delivery services, is an excellent example of a prominent company heavily involved in the international supply chain and containerized freight security policies as a result. UPS is the world's ninth largest airline and the railroad's biggest customer. With approximately 300 jets and 80,000 vehicles at its disposal, UPS is thoroughly enmeshed in the politics and practices of shipping containerized freight by all modes of transport.

Some insights from our interviews with UPS personnel include the perception of "100% scanning" and how that translates into practice, the perception of costs for new security programs and the resulting implications for competitiveness, and the perception of trusted-traveler programs. First, for the 100% scanning initiative, UPS representatives felt confident that the implementation of SFI would not be as strict as the initial letter of the law proposed. This was because the language of "inspection," "screening," and "scanning" had been often confused during the process of legislation, and UPS knew of a great deal of protest against 100% scanning that should likely modify the practices of the legislation. Interviewees were quick to agree that 100% *inspection*, in the form of information collecting and other non-intrusive methods, was certainly a sensible idea, but felt in alliance with other organizations that 100% scanning was unreasonable and would impose a significant barrier to the industry. Second, the interviewees were not greatly concerned with costs associated with new security policies, such as C-TPAT, advance manifests, etc. This was primarily due to the company's previous operating methods and mandates, which already contained some elements of what the new protocols required (detailed information on contents, shippers, handlers, and personnel). The main cost that would have to be absorbed was a pilot certified shipper program, similar to a program in the EU called "known consigners." Interviewees were hesitant to say that this cost was worthwhile, given the logic of C-TPAT. They also stated that the idea of a centralized database for known shippers would not work for businesses because of privacy issues surrounding pricing and business relationships. Third, UPS felt strongly that C-TPAT was a solid program in both formulation and implementation. Interviewees believed that they had received enough information and been invited to participate in C-TPAT development sessions through their memberships in shipping organizations (such as XLA), and felt equally strongly that initiatives building off of public-private relationships would be the most successful for advancing security policies. They also stated that the inherent competitive nature of C-TPAT – where businesses voluntarily decide to upgrade their security practices and meet higher standards of security in exchange for privileged procedural benefits at various points of entry into the United States. Those interviewed believed this was an excellent precedent to set for future security initiatives (Industry Interviews 2007).

The cumulative information from the UPS interviews showed that businesses cannot escape the competitive nature of their environment if they are to maintain their own existence. This is a point that cannot be emphasized enough when considering security policies designed to protect imports to the United States. All of our interviews with private industry taken together revealed that trade and security do not need to be competing goals for national security, and can in fact co-exist relatively harmoniously with a great deal of collaboration. In this sense, detailed information and risk management in the form of screening is key for all actors involved.

Conclusion

Recognition of private sector efforts is important due to the perennial tension between the competing needs of heightened security and economic efficiency of trade. Security is an evident part of the mainstream supply chain paradigm, and security can also become a driver for trade facilitation (Banomyong 2005). Theories of international relations more often than not tend to treat economic security and defense security as two separate worlds within a state's national security. The reality – particularly for global trade and modern states' reliance on importing and exporting – is that economic security cannot and should not be treated as distinct from any major form of national security in order for policy design to remain effective and efficient. Given that security concerns are now a pressing issue in the passage of trade and containerized freight, prevention and monitoring measures must necessarily be compatible with high economic performances. This is particularly important for "just-in-time" and "door-to-door" shipping services that require a high security level coupled with low inventory level and efficient movements between several points of origins and destinations (Ibid.).

Efficiency and accountability are the two overarching areas where defense security meets economic security for general national interest. Many new security policies contain inherent logistics costs for the private sector to absorb. This is true for data management and software systems, such as for freight forwarders to provide the correct electronic advance manifests to CBP. This is also the case for staffing and training in multiple areas, such as along land borders and to maintain the TWIC program. Similarly, developing infrastructure to meet new security policies, such as for handling radiation portals and the material resulting from their use at various locations, also necessitates absorbing significant costs over an extended period of time.

Generalizable contingency plans ought to be developed and implemented to manage a catastrophic incident in the form of a terrorist attack if one were to occur. Such plans need to go beyond the immediate shutdowns and alerts to account for trade blockages and slowdowns, and need to be designed to minimize economic losses – in particular, cargo waiting to be imported. Government agencies and public officials should continue to formulate and implement such plans in a cooperative manner with industry leaders, since such collaborative ventures have shown significant results in timely and effective security policies. This is true for all new security policies relating to containerized freight and all imports to the United States.

This chapter explored the main issues uniting public and private stakeholders in container security thought and practice, using first-hand interviews between the authors and important actors in business, government, and organized interests. At first glance, the priorities of safety, risk, and security to national defense interests bristle against the priorities of cost and time for economic interests. The danger of increased supply chain security is higher logistics costs, which in turn exert negative pressure on economic growth for the US economy by slowing down the actual movement of trade and by limiting the operational scope of companies involved in importing freight to the United States. For this reason policy makers need to continue to involve the private sector whenever possible in formulating risk assessment measures so as to avoid unnecessary barriers to trade. The positive developments that have occurred to date – where positive indicates a general consensus that security practices are tighter and that the policy works well for the private sector too, such as C-TPAT – illustrate that the longer-term consequences for heightening supply chain security could be beneficial for all stakeholders involved. Certified and recognized operators will enjoy smoother importing procedures, raising competitive stakes for other legitimate actors seeking to maintain their footing in the industry. Greater security, in the longer term, can just as easily lead to increased efficiency and stronger trade relationships, thus serving the purpose of all elements of national security. Having examined the domestic and international politics of containerized freight security, as well as the difficult issues of balancing economic and national security, in the next chapter we evaluate port operations at 17 domestic and international seaports.

Bibliography

Albright, Brian. February 2004. "New Cargo Security Regulations Present Challenges to Shippers, Carriers: Advance Manifest and Food Safety Rules Could Increase Safety and Cost of Cross-border Shipments," *Frontline Solutions*, February 2004, Bnet, available at http://findarticles.com/p/articles/mi_m0DIS/is_2_5/ai_113907155/?tag=content;col1.

ALPHALINER. May 2009. "Top 100 – How it Works?," available at http://www. axs-alphaliner.com/top100/AXS-Alphaliner-TOP100.pdf.

American Association of Port Authorities (AAPA) Survey. 2008. "North American Port Container Traffic," available at http://aapa.files.cms-plus.com/Statistics/ NORTHAMERICANPORTCONTAINERTRAFFIC2008.pdf.

American Association of Port Authorities (AAPA). 2009. "Port Industry Information: Trade and Economic Growth," available at http://www.aapa-ports.org/Industry/content.cfm?ItemNumber=1024&navItemNumber=1027.

Andreas, Peter. 2003. "A Tale of Two Borders: The US-Mexico and US-Canada Lines After 9/11," *The Center for Comparative Immigration Studies*, University of California, San Diego. Working Paper No. 77, available at http://ccis.ucsd. edu/PUBLICATIONS/wrkg77.pdf.

Baldwin, David A. 1993. "Neoliberalism, Neorealism, and World Politics," in D.A. Baldwin (ed.), *Neorealism and Neoliberalism: The Contemporary Debate* (New York: Columbia University Press), 3-27.

Banomyong, Ruth. 2005. "The Impact of Port and Trade Security Initiatives on Maritime Supply-Chain Management," *Maritime Policy Management*, Vol. 32, No.1, 3-13.

Bartholomew, Doug. March 2005. "Cargo Crunch! Manufacturers are bringing sourcing back to North America, using more air freight and building inventories as a response to tie-ups at West Coast Ports," *Industry Week*, available at http:// www.industryweek.com/articles/cargo_crunch_9980.aspx.

Customs and Border Patrol (CBP). December 2007. "C-TPAT Overview," available at http://www.cbp.gov/xp/cgov/trade/cargo_security/ctpat/what_ctpat/ctpat_ overview.xml.

Customs and Border Patrol (CBP) Press Release. January 2008. "CBP Issues Proposed Rule Requiring Additional Cargo Information," available at http:// www.cbp.gov/xp/cgov/newsroom/news_releases/archives/2008_news_ releases/jan_2008/01022008.xml.

Flynn, Stephen E. January/February 2002. "America the Vulnerable," *Foreign Affairs*, Vol. 81, No. 1, 60-74.

Gilpin, Robert. 1987. *The Political Economy of International Relations* (Princeton, NJ: Princeton University Press).

Keohane, Robert O. 1984. *After Hegemony: Cooperation and Discord in the World Political Economy* (Princeton, NJ: Princeton University Press).

"Longshore Stoppage Closes US Pacific Coast Ports," June 2008. *The Cal Trade Report*, available at http://www.caltradereport.com/eWebPages/front-page-1209668183.html.

McLaughlin, Lindsey. March 2006. "The ILWU Goes to Washington," *International Longshore and Warehouse Union*, available at http://www.ilwu. org/dispatcher/2006/01/2006-01-washrpt.cfm.

Morgenthau, Hans J. 1992. *Politics Among Nations: The Struggle for Power and Peace* (5th Edition, revised) (New York: Knopf).

Port of Tacoma. 2006. "From Here to There: Supply Chain Security to the Port of Tacoma," available at http://staging.aapa.files.cms-plus.com/PDFs/supply_chain_security_example.pdf?nav ItemNumber=1100.

Schonberger, Richard J. 1982. *Japanese Manufacturing Techniques: Nine Hidden Lessons in Simplicity* (New York: Free Press).

US Census. 2009. "Top Ten Countries With Which the US Trades," August 2009, available at http://www.census.gov/foreign-trade/top/dst/2009/08/balance.html. Retrieved October 16, 2009.

US Census Bureau Foreign Trade Statistics. 2008a. "Trade in Goods (Imports, Exports, and Trade Balance) with Canada," available at http://www.census.gov/foreign-trade/balance/c1220.html#2008.

US Census Bureau Foreign Trade Statistics. 2008b. "Trade in Goods (Imports, Exports, and Trade Balance) with Mexico," available at http://www.census.gov/foreign-trade/balance/c2010. html#2008.

Waltz, Kenneth. 1979. *Theory of International Politics* (Boston: McGraw-Hill).

Wendt, Alexander. 1999. *Social Theory of International Politics* (New York: Cambridge University Press).

Yardley, William. 2008. "US Dock Workers Skip Work to Protest Iraq War," *The New York Times*, 2 May 2008.

Chapter 7

Assessing Seaport and Container Security Around the World[1]

On a daily basis, goods are produced in all corners of the globe and transported to a hub of international commerce where they are packed into large cargo containers, often with goods produced by others and in different geographic areas. These containers are then loaded onto enormous seafaring vessels that potentially layover at numerous seaports, loading and off-loading goods, before reaching their final destination. As has been demonstrated in earlier chapters, this transportation chain that supplies our homes, offices, schools, communities and numerous other entities with the materials and items we need and desire may also be exploited to transport and deploy dangerous and deadly goods for nefarious purposes; putting humans around the world at risk and endangering our global system of trade and commerce. We have argued that the security of containerized freight and ports of entry and exit is important for global and national security efforts. We now demonstrate one way we can enhance such security efforts with an assessment tool for evaluating the safety and security of seaport operations around the world.

Given the transnational nature of containerized freight security, it is crucial that port security issues are understood in a multilateral and interdependent framework. Although no one particular system or set of measures will serve the security needs of every single seaport in operation around the world, some level of compatibility is essential to ensure that criminal activities involving cargo containers and their movement are not lost in a sea of loopholes and a mixture of measures that are unmatched from port to port. As with any other global or transnational problem, such as weapons proliferation, drug or human trafficking, or climate change, multilateral action is essential to effectively address, manage and minimize potential negative effects (Ostrom 1990; Ruggie 1993; Sandler 2004; Axelrod 2006). Seaports and the secure movement of containerized freight are only as safe and strong as the weakest link in the supply chain. As the various international initiatives regarding container and seaport security have demonstrated, collective action and comprehensive and compatible security

---

1 This chapter is based on an article the authors published in the *Journal of Homeland Security and Emergency Management*. See Suzette R. Grillot, Rebecca J. Cruise and Valerie J. D'Erman, 2009. "National and Global Efforts to Enhance Containerized Freight Security," *Journal of Homeland Security and Emergency Management*, Vol. 6, No. 1, available at http://www.bepress.com/jhsem/vol6/iss1/51/.

systems are necessary to address the vulnerability of our ports and ultimately enhance the security of our global community.

How do we know whether multilateral security measures are compatible and effective? International agreements such as the ISPS (see Chapter 4) are clearly an important place to begin the development of compatible and collective port security activities, but such agreements are only the beginning. Individual countries and their respective officials responsible for port and container security must develop and implement the relevant procedures, plans and actions necessary to ensure compliance with such international agreements. And ultimately, to know whether security measures are indeed compatible and effective, to prevent the improper use of the global system of containerized freight movements, we must assess and evaluate individual port procedures, plans and actions – to highlight strengths and address weaknesses in the global supply chain.

Our research on the politics, policies and practices governing US container security at home and international security protocols in operation abroad (in Asia and Europe primarily) led to the development of a list of 12 elements we believe are crucial for the operation of safe ports and the secure movement of containerized freight. Using these 12 elements, we created an assessment tool that emphasizes aspects of seaport infrastructure, containerized freight documentation, and international coordination and collaboration among seaport officials and operators. Adherence to these elements by all parties helps to synchronize global port policy and ensures that all actors are working towards the same goals regarding seaport and container security around the world. Ultimately, this global assessment tool allows us to compare ports across the globe and evaluate their strengths and weaknesses so that successful and strong elements may be maintained and enhanced and gaps in policy and practice may be eliminated.

How and Why We Evaluate Policies and Programs

For nearly as long as there have been official policies and public or private programs, there have been efforts made to determine their effectiveness. In recent years, in particular, there has been a surge in literature focused on the role evaluation plays in the policy-making process. Moreover, government agencies and private foundations have increased their requirements for program evaluation for those who receive funding to develop policies and programs. Assessment and evaluation, therefore, are important elements of policy and practice across the policy spectrum. Although assessment methods and instruments may vary, as might the specific focus, goals and outcomes of assessment activities, analysts, officials and experts have heightened their attention to policy and program evaluation in an effort to enhance policy and program effectiveness.[2] In fact, policy evaluation is growing in areas such as the environment, education, social work and homeland security (Leroy and Crabbe 2008; Ginsberg 2000; Mingat, Tan, and Sosale 2003; Pinkowski 2008).

The area of assessment that has most influenced the development of our seaport and container security model is nonproliferation policy evaluation. After the collapse of the Soviet Union and the end of the Cold War in the early 1990s, the United States government and its allies quickly began to focus on the potential global spread of weapons of mass destruction – particularly nuclear weapons flowing out of the former Soviet region (see Chapter 3 for more specifics on US nonproliferation policy). As weapons control policies began to emerge in the United States, Europe, Asia and elsewhere, efforts to assess their compatibility and overall effectiveness emerged as well. As with other security elements in the international community, nonproliferation policies are only as effective as the weakest link across the globe. Although one country may develop the mechanisms necessary to control access to and acquisition of weapons of mass destruction, if another country that possesses the same or similar weapons capability does not establish similar or compatible controls, the overall nonproliferation effort is weakened.

To study the effectiveness of nonproliferation policies and practices, the Center for International Trade and Security (CITS) at the University of Georgia developed an analytical tool and assessment method for evaluating the development of nonproliferation export controls around the world. Beginning with national export control development in the former Soviet Union, the project grew to focus on important nuclear supplier countries in nearly every region.[3] Ultimately, the CITS team identified the necessary ingredients of an effective national export control system to prevent the unchecked spread of nuclear weapons and their component parts, and established a process to evaluate whether and to what extent these ingredients are in place and at work. Similar to the spread of weapons of mass destruction, the unchecked flow of containerized freight poses

---

2   For general program evaluation discussions, see Evert Vedung. 2000. *Public Policy and Program Evaluation*; Melvin M. Mark, Gary T. Henry and George Julnes. 2000. *Evaluation: An Integrated Framework for Understanding, Guiding and Improving Policies and Programs*; Carol H. Weiss. 1997. *Evaluation*, 2nd Edition; and Joseph S. Wholey, Harry P. Hatry and Kathryn E. Newcomer (eds), 2004. *Handbook of Practical Program Evaluation*. Regarding evaluation methods, see Stuart S. Nagel. 2001. *Handbook of Public Policy Evaluation*; and Peter H. Rossi, Mark W. Lipsey and Howard E. Freeman. 2003. *Evaluation: A Systematic Approach*.

3   For specifics on the original CITS assessment efforts, see Gary K. Bertsch and Suzette R. Grillot (eds), 1998. *Arms on the Market: Reducing the Risk of Proliferation in the Former Soviet Union*, especially pp. 11-13. For additional assessment studies, see Michael D. Beck, Richard T. Cupitt, Seema Galhaut and Scott A. Jones. 2003. *To Supply or Deny: Comparing Nonproliferation Export Controls in Five Key Countries*.

140 *Protecting Our Ports*

significant threats to global security. Like the efforts to assess nonproliferation export control policies and programs, therefore, our effort is to assess port and container security policies and programs as such evaluations highlight areas of weakness and allow us to address gaps in practice around the world so that we may strengthen our security environment.

Elements of a Secure Containerized Freight System

To ensure the security of containerized freight and its global movement, there are a number of policies, practices and procedures that should be in place and functioning effectively at seaports around the world. These elements (or ingredients) of a comprehensive containerized freight security system include all the necessary components required to maximize security (see Table 7.1). Based on a year long investigation where we interviewed a number of port security experts, policy-makers and practitioners, we developed a list of critical elements relevant for a comprehensive containerized freight security system. We present these 12 essential features of a secure seaport below. Using these elements, we can determine how well any seaport meets these various requirements, indicating the level of security of that point in the supply chain.

We divided the elements of a global containerized freight security system into three areas: (1) infrastructure, (2) documentation, and (3) coordination. Infrastructure refers to the various rules, regulations and physical security measures developed to enhance the security of the port and the goods that transport through it. Port security architecture should include policies and procedures that detail the responsibilities of authorities and personnel at every point of the supply chain, as well as delineate and describe the physical methods used to detect and handle dangerous items entering and exiting port facilities. Furthermore, officials should develop policies and procedures regarding responses to terrorist and other types of critical incidents within port areas, as well as plans for recovering and even re-routing trade and commercial activities during and after any kind of traumatic event that disrupts port operations.

Documentation refers to the records and manifests used to trace and track cargo containers as they move through the supply chain, entering and exiting ports and traveling toward their final destination. Officials should use shipping documents to verify the origination of goods and the reliability of producers, exporters, transporters, shippers, handlers and importers. Finally, the interdependent nature of the global economy requires that all parties involved in international trade communicate, coordinate, cooperate, and collaborate at very high levels. Therefore, coordination refers to the various and numerous activities involving information sharing, joint practices and training exercises, and interagency and inter-party communication, as well as collaborative and coordinated enforcement of rules and regulations and a system of accountability that requires collective action. Ultimately, the security of port facilities and the safe movement of containerized freight require open and regular communication and coordination among, within, across and between all the varied and relevant actors in both the public and private spheres.

Effective and secure movements and operations regarding containerized freight necessitate a high level of adherence to and compliance with these relevant elements at all ports of entry and exit where cargo containers travel. The strength and security of global trade reflects the weakest link in the supply chain. Therefore, a comprehensive and compatible system of port and container security around the world and across all the various parties is necessary. Our model outlining the 12 elements of a global container security system provides us with an assessment tool necessary for the evaluation of port and containerized freight security around the world. The model also provides us with information needed to target assistance efforts and enhance specific aspects of the global supply chain.[4]

What follows is a description of the 12 elements of global port and container security, as well as a discussion of measurement of the elements. The assessment questionnaire we used to evaluate port security in the United States, Europe and Asia is available in the Appendix, as are the assessment scores. Our discussion of strengths and weaknesses based on our seaport assessments highlights the areas where port security is quite well established, as well as the areas where gaps exist and must be closed.

Infrastructure

Policies, Regulations and Laws

The first step toward a secure supply chain and the secure movement of containerized freight is the creation of policies, regulations, rules and laws that outline the legal commitments and obligations of governments and businesses regarding the use and movement of cargo containers and ports of entry and exit. The various policies, regulations, rules and laws should outline legal authority and delineate actors and their responsibilities regarding containerized freight security. These documents should also appoint a governing agency that is responsible for

---

4 The model we have developed to assess port and container security is certainly not without flaws, but is a basis for evaluating security measures relevant for port operations and the movement of containerized freight at individual ports of entry and exit as well as for collective comparisons in an effort to identify strengths and weaknesses. Other methods for evaluation may be in place to do this, but this research team is unaware of any pre-existing, systematic methods for assessing port and container security. Moreover, there may be important security elements in addition to the 12 we have highlighted, but based on existing agreements, policies, practices and procedures, these 12 elements appear to cover the overwhelming majority of best port and container security practices.

enacting and enforcing laws regarding port security. Such a body should clearly state what programs will be put in place, how they will be operated, and who will be responsible for given aspects of port and container security. The policies and regulations must be implemented and contain an oversight mechanism so that agencies, actors and personnel are held accountable for their activities. Such an oversight mechanism might be a multiple agency process for checking and balancing the work of each counterpart.

Targeting System, Information Data Base, Threat Assessment

Containers traveling the global supply chain must be monitored and targeted for security checks based on threat assessment. Because it is inefficient and detrimental to global trade to manually scan all containers, a system for recognizing anomalies and targeting suspicious cargo containers must be in place. Although customs, border control and port authorities withhold specifics regarding exactly what kind of data they collect and use to assess the threat of particular cargo containers, they admit in general that they maintain and refer to records such as cargo manifests, original source of goods, transit and transshipment locations, destination information, end-user and end-use information, and shipper and shipping histories. Cross-referencing this data, which may cover decades of shipping activities, is the most efficient and effective method to search containers and highlight "at risk" containers that would be tagged for special review. It is also important to gather data from various sources, that they are triangulated to assure efficiency, and that they represent the most recent assessment of threats. The Automated Targeting System (ATS), for example, is used by US officials to identify and target suspicious containers for isolation and review. US officials do not offer specifics about the data they collect and include in their ATS database, but some have criticized that it only flags about 2-3% of all containers entering the United States, requiring that additional intelligence and information programs be used to ensure that all potentially dangerous cargo containers are found (Wein, Wilkins, Baveja and Flynn 2006, 1377-1393).

Physical Security Measures and Detection Devices

The world's seaports are not necessarily isolated in a way that prevents unauthorized access to port facilities and goods flowing through them. Most ports have large land areas that are accessible in many places. Moreover, many ports are located in or near heavily populated areas. Therefore, the physical security of port spaces and the materials that are entering and exiting usually 24 hours a day, 7 days a week, 52 weeks a year is essential (Frittelli 2008, 11-42). Recognizing this vulnerability, ports properly adhering to the ISPS code (see Chapter 4) are required to take infrastructural security seriously. Before admitted as ISPS members, ports must complete a facility assessment indicating weaknesses and possible security breaches. They must then indicate how they will remedy the situation and must act to do so under the constant possibility of surprise visits from IMO officials.[5] Most importantly, ports must show how they plan to monitor and secure access to the facility and how they will monitor cargo and people at the port.

Therefore, this element involves three aspects of physical security and detection. First, ports of entry and exit themselves should be highly secure areas. Secure fencing should be evident and security measures (such as guards, surveillance equipment, and other physical barriers) should be in place to limit access to port property and containerized freight. Second, containers themselves should incorporate physical security measures, such as seals, that prevent and identify tampering. Third, once a targeting system has identified high-risk cargo/containers, there must be a means of physically examining that cargo. Appropriate technology is vital so as to efficiently and effectively search suspect containers. Radiation portals, x-ray and gamma-ray machines, or other types of detection devices should be available. Manual, physical checks of cargo must also be possible if and when technological results are inconclusive or are not sufficient.

Training of Port Personnel and Officials

Technology enhances our detection and security capabilities, but it is never a replacement for human observation and experience. Therefore, it is imperative that personnel involved in shipping and port operations be trained to recognize suspect activities, questionable cargo, and appropriate security procedures. Personnel and officials working all along the supply chain and involved in the movement of containerized freight in and out of ports should receive continual training on the security systems that they are operating and should be kept up to date on technological advancements. Training should be implemented to incorporate relevant agencies, officials, and port personnel and it should be monitored from one agency and office to another so that multiple actors are aware of and overseeing training activities. The Asia Pacific Economic Cooperation (APEC) organization, for example, has developed joint training activities for Asian ports so that officials and personnel share experiences and best practices related to the implementation of the ISPS code (APEC Port Services).

Response and Recovery Plans

In the event of a terrorist or other traumatic event at a port of entry or exit, port operations should incorporate rapid response and recovery plans. The closing of even one terminal in a port can have dire security and economic consequences.

---

5   As noted in Chapter 4, final ISPS certification ultimately comes from the individual governments, not the IMO.

Should such an event occur, from terrorist or natural activities, there must exist a plan of action to respond to the incident, re-route incoming cargo as needed, and begin procedures for the recovery of port operations as swiftly and effectively as possible. Although port personnel and officials may be caught off guard depending on the type of incident, they should be prepared to implement well-outlined and practiced plans to prevent the effects of the incident from spreading and to prevent long-term effects of a closed or damaged port.

In the United States, for example, the Maritime Transportation Security Act (MTSA) requires a National Maritime Transportation Security Plan "for efficient, coordinated and effective action to deter and minimize damage from a transportation security incident" (Pinto and Talley 2006, 277). Moreover, the Homeland Security Presidential Directive 13 issued in December 2004 states that "expediting recovery and response from attacks within the maritime domain is one of six core elements of US policy for enhancing the security of this domain" (Pinto and Talley 2006). Also, the SAFE Port Act of 2006 attempts to streamline port response and recovery plans. For ISPS members, the requirements are slightly more flexible. ISPS ports must have plans for responding to a number of possibilities. They must indicate a line of communications and reaction. However, there is no requirement addressing redirection plans.

Documentation

Manifests, Certificates, and Verification

The use of container manifests, cargo information such as producer, exporter, importer, shipping and shipper information, and certificates of import and export enhances the level of port security by increasing the ability to monitor and verify the global movement of containerized goods. Manifests, cargo process information, and certificates play a significant role in assessing and targeting goods as they can be used to quickly assess the contents of containers, which can be checked and verified using technological (e.g. gamma ray) readings. Manifests, cargo information and certificates also provide a paper trail should there be a problem with a particular container and the supplier and/or end-user needs to be investigated. Officials should verify all manifests, cargo information and certificates for authenticity, and there should be a process for cross-referencing documents along the supply chain. A program to verify the receipt of goods by the rightful owner also prevents the diversion of goods to questionable end-users.

Background Checks and Identification Cards

All personnel that are involved in the movement of goods through the supply chain should undergo a thorough review before employed to work with containerized freight – from those that transport goods to port facilities and those that place goods into containers to personnel that ship containers overseas and those who pick up goods at ports of entry and deliver cargo to its final destination. Port personnel and all employees who come into contact with containers (e.g. drivers, equipment operators, etc.) should undergo background checks that are updated on a regular basis. Moreover, personnel should be issued proper identification cards that are harmonized to the extent they can be to prevent fraud and forgery of identification cards and, therefore, improper access to port facilities and containerized freight operations.

Cooperation and Coordination

Communication and Coordination Among Government Agencies and Officials

All domestic government agencies involved with the security and movement of freight along the supply chain must have open communication and a high level of cooperation among them. Regular interaction, coordination, and sharing of information among relevant agencies and their officers enhances all their activities, ensures an appropriate division of labor, and prevents unnecessary duplication and waste. Because the temptation does exist for coordination problems among different agency "cultures," an oversight mechanism in the form of an interagency council or regular interagency meetings should exist to prevent turf battles and to facilitate interagency decision-making.

Government and Business Cooperation and Coordination

Because private businesses are financially invested in the supply chain and depend on the smooth, efficient and secure movement of goods around the world, their participation is critical. Therefore, programs and partnerships between governments and business entities (such as C-TPAT in the United States) help to ensure the security of freight and ports. Bringing the business community into the security process allows for their concerns to be heard and addressed and makes them even more invested in the structure of the supply chain. Secure shipping of containerized freight should be a mutually beneficial public/private partnership. The more often government officials and business entities interact, share information, coordinate their security activities and cooperate on the development and implementation of security measures, the more secure the supply chain will be, the more profitable

146 *Protecting Our Ports*

businesses will be, the more effective governments will be, and the more secure and safe consumers will be.

International Cooperation and Coordination

The global container supply chain is interconnected at a number of ports of entry and exit around the world. The supply line is only as secure as its weakest port. Therefore, the security of all containerized freight is determined by the security of all ports. To this end, programs and partnerships between countries should exist in an effort to share new technologies, arrange for and implement joint training exercises, and ensure the adoption of common, harmonized security measures around the world. This requires bilateral and multilateral interactions and exchanges on all aspects of policy, procedure and implementation of supply chain security. It requires open communication and cooperation among a large number of international actors adhering to internationally accepted norms and procedures. Discussions and declaration emerging within international organizations such as the WCO, IMO, EU and ASEAN, for example, demonstrate the kind of transnational interaction and cooperation that has emerged on the port security issue (Bradford 2005, 63-86).

Information Sharing and Privacy Protection

Information about producers, suppliers, shippers, exporters, importers and goods is the key to a secure containerized freight system. Therefore, all relevant actors must share information with other relevant parties along the supply chain in order to detect potentially dangerous transactions. Commercial agents must provide manifest information that is accurate and they must be willing to share it with security officials. Because this requires commercial agents to provide proprietary information, there must also exist procedures and processes for protecting such commercial information so that it is only used for security purposes. The development of a "trusted enclave" where proprietary information can be shared and audited for proper use by a trusted third party may enhance the sharing of sensitive commercial information and, therefore, the security of containerized freight operations. One example of information sharing includes the US Coast Guard's maritime domain awareness (MDA) program. This program "involves fusing intelligence information with information from public, private, commercial, and international sources to provide a more complete picture of potential maritime security threats" (Frittelli 2008, 23).

Enforcement of Rules, Regulations and Laws and Accountability for Violations

It does little good to implement policies that aim to secure containerized freight and port operations if there is no means of enforcement. This element requires the existence of diligent police and investigative authorities that can, and do, enforce

Assessing Seaport and Container Security Around the World   147

Table 7.1   **Elements of a Secure Containerized Freight System in Brief**

ELEMENTS	DESCRIPTION
Infrastructure	
Policies, Regulations and Laws	Official agreements and documents that detail legal responsibilities for all actors involved in containerized freight activities.
Targeting System, Information Data Base, Threat Assessment	Collection and use of relevant cargo information, such as container contents, manifests, material sources, shipper and shipping histories, transshipment and transit activities, to target high risk containers for examination.
Physical Security Measures and Detection Devices	Fences, guards, surveillance cameras, physical barriers and detection equipment in place and in use at ports of entry and exit; seals in use on containers throughout the transit process.
Personnel and Official Training	Training programs specifically designed for personnel and officials who are involved in container cargo movements and port operations.
Response and Recovery Plans	Procedures in place at ports of entry and exit that are implemented in the event of a terrorist or other violent incident so that emergency responders are deployed, trade is re-routed and recovery begins.
Documentation	
Manifests, Certificates and Verification	Documents related to the contents of containers, their origination, handling and destination, as well as certificates of import and export, used to monitor and verify sources and purposes of goods transported via cargo container.
Background Checks and Identification Cards	Personnel and officials responsible for the flow of containerized freight undergo criminal background checks and are issued standardized identification cards that are shown to access port facilities and cargo areas.
Coordination	
Communication and Coordination among Government Agencies and Officials	Relevant domestic agencies and actors participating in the secure movement of containerized freight along the supply chain engage in regular communication, cooperation and collaboration at all levels.
Government and Business Cooperation and Coordination	Implementation of programs to partner governments and businesses involved in the global movement of containerized freight.
International Cooperation and Coordination	Bilateral and multilateral interactions and exchanges between countries in an effort to establish common practices, engage in joint exercises and harmonize security measures around the world.
Sharing of Information and Protection of Privacy	Public and private actors involved in the transportation of goods via containerized freight at every stage of the supply chain, as well as officials responsible for oversight, share information about producers, shippers, exporters, importers, goods, materials and methods in an effort to enhance knowledge at all levels and prevent, manage and minimize dangerous and deadly transactions.
Enforcement of Rules, Regulations and Laws and Accountability for Violations	Appropriate authorities tasked with policing and investigating activities along the supply chain, prosecuting breaches of the law, and punishing those convicted of criminal and/or civil violations.

security measures. This also requires a process for prosecuting and punishing those who are found guilty of breaking port and container security laws, rules or regulations, including both criminal and civil liabilities. Punishment might include an increased number of container checks, loss of green-lane privileges, financial fines and penalties, as well as prison sentences. Officials must hold those who violate security policies accountable for breaches to the full extent of the law.

Measuring Port Security

The 12 elements of a secure global container security system and the corresponding questionnaire (see Appendix) provide us with a tool to investigate local and international ports and gauge their degree of security. Assessing ports on the basis of these elements allows us to highlight strengths and weaknesses of seaport links in the supply chain. Security measures may also be compared and contrasted from seaport to seaport and throughout the supply chain in an effort to highlight gaps and ultimately enhance harmonization.

We visited and assessed a total of 17 seaports in the United States, Europe and Asia.[6] Our intent was to observe operations at a number of the world's largest and most important ports (e.g. Rotterdam, Antwerp, New York/New Jersey, Los Angeles, Singapore, Tokyo and others). We also sought to include a few smaller ports in our investigation (New Orleans, Thessaloniki and Taicang, for example). Our case selection, therefore, was not random, but purposeful. Nonetheless, based on our targeted selection we believe that our port assessments are fairly representative. However, while we may certainly draw conclusions about the ports we visited and assessed, and we can generalize somewhat to the regions included in the study, we are hesitant to make broad, sweeping generalizations about global seaport security based on these evaluations. What we are able to do is become more aware of areas where there seems to be a lack of attention, and of areas where a number of ports are shoring up security measures. This gives us, and potentially future researchers, results to further develop, test and implement.

With our assessment tool created, we personally toured and met with representatives at global seaports and ranked their compliance with the elements of a secure seaport. While officials were aware of our research task, they did not see nor complete the assessment instrument. The research team conducted the evaluations based on observations at the port, interviews with port authorities,

---

6 In the United States, ports include New York/New Jersey, Seattle, New Orleans and LA/Long Beach. In Asia ports include Taicang, China; Yangshan, China; Hong Kong, Singapore and Tokyo, Japan. In Europe ports include Rotterdam, The Netherlands; Hamburg, Germany; Antwerp, Belgium; Gdansk, Poland; London, England; Duress, Albania; Thessaloniki, Greece and Athens, Greece.

documents regarding official policy and procedures, and published port materials. Personal observations at port facilities are, however, most important source of our data. Even small seaports operate on a rather sizeable scale – and the large seaports are simply massive facilities. The general public, typically not having access to port and shipping operations, has little understanding of the significant activities involved in safely transporting their products and materials into, through, and out of their local communities, much less their country. While seaports should not be open for public observation, it is difficult for the public to understand the enormity of port and shipping procedures and to appreciate the immense challenges port officials and shipping companies face in terms of maintaining a secure and safe supply chain. Similarly, without gaining access to various seaports in an effort to assess port security measures on the ground, research on the subject would be of far less value.

In terms of measurement, the 12 elements elaborated in our assessment tool are scored on a scale from 0 to 3 (0 1 2 3). A score of 0 suggests that no evidence of the element exists at the port under consideration. Minimal development of an element, typically meaning that there may be some sort of policy in place, but little to no implementation of the policy, results in a score of 1. When an element has been developed beyond policy with some sort of procedure or institutionalized practice in place, a score of 2 is warranted. Finally, a score of 3 suggests that the element is completely developed and is being fully implemented. Based on personal visits to 17 seaports, dozens of interviews and the collection of numerous documents, we were able to determine which of the ports we evaluated were most secure and which ports raised concerns. Our assessments allowed us to identify gaps and weaknesses across and within ports, from which we offer recommendations regarding the targeting of assistance and the facilitation of further action.

Ultimately, the goal is to enhance supply chain security and the intermodal movement of containerized freight by improving and strengthening those elements that received low marks. A comprehensive approach is a must, and this model provides us the assessment tool needed to develop and enhance comprehensive and compatible security measures at seaports around the world.

Strengths and Weaknesses of Seaport Security

An assessment of 17 domestic and international seaports in the United States, Asia and Europe highlight some areas in which port security is flourishing as well as some areas that need improvement (see the seaport assessment scores in the Appendix). In general, there is a relatively high level of compatibility across the 17 ports we evaluated. Most of the world's largest and busiest ports scored into the 90th percentile, suggesting that many of the highest volume seaports have taken appropriate and important steps to establish needed measures regarding the security of containerized freight. A few of the smaller or less developed ports may need additional time, and perhaps more resources, to enhance their evaluation scores. Taken together, however, the assessments allow us to draw attention to a number of strengths as well as weaknesses in seaport operations. Ultimately, raising awareness of where port security measures are well developed and implemented and where measures require additional attention provides much needed information useful for strengthening security efforts.

The good news is most obvious in the scores of the first element: policies, regulations and laws. Every port we visited and evaluated had established a number of policies, regulations, rules and laws regarding port security authorities and practices. Japan's 2004 Law for the Security of Ships and Port Facilities is just one such policy. Moreover, each port referred to an oversight agency that was responsible for ensuring effective implementation of relevant policies and laws. For example, in the US this is CBP, in Greece the agency is the Ministry of Mercantile Marine, and the Ministry of Land Infrastructure and Trade serves the same purpose in Japan. Port officials regularly analyze their security procedures and continually seek ways to address challenges, fix weaknesses and generally improve security at their individual ports. In fact, designated security officers are quite often present throughout the port to monitor, evaluate, verify and strengthen security efforts. Furthermore, police forces, such as in Rotterdam, and specific government agencies, such as the Immigration Customs Enforcement agency in the United States, have been designated with the authority in all ports visited to investigate port and cargo activities as well as enforce relevant port security policies, laws and regulations

Moreover, evaluation scores for physical security measures at these 17 ports are also quite high. Nearly every port assessed had in place the required fencing, guard posts and lighting, as well as surveillance cameras and various detection devices that alerted port personnel if an intruder had entered secure port areas. Our own experiences with conducting research at port facilities highlights the strength of physical security measures regarding port entry and exit. At all ports investigated for this study, we had to go through several layers of contacts in order to gain permission to enter the seaport area. Most often we were met at a designated port entrance and our identification was checked and scrutinized. We were escorted through and around port facilities and provided enviable access, but were never allowed to wander through the facilities and conduct analysis on our own. We observed potential points of entry and exit at each seaport and watched as other visitors, employees, drivers and authorities were screened as they entered or left port areas. We also observed the surveillance rooms where security officers constantly monitored port facilities and activities via video camera. In nearly all cases, with the exception of only the Port of Duress in Albania, physical security efforts were of high caliber. And even in Albania, physical security measures are much improved from previous years. Of all ports visited for this study, it is the Port of Duress that we have actually visited in prior years for previous projects. In 2003, for example, the Port of Duress had no fences, no cameras, no guards, no physical security measures of any kind. In 2003 we observed random individuals enter the port area and rummage through scrap materials at will. In 2008, this was not the case. The port had developed nearly all of the necessary requirements (fencing, guards, surveillance) to control access to the port and the goods and materials that flow through it.

In addition to physical access, nearly all ports had implemented procedures to ensure that containers were physically safe and secure and that container seals were regularly checked. Basic ISPS requirements regarding the physical security of port facilities, in other words, were in place and officials were aware of their importance. Many ports, in fact, had moved beyond ISPS minimum requirements to implement state of the art technologies and the latest forms of non-invasive detection devices such as x-ray, gamma-ray and radiation machines. This was seen often in European ports which are required to comply, or work toward complying, with EU Directive 2005/65 (see Chapter 4), which states that all EU ports need to take steps to act as if they were at ISPS level II security (heightened risk – fewer allowed into the port facility, greater scrutiny of documents and persons). The largest ports have met these requirements: Rotterdam, Hamburg, Antwerp and London. Seaports in Southeastern Europe – Albania (not an EU port), Thessaloniki and Piraeus – appear to be making some progress. US domestic ports and Asian ports also ranked quite high on this element.

Also regarding infrastructure, nearly all ports have developed and have on hand emergency response plans in the event of a traumatic incident at the port. Moreover, most ports regularly train their personnel how to respond to incidents of all kinds and run drills so cargo handlers are familiar with procedures. A number of possible scenarios regarding problems and disturbances at ports involving ships, containers, or port facilities themselves are often included in the plans and preparations, as are a number of different actors and agencies that may be involved in any type of incident. At the Port of Rotterdam, for example, the Port Authority, Customs, Rotterdam Police, the Harbor Master and even the Fire Department and the Navy are all included in contingency plans – and these authorities are involved in training and relevant drills on a regular basis. Should there be a weather delay in Rotterdam, the Harbor Master and the Port Authority have drawn plans for a joint response. If a port terminal closes due to a fire, there is a plan in place to open the port to the fire department while the Harbor Master helps hold off or redirects shipping traffic. While contingency plans are guarded, most ports we visited drafted similar response and recovery protocols.

As detailed in Chapter 3, interaction among and cooperation between agencies within states, particularly in the United States, is quite well developed. Domestic agencies in all countries visited have been identified as the appropriate authorities to oversee port and container security efforts. Jurisdictions, responsibilities, and relevant divisions of labor have largely been outlined and delineated in all countries evaluated. The sharing of information also received relatively high scores as port officials speak and meet often with one another, pass on latest updates relevant to their work, engage in joint activities, and interact regularly regarding port security operations and secure port and shipping procedures. Unfortunately, however, most of this information sharing is taking place within governments and among domestic actors involved in port and container security. Marks for international cooperation were not nearly as high as they should be. As discussed in Chapters 4 and 5, international cooperation and collaboration on port and container security is taking place, and a number of programs have been implemented to enhance coordination among players around the world. However, various obstacles remain regarding the reception of US mandated security measures and externally driven security concerns that seemingly benefit one player in the global community, the United States, more so than any other partner. The Secure Freight Initiative calling for 100% scanning technology for use on all containers heading for the United States by 2012 is one such policy causing concern among international seaports operators.

Although the overall assessment scores for the 17 seaports we visited were quite positive, there remains much room for improvement. One area in particular requires attention – the development of redirection plans in the event of a violent incident at a port. While most ports have in place plans for responding to and recovering from terrorist or other kinds of traumatic events at the port, few have concrete plans for redirecting incoming vessels. The Port Authority at the Port of London, for example, would attempt to redirect shipping traffic if the port was to close, but no policy, procedure or specific plan is in place to guide and facilitate the process. Most likely, ships would be left alone to search for another port that could accommodate their size and load, which then complicates the smooth operation of the supply chain. In a geographically close area like Europe, this may not be as big of an obstacle as it would be in regions where seaports and countries are more distant. This seemed to be the case when the Port of New Orleans had to be shut down for Hurricane Katrina. Because of the lack of a specific redirection plan, incoming ships had to determine their redirection independently and more or less scramble to find another port for docking.[7] Of course, port operators do explain why it is difficult to have a standardized plan for redirection. US officials along the West Coast, for example, argue that an incident involving West Coast ports would leave ships stranded for some time as most of the world's largest ships off load in ports such as LA/Long Beach and are too big to redirect through the Panama Canal to an East Coast port. Other officials around the world suggest that no one redirection plan can serve the needs of all types of ships and cargo, so flexibility in the event of port incidents will always be necessary.

An additional weakness at all ports assessed for this study is the use of a third party or "trusted enclave" to facilitate the collection, storage and use of

---

7 In weather related incidents there is often some preparation time, with a terrorist event the closedown would be immediate and unexpected.

cargo and shipping data relevant for security concerns. Because much of the data used for targeting potentially risky cargo containers involves proprietary information (see Chapter 7), an unaffiliated, trusted third party could serve as a means of monitoring the collection and use of the data for appropriate purposes. This practice, however, is not in place at any port we visited. The United States has begun an investigation into whether the establishment of such a practice would be beneficial, but at this point no port includes a third party in the data management process. Former Homeland Security Deputy Secretary, Michael Jackson, was a major proponent of the third party concept, but with his departure in October 2007, interest in the program has clearly declined. While private enterprise continues to be concerned about the use and control of private information related to trade activities, those we interviewed in the private sector were relatively unenthused about a third party, "trusted enclave" data process. Moreover, officials working at international ports were seemingly unaware and relatively unsupportive of third party data proposals. One overseas official referred to the idea as "a database in the sky," citing concerns with cost, what kinds of data would be stored, who would have access, and who should monitor the process. Although some officials were intrigued by the third party idea in theory, nearly everyone interviewed was skeptical given questions about plausibility, feasibility and desirability.

In the area of research and development we see very mixed results. Some ports actively encourage and incentivize research development regarding better security measures and more secure port and container activities. At the Port of Hamburg, there is an institutionalized system of bonuses for officials who create new and useful ideas for the enhancement of security procedures. However, all ports could use improvement in this area. There can be no substitute for the training, experience and intuition of port personnel and officials, but research on ways to improve security measures and enhance the work of individuals involved in the secure movement of containerized freight is essential. The most promising research and development, has actually emerged in the private sector where companies are working to find better ways to protect their goods from being stolen somewhere along the supply chain. The Heineken beer company is quite proficient in this regard. Officials at the Port of Rotterdam explained that Heineken has been a major contributor to the development of new container and seal technology. Heineken, and other large companies, ship millions of dollars worth of their product each year. Therefore, it is in their interest to take steps to ensure that their product reaches shelves around the world without tampering. In fact, theft prevention is the primary motivation behind most if not all private business security activities. Merging research and development on anti-theft devices and practices with R&D on anti-terrorism or anti-violence efforts would be ideal.

The verification of cargo and shipping data and documents is always a challenge. Unfortunately, those seeking to engage in fraudulent and potentially dangerous activities involving the movement of containerized freight do so with the use of false documents and information. Most port operators and officials are unable to thoroughly vet and check the authenticity of relevant data and documentation. Some ports attempt to cross reference their data with records held in other areas and by other ports in an effort to catch inconsistencies and anomalies, but a number of ports (Taicang, Yangshan, Duress, Pireaus and Thessaloniki) were less able to commit the time and human and financial resources to such "fact checking." It is notable, that the ports falling short on this element tend to be smaller ports. Many officials suggested that they have difficulty identifying best practices and methods for verifying the authenticity of documents, but believe that as more and more shipping activity is managed online using electronic capabilities, new and better methods are becoming more available and will enhance efforts to prevent fraudulent and potentially dangerous activities. These advancements should help smaller ports that might be resource strapped. For some ports, however, (Thessaloniki in particular) concerns with verification were simply absent. For them, checking the authenticity of documents was not necessarily a matter of resource commitment, but that it just was not necessary or reasonable.

Two significant areas of weakness in seaport security concern the existence and effectiveness of joint training exercises and the distribution and use of universal identification cards for port personnel. While many port facilities organize and implement joint security training activities, it is not apparent that all personnel involved in the movement of containerized freight are included in such training programs. In some cases, each individual agency or office with responsibilities concerning secure freight shipments train their own personnel independently without engaging in collective efforts to prevent duplication and to ensure compatible practices. This is of particular concern in Asia and Southeastern Europe. This was evident at the Port of Yangshan, where some of the larger companies provide job, and to some degree safety, training for employees, but there was no effort to do cooperative training exercises between agencies. The situation at the Albanian Port of Duress is similar where security training for port employees, though not truck drivers who enter port facilities, occurs but is not taking place in cooperation or collaboration with relevant agencies. US officials and international organizations such as the WCO and IMO as well as the EU have either required or encouraged joint training exercises concerning port and container security. It is not clear, however, that many of the ports visited were actually following such prescriptions.

Moreover, identification cards were of major concern at most ports. Although every port we evaluated had some process for checking who enters the port area and who handles and manages containerized freight, in many cases (particularly in Southeastern Europe) the identification process is not universal and does not involve all individuals that come into contact with ports, ships and cargo containers. In some instances truck drivers are given identification cards by just showing a drivers license (e.g. Taicang) and in others there is no real monitoring of cards (e.g. Duress and Yangshan). The larger ports certainly handle the identification process better than smaller ports, but there is room for improvement on this issue at all levels.

The United States has been pushing for universal identification cards for those with access to domestic ports. First authorized through MTSA, The SAFE Port Act of 2006 further advanced the concept and included a provision for the Transportation Worker Identification Credential (TWIC), which went into mandatory affect in April 2009 (One Week Until TWIC Implementation 2009). Under the requirement, all "maritime transportation works, including terminal employees, longshoremen, truck drivers, vendors, agents and contractors will be required to have a TWIC card" (Ibid.). Even in the United States, this has not been without controversy (see Chapter 2).

An additional glaring weakness in the seaport assessments is the lack of programs for government and business partnerships. As indicated above, government and business relations regarding port and container security are essential. Both public and private entities have a stake in secure freight transportation, and both public and private enterprises have a role to play. Most ports suggest that they have positive relations with their relevant business communities and that local private actors are involved in and informed about issues regarding secure port initiatives and efforts. Programs such as C-TPAT in the United States and AEO in the European Union (see Chapters 4 and 5), for example, facilitate government-business interactions on security measures and assist shippers in the movement of containerized freight through the supply chain. However, some port officials interviewed for this study were not familiar with these programs. Though enacted in January 2008, and discussed for a number of years previously, few of the officials at the European ports we visited knew much about the AEO program or how it would affect their operations. This was especially interesting, given that we conducted many of these interviews after AEO implementation.

One final area of weakness at a number of ports assessed concerns the issue of background checks for port personnel and officials. In the United States there is a routine practice of ensuring that all personnel and employees that enter port facilities and manage containerized freight (such as truck drivers, machine operators, merchant marines, agency officials, etc.) undergo a thorough background check to prevent hiring individuals with certain criminal records in important port and container operations. These background searches are updated in the United States on a regular basis and are reviewed at any time a driver's cargo, for example, triggers an alarm after exiting through a radiation portal. Background searches in some European countries, however, are much more problematic. Countries like Belgium and The Netherlands, for example, have strict laws regarding the protection of individual privacy, including one's criminal history. Although it is certainly possible to conduct a background check is such countries, doing so is quite costly and there typically must exist unusual circumstances or some kind of suspicion to warrant a check into someone's background. Therefore, it is nearly impossible to check the background of every employee who is involved in port operations. Japanese ports are similarly constrained as the laws of the country also protect privacy in this regard.

Conclusion

With so many positive developments regarding port and container security at these 17 ports around the world, there is much to be optimistic about regarding the security of our seas, ports and national and international landscapes. First, the level of awareness about port and container security issues around the world is substantial. Port officials and personnel on three continents are seemingly committed to enhancing supply chain security and preventing the use of cargo containers for terrorist or other deadly and destructive activities. The governments responsible for these 17 seaports have developed policies, rules, laws and regulations that address port and container security needs. Port operators have installed various physical security barriers and measures to prevent unauthorized access to port areas and to limit access to containerized freight. Domestic agencies involved in port and container security efforts have established a relatively high level of cooperation, communication and collaboration in order to strengthen their respective programs and eliminate, or at least minimize, duplication, waste and turf battles. Finally, port authorities have created and implemented response and recovery plans so that they may effectively respond to and recover from a terrorist or other kind of violent event involving port facilities. There has, therefore, been much progress regarding port and container security in recent years.

Despite the numbers of successes, there remain serious concerns. Ports should do better to develop at least preliminary redirection plans in the event of a violent incident where there is an effect on port operations. Port officials can do more to encourage the sharing of proprietary information relevant for security purposes. Whether such information sharing is enhanced using a third party, trusted enclave or not, it is important to strengthen the appropriate distribution, access, monitoring, verification and use of sensitive data. Research and development activities on security measures are also relatively weak, as are joint training opportunities, the creation and use of universal identification cards, the use of background checks, the ability of port authorities to verify the authenticity of important documents and the partnerships between government and business. All of these elements exist to varying degrees across the ports assessed here, but all require additional attention and ultimately necessitate harmonization. Moreover, ports cannot neglect those elements that are more evident. Involved agents must work to undertake an overall effort to develop, maintain and strengthen all aspects of port and container security.

Ultimately, with the development of this assessment tool we are better able to gauge the effectiveness of port and container security measures around the world. Because compatible, multilateral measures are a must to enhance and ensure the security of containerized cargo wherever it may go, we must evaluate individual efforts, programs, policies and practices in order to identify weaknesses and close gaps. Only through consistent and regular attention to port and container security efforts are we likely to prevent, manage and minimize dangerous consequences involving ports and containerized freight. International commerce and human security depend on the safe and secure movement of goods through the global supply chain. Assessment of the secure cargo process is, therefore, essential.

APPENDIX

Assessment Questionnaire

Infrastructure

1. *Policies, Regulations and Laws*
Is there a governing agency that outlines rules, regulations and policies in regards to containerized freight flow?

| 0 | 1 | 2 | 3 |

Are responsibilities of involved actors clearly delineated by said body?

| 0 | 1 | 2 | 3 |

Is there an oversight mechanism in place?

| 0 | 1 | 2 | 3 |

Are operations analyzed and evaluated in an effort to identify challenges and obstacles?

| 0 | 1 | 2 | 3 |

Comments:
Policy Score:

2. *Targeting System/Information Data Base/Threat Assessment*
Is there an up to date and efficient system of targeting anomaly containers?

| 0 | 1 | 2 | 3 |

Is an information data base in place that includes information on manifest cargo, origination, transit and destination information and shipping/shipper histories?

| 0 | 1 | 2 | 3 |

Is targeting information cross referenced against other sources of information?

| 0 | 1 | 2 | 3 |

Comments:
Targeting Score:

3. *Physical Security Measures and Detection Devices*

Are ports of entry/exit physically secure (evident fencing, guards, surveillance equipment etc.)?

| 0 | 1 | 2 | 3 |

Are containers physically secure (seals, tamper detection etc.)?

| 0 | 1 | 2 | 3 |

Is appropriate technology (x-ray, gamma ray etc.) used to examine "suspect" and random cargo?

| 0 | 1 | 2 | 3 |

Are manual, physical checks of containers done when necessary?

| 0 | 1 | 2 | 3 |

Are research and development activities taking place to enhance capabilities?

| 0 | 1 | 2 | 3 |

Comments:

Physical Security Score:

4. *Training*

Do port personnel receive appropriate and reoccurring training on port security technology and policies?

| 0 | 1 | 2 | 3 |

Does this extend to all personnel involved with the flow of freight?

| 0 | 1 | 2 | 3 |

Does collaborative training occur among involved agencies?

| 0 | 1 | 2 | 3 |

Are training practices monitored by external agent?

| 0 | 1 | 2 | 3 |

Comments:

Training Score:

5. *Response and Recovery*

Are rapid response and recovery plans in place and prepared for?

| 0 | 1 | 2 | 3 |

Is there a redirection plan in place in the event of port or terminal close down?

| 0 | 1 | 2 | 3 |

Comments:

Response and Recovery Score:

Assessing Seaport and Container Security Around the World 159

Documentation

6. *Manifests, Certificates, and Verification*
Are cargo manifests and import/export certificates used to trace the movement of goods as a means of targeting suspicious containers?

| 0 | 1 | 2 | 3 |

Are manifests and import/export certificates verified for authenticity?

| 0 | 1 | 2 | 3 |

Comments:
Manifests Score:

7. *Background Checks and Identification Cards*
Do all personnel involved in the movement of goods along the supply chain under go an extensive background check and personal review?

| 0 | 1 | 2 | 3 |

Are all personnel along the supply chain issued identification cards which are monitored?

| 0 | 1 | 2 | 3 |

Comments:
Checks and IDs Score:

Communication, Cooperation and Coordination

8. *Interagency Communication and Coordination*
Is there regular interaction, coordination and information sharing among relevant agencies?

| 0 | 1 | 2 | 3 |

Is there an oversight mechanism in place to limit "turf battles" and facilitate inter-agency decision-making among involved agencies?

| 0 | 1 | 2 | 3 |

Comments:
Communication Score:

9. *Government and Business Cooperation and Coordination*
Are programs and partnerships in place, which foster positive relationships between private businesses and government?

| 0 | 1 | 2 | 3 |

Comments:
Government/Business Score:

160 *Protecting Our Ports*

10. *International Cooperation and Coordination*
Does the port (country) participate in programs/partnerships with other countries, which results in the sharing of new technologies, encourages collaborative training exercises and leads to the harmonization of global port security policies?

    0   1   2   3

Does port (country) participate in bilateral/multilateral partnerships along all aspects of policy, procedure and implementation of supply chain security?

    0   1   2   3

Does port (country) openly communicate with other actors/countries involved in the transfer of international freight?

    0   1   2   3

Comments:
International Cooperation Score:

11. *Information Sharing and Privacy Protection*
Is security information shared among all actors (governmental agencies, shippers and business entities) involved in the movement of freight?

    0   1   2   3

Do commercial agents provide accurate and detailed information with security officials?

    0   1   2   3

Is there a secure means of protecting proprietary information provided by business entities?

    0   1   2   3

Is there a third party (trusted enclave) responsible for monitoring and storing proprietary information?

    0   1   2   3

Comments:
Information Sharing Score:

12. *Enforcement and Accountability*
Are security rules, policies and procedures enforced by a policing and investigatory body(s)?

    0   1   2   3

Is there a means for punishing law breakers?

    0   1   2   3

Comments:
Enforcement Score:

Port Score:

Infrastructure:
Documentation:
Coordination
TOTAL

Seaport Assessment Scores

Port	New York/Jersey	Seattle	New Orleans	LA/Long Beach	Taicang	Yangshan
Region	N. Am- E. Coast	N. Am- W. Coast	N.Am- Gulf	N. Am- W. Coast	Asia- China	Asia- China
Size	Large	Medium	Small	Ex. Large	Medium	Large
Visit	10.11.06	10.24.06	1.5.07	5.25.07	10.10.07	10.12.07
CSI Port?	NA	NA	NA	NA	No	No
1: Policies, Regulations and Laws						
Is there an agency that outlines rules, regulations and politics?	3	3	3	3	3	3
Are responsibilities delineated by said body?	3	3	3	3	3	3
Is there an oversight mechanism in place?	2	2	2	2	3	3
Are operations analyzed to identify challenges/obstacles?	3	3	3	3	2	2
2: Targeting/Data Base/ Threat Assessment						
Up to date, efficient targeting system	3	3	3	3	1	2
Data set that includes manifest, origination, histories etc.	3	3	3	3	1	2
Is targeting info. cross referenced with other sources?	3	3	3	3	1	1
3: Physical Security/ Detection Devices						
Ports physically secure? Fencing, guards, cameras?	3	3	3	3	3	3
Containers secure? Seals, tamper detection	3	3	3	3	3	3
Technology used to examine suspect and random cargo?	3	2	1	3	0	2
Are manual checks done when needed?	3	3	3	3	3	3
Is R&D taking place	3	3	3	3	1	2
4: Training						
Port personnel get appropriate training?	3	3	3	3	3	3
All personnel in freight flow?	2	2	2	2	3	3
Joint training among agencies?	3	3	3	3	0	0
Training is monitored by external agent?	2	2	2	2	0	0
5: Response & Recovery						
Are plans in place and prepared for?	3	3	3	3	3	3
Is there a redirection plan?	1	1	1	1	3	3
6: Manifests/Certificates & Verification						
Import/Export certificates used to trace goods?	3	3	3	3	2	3
Are they verified for authenticity?	2	2	2	2	0	0
7: Background Checks/ID cards						
All personnel undergo background check?	3	3	3	3	1	2
ID cards that are monitored?	3	3	3	3	1	2
8: Inter-agency Communication/ Coordination						
Regular interaction and info. sharing among agencies?	3	3	3	3	3	3
Oversight mechanism to limit turf battles?	3	3	3	3	3	3
9: Gov. & Business Coordination						
Programs to enhance private/gov. relationships?	3	3	3	3	1	2
10: International Cooperation						
Country participates w/ other countries to harmonize policies?	3	3	3	3	0	2
Bilateral & Multilateral partnerships?	3	3	3	3	1	2
Open communication with other actors?	3	3	3	3	0	2
11: Info. Sharing and Privacy						
Is info. shared among all actors?	3	3	3	3	2	2
Commercial agents give accurate info?	3	3	3	3	2	2
Means of protecting information?	2	2	2	2	2	2
3rd party monitoring proprietary info?	1	1	1	1	0	0
12: Enforcement & Accountability						
Are policies enforced by investigatory body?	3	3	3	3	2	2
Means of punishment in place?	3	3	3	3	2	2
Port Score						
Infrastructure x/54	91%	88%	87%	91%	67%	76%
Documentation x/12	92%	92%	92%	92%	33%	58%
Coordination x/36	92%	92%	92%	92%	50%	67%
Total x/102	**91%**	**90%**	**89%**	**91%**	**57%**	**71%**
	A-	**A-**	**B+**	**A-**	**F**	**C**

Port	Hong Kong	Singapore	Tokyo	Rotterdam	Hamburg	Antwerp
Region	Asia-China	Asia-Singapore	Asia-Japan	N. Europe	Europe-Baltic	Europe-N
Size	Large	Ex. Large	Large	Ex. Large	Large	Large
Visit	11.06.07	11.9.07	12.5.07	10.30.07	2.21.08	3.27.08
CSI Port?	5/5/03	3/10/03	5/21/04	9/2/02	2/9/03	2/23/03
1: Policies, Regulations and Laws						
Is there an agency that outlines rules, regulations and politics?	3	3	3	3	3	3
Are responsibilities delineated by said body?	3	3	3	3	3	3
Is there an oversight mechanism in place?	3	3	3	3	3	3
Are operations analyzed to identify challenges/obstacles?	3	3	3	3	3	3
2: Targeting/Data Base/ Threat Assessment						
Up to date, efficient targeting system	3	3	3	3	3	3
Data set that includes manifest, origination, histories etc.	3	3	3	3	3	3
Is targeting info. cross referenced with other sources?	3	3	3	3	3	3
3: Physical Security/ Detection Devices						
Ports physically secure? Fencing, guards, cameras?	2	3	3	3	3	3
Containers secure? Seals, tamper detection	3	3	3	3	3	3
Technology used to examine suspect and random cargo?	3	3	3	3	1	3
Are manual checks done when needed?	3	3	3	3	3	3
Is R&D taking place	3	3	3	3	3	3
4: Training						
Port personnel get appropriate and reoccurring training?	3	3	3	3	3	3
All personnel in freight flow?	3	3	3	2	3	3
Joint training among agencies?	2	3	3	3	3	3
Training is monitored by external agent?	2	3	3	3	3	3
5: Response & Recovery						
Are plans in place and prepared for?	3	1	3	3	3	3
Is there a redirection plan?	3	1	3	2	2	2
6: Manifests/Certificates & Verification						
Import/Export certificates used to trace goods?	3	3	3	3	3	3
Are they verified for authenticity?	2	2	3	2	2	2
7: Background Checks/ID cards						
All personnel undergo background check?	3	3	1	1	2	1
ID cards that are monitored?	3	3	3	3	3	3
8: Inter-agency Communication/ Coordination						
Regular interaction, coordination and info. sharing among agencies?	2	3	3	3	3	3
Oversight mechanism to limit turf battles?	2	3	3	3	3	3
9: Gov. & Business Coordination						
Programs to enhance private/gov. relationships?	3	3	1	3	3	3
10: International Cooperation						
Country participates w/ other countries to harmonize policies?	3	3	3	3	3	3
Bilateral & Multilateral partnerships?	3	3	3	3	3	3
Open communication with other actors?	3	3	3	3	3	3
11: Info. Sharing and Privacy						
Is info. shared among all actors?	2	2	3	3	3	3
Commercial agents give accurate info?	2	2	3	2	2	2
Means of protecting information?	3	3	3	3	3	3
3rd party monitoring proprietary info?	0	0	0	0	0	0
12: Enforcement & Accountability						
Are policies enforced by investigatory body?	3	3	3	3	3	3
Means of punishment in place?	3	3	3	3	3	3
Port Score						
Infrastructure x/54	94%	92%	100%	96%	96%	98%
Documentation x/12	97%	97%	83%	75%	83%	75%
Coordination x/36	81%	81%	81%	89%	89%	89%
Total x/102	89%	90%	93%	91%	91%	92%
	B+	A-	A-	A-	A-	A-

Port	Gdansk	London	Albania	Thessaloniki	Athens
Region	Europe-North Sea	UK-River Themes	SEE-Adriatic	SEE-Med	SEE-Med
Size	Medium	Large	Small	Small	Medium
Visit	7.16.08	7.20.08	6.2.08	6.6.08	6.10.08
CSI Port?	No-soon	No	No	No	7/27/04
1: Policies, Regulations and Laws					
Is there an agency that outlines rules, regulations	3	3	3	3	3
Are responsibilities delineated by said body?	3	3	3	2	2
Is there an oversight mechanism in place?	3	3	3	2	2
Are operations analyzed to identify challenges?	3	3	2	2	2
2: Targeting/Data Base/ Threat Assessment					
Up to date, efficient targeting system	3	3	1	3	3
Data set that includes manifest, origination, histories etc.	3	3	1	2	2
Is targeting info. cross referenced with other sources?	3	3	0	0	0
3: Physical Security/ Detection Devices					
Ports physically secure? Fencing, guards, cameras?	3	3	2	3	3
Containers secure? Seals, tamper detection	3	3	3	3	3
Technology used to examine suspect and random cargo?	3	2	1	3	3
Are manual checks done when needed?	3	3	3	3	3
Is R&D taking place	1	3	1	0	0
4: Training					
Port personnel get appropriate and reoccurring training?	3	3	3	3	2
All personnel in freight flow?	3	3	2	2	2
Joint training among agencies?	3	3	0	1	1
Training is monitored by external agent?	3	3	0	2	2
5: Response & Recovery					
Are plans in place and prepared for?	3	3	3	3	3
Is there a redirection plan?	1	2	1	1	1
6: Manifests/Certificates & Verification					
Import/Export certificates used to trace goods?	3	3	3	3	3
Are they verified for authenticity?	2	2	0	2	1
7: Background Checks/ID cards					
All personnel undergo background check?	3	3	1	3	3
ID cards that are monitored?	3	3	1	1	3
8: Inter-agency Communication/ Coordination					
Regular interaction, and info. sharing among agencies?	3	3	3	2	2
Oversight mechanism to limit turf battles?	2	3	1	2	2
9: Gov. & Business Coordination					
Programs to enhance private/gov. relationships?	3	3	0	0	0
10: International Cooperation					
Country participates with others harmonize policies?	3	3	1	3	3
Bilateral & Multilateral partnerships?	3	3	1	2	2
Open communication with other actors?	3	3	0	2	2
11: Info. Sharing and Privacy					
Is info. shared among all actors?	2	3	2	2	2
Commercial agents give accurate info?	3	3	2	2	2
Means of protecting information?	3	3	2	3	3
3rd party monitoring proprietary info?	0	0	0	0	0
12: Enforcement & Accountability					
Are policies enforced by investigatory body?	3	3	2	3	3
Means of punishment in place?	3	3	2	3	3
Port Score					
Infrastructure x/54	93%	96%	59%	70%	69%
Documentation x/12	92%	92%	42%	75%	83%
Coordination x/36	86%	92%	44%	67%	67%
Total x/102	**90%**	**94%**	**52%**	**70%**	**70%**
	A-	A	F	C-	C-

Bibliography

APEC Port Services, available at http://www.apecpsn.org/Thumbnails/2009 421180841162.pdf.

Axelrod, Robert. 2006. *The Evolution of Cooperation* (New York: Basic Books).

Beck, Michael D., Richard T. Cupitt, Seema Galhaut and Scott A. Jones. 2003. *To Supply or Deny: Comparing Nonproliferation Export Controls in Five Key Countries* (The Hague, The Netherlands: Kluwer Law International).

Bertsch, Gary K., and Suzette R. Grillot (eds), 1998. *Arms on the Market: Reducing the Risk of Proliferation in the Former Soviet Union* (New York: Routledge).

Bradford, John F. 2005. "The Growing Prospects for Maritime Security Cooperation in Southeast Asia," *Naval War College Review*, Vol. 58, No. 3, 63-86, available at http://www.southchinasea.org/docs/Maritime%20security%20cooperation %20in%20Southeast%20Asia.pdf.

C-TPAT in the United States, see http://www.cbp.gov/xp/cgov/trade/cargo_ security/ctpat/what_ctpat/ctpat_overview.zml.

Frittelli, John F. 2008. "Port and Maritime Security: Background and Issues for Congress," in Jonathan P. Vesky (ed.), *Port and Maritime Security* (New York: Nova Science Publishers, Inc.), 11-42.

Ginsberg, Leon H. 2000. *Social Work Evaluation: Principles and Methods* (Boston: Allyn and Bacon).

Grillot, Suzette R., Rebecca J. Cruise and Valerie J. D'Erman. 2009. "National and Global Efforts to Enhance Containerized Freight Security," *Journal of Homeland Security and Emergency Management*, Vol. 6, No. 1, available at http://www.bepress.com/jhsem/vol6/iss1/51/.

Leroy, Pieter and Ann Crabbe. 2008. *The Handbook of Environmental Policy Evaluation* (London: Earthscan Publications Ltd.).

Melvin, Mark M., Gary T. Henry and George Julnes, 2000. *Evaluation: An Integrated Framework for Understanding, Guiding and Improving Policies and Programs* (San Francisco, CA: Jossey-Bass).

Mingat, Alain, Jee-Peng Tan and Shobhana Sosale. 2003 *Tools for Education Policy Analysis* (Washington, DC: World Bank Publications).

Nagel, Stuart S. 2001. *Handbook of Public Policy Evaluation* (Thousand Oaks, CA: Sage Publications).

"One Week Until TWIC Implementation," April 7, 2009, available at http://uscgla. blogspot.com/2009/04/one-week-until-twic-implementation.html.

Ostrom, Elinor. 1990. *Governing the Commons: The Evolution of Institutions for Collective Action* (Cambridge: Cambridge University Press).

Pinkowski, Jack. 2008. *Homeland Security Handbook* (Boca Raton, FL: CRC Press).

Pinto, C. Ariel, and Wayne K. Talley. 2006. "The Security Incident Cycle of Ports," *Maritime Economics & Logistics*, Vol. 8, No. 3, 267-286.

Rossi, Peter H., Mark W. Lipsey and Howard E. Freeman. 2003. *Evaluation: A Systematic Approach* (Thousand Oaks, CA: Sage Publications).

Ruggie, John Gerard (ed.). 1993. *Multilateralism Matters* (New York: Columbia University Press).

Sandler, Todd. 2004. *Global Collective Action* (Cambridge: Cambridge University Press).

Vedung, Evert. 2000. *Public Policy and Program Evaluation* (New Brunswick, NJ: Transaction Publishers).

Wein, Lawrence M., Alex H. Wilkins, Manas Baveja and Stephen E. Flynn. 2006. "Preventing the Importation of Illicit Nuclear Materials in Shipping Containers," *Risk Analysis*, Vol. 26, No. 5, 1377-1393, available at http:// dimax.rutgers.edu/~smcginit/Resources/Wein.pdf.

Weiss, Carol H. 1997. *Evaluation*, 2nd Edition (Upper Saddle River, NJ: Prentice-Hall).

Wholey, Joseph S., Harry P. Hatry and Kathryn E. Newcomer (eds). 2004. *Handbook of Practical Program Evaluation* (San Francisco, CA: Jossey-Bass).

Chapter 8

Conclusion

There has been a great deal studied, evaluated, discussed and written about the September 11, 2001 attacks in the United States and the ramifications of that horrific day on almost all aspects of life. Nearly a decade later, it may not be accurate to suggest that 9/11 changed everything in the country, but in the area of containerized freight security it did indeed have a significant impact. Looking at the larger issues of security and defense, and the related issue of port and containerized freight security, the United States has drastically shifted its focus over the last decade. In this book we highlighted the development of domestic and international efforts to secure the transportation of containerized freight, and most specifically the enhancement of security at seaports around the world. In particular we focused on examining the actors, agencies, policies and procedures involved in freight security at home and abroad. We also addressed several specific issues that affect freight security: the domestic political process in the United States, the role of interagency interaction, the impact of US leadership on the international politics of port security, the development of an international maritime security regime, the necessity of evaluating port security procedures, and the relationship between economic and national security.

In this concluding chapter we summarize the lessons learned from our research, highlighting the strengths and weaknesses of attempts to enhance the security of containerized freight as it travels throughout the global supply chain. We build on the book's analysis by offering practical implications of our findings as well as the broader theoretical implications that are useful for future research on the issues of freight and port security and beyond. Finally, we present recommendations for filling current gaps in port and container security operations and meeting future challenges regarding this important area of national security.

Primary Lessons Learned

Seaports in the United States and Abroad are More Secure Than We Might Think

There have been those in the media and in political life that are quick to draw attention to the inefficiencies and ineffectiveness of port and containerized freight security. Most notable is Stephen Flynn (2004) who properly highlighted numerous important weaknesses in US port security operations that contribute to US vulnerability. However, Flynn's work and that of others who have addressed these issues do not well outline the many positive advancements in the area of port and container security that have emerged in the last decade. Moreover, there has often been a misrepresentation of the port security issue. For example, it is not uncommon to see media reports that raise concern over the fact that only an estimated 2% of containers entering US seaports are searched. Most people upon reading that statement would rightly be concerned. However, what many of those reports fail to state is that today, 100% of containers entering the US via seaports are screened and a significantly high number are also scanned using radioactive portals. The 2% that is often referenced in reports pertains to containers that do not pass the scanning and screening measures and require manual physical inspection. It would be undesirable, and nearly impossible, to require a higher manual inspection rate, and one can only imagine the economic calamities that would occur should 100% of containers entering this country be intrusively searched. Those same readers who are undoubtedly concerned when they read the 2% figure, may be much more disgruntled if goods were not delivered in a reasonable amount of time to their department and grocery stores.

One of the main strengths of the new politics of container security has been the recognition of the risks that seaport management and the passage of containerized freight pose for attacks on US soil, due to the numerous points of vulnerability for containers traveling internationally through the supply chain. The complexity of the intermodal system and the volume of freight that passes through US seaports warrant increased attention to the monitoring and accountability systems controlling for the presence of dangerous cargo. A related strength is the separation and identification of the different probable threat scenarios for each mode of transport and each point of entry to the United States (air, land, sea), and the parceling of layered defenses (or, in the case of air transport, the streamlining of policy) for each form of transport. This identification avoids the clutter and mishaps of treating all points of entry and all modes of transport the same way, and is an important step in enhancing the monitoring of container security.

The fact is a lot of progress has been made regarding the protection of ports and containerized freight in the United States and around much of the world. Most members of the international community now recognize and accept the importance of monitoring and securing freight, even if they have done so because the United States has required it. Moreover, new policies and agreements, such as ISPS and the SAFE Frameworks of Standards, and programs like CSI and C-TPAT have served to enhance security and diminish the likelihood of a terrorist incident involving a port or container. Though challenges remain, it is important to recognize that in a relatively short period of time significant programs and policies have been developed and implemented. Not a single official, representative or analyst we spoke with throughout the course of conducting research for this study in the US, Europe or Asia stated that ports or containers were more secure before September 11, 2001.

Conclusion 167

Port and Container Security Has Become a Political Rather Than Pragmatic Issue

Despite the number of port and container security successes and the strengthening of US and international ports, we have also witnessed a number of instances where freight security became highly politicized. With the heated debates about and fallout from the SAFE Port Act, the 9/11 Commission Act, the Secure Freight Initiative, and Dubai Ports World, it was clear that politicians attempted to gain some political leverage or electoral advantage by raising alarm about and hyping up port security issues and programs. Politicians and members of the media capitalized on the frazzled mindset of the American public following 9/11 and throughout the initial years of the wars in Afghanistan and Iraq to capitalize on fear. Specifically, in the new, uncertain post-9/11 environment, American officials and citizens alike began to view the international system in terms of possibilities rather than probabilities, emphasizing worst case scenario thinking. This focus on what might be possible rather than probable built on the fear of additional terrorist attacks and activities and contributed to the paranoid nature of American foreign policy in the post-9/11 period. Although enhanced security policies after September 11 were a must, for numerous reasons, the extent to which the politics of fear instead of the pragmatics of policy and process motivated much of what occurred in terms of port and container security in the early post-9/11 era is considerable. US counterparts around the world recognized the politics rather than the pragmatics of the issues and eventually became somewhat hesitant to comply with US demands – not only on the port and container security issue, but on a number of other issues as well. Therefore, minimizing the politics and enhancing the practicalities of port and container policies and procedures has to become the focus.

The Large Number of Port and Container Security Actors are Very Active

It should be clear by now that the actors, agents and agencies involved in the global transport of goods, and specifically with port and containerized freight security, are incredibly numerous. Moreover, it is clear that the multitude of actors represent many different interests, both public and private. In Chapters 2 and 4 we outlined the various domestic and international actors interested and involved in port and container security. We also delineated the various programs that have been advanced to coordinate security measures and build domestic and global partnerships. Moreover, in Chapters 3 and 5 we explored how the various interested parties interact and the development of such cooperation over the past decade. As was demonstrated throughout the book, this range of actors is not only a factual feature of port and container activities, but a necessity for increasing security given the need to attack potential threats from a number of different angles, perspectives, locations and levels. The large number of relevant parties, of course, can make and has made it difficult to make progress on the issue. However, the United States has clearly sought to work within this complex environment and manage the difficulty to gain a security advantage. A multi-layered defense would not be feasible otherwise.

One particular improvement in recent transportation security policy implementations is the reorganization of agencies under the DHS umbrella. While many entities existed previous to 9/11, the definition of DHS offered a means to assign security responsibilities more formally and to define the borders of each agency's jurisdiction (as with the division of duties between CBP and the USCG regarding a ship coming to port). DHS remains under heavy scrutiny for its salience and effectiveness, but the reorganization did clarify the points of weakness in container security and began a roadmap to devise solutions. This is not to say that DHS in its entirety is a success. CBP and the USCG have both inherited new missions post-9/11, and are underfunded and understaffed to do so effectively. As new agencies within DHS, the TSA and ICE have necessarily experienced steep learning curves and have suffered organizational and procedural difficulties as a result – and the expectations assigned to these new agencies have perhaps been unforgiving.

US Leadership Domestically and Internationally is Necessary, Yet Problematic

As demonstrated in Chapter 3, interagency communication, coordination, cooperation and collaboration are essential for the successful prevention of terrorist and other dangerous activities using ports and cargo containers. Interagency interaction, however, does not come easily and in many cases is lacking. Although a history of interagency action on national security issues, and particularly regarding nuclear nonproliferation concerns, has positively affected post-9/11 interagency activities focused on port and container security, confusion about agency roles, a lack of organization, competing missions, and personality conflicts continue to get in the way of higher levels of interagency communication, coordination, cooperation and collaboration.

In addition to domestic cooperation, significant levels of international cooperation are also necessary to strengthen port and container security and prevent destabilizing and dangerous activities involving the global supply chain. Security threats concerning ports and cargo containers are obviously transnational in nature and, therefore, require transnational action. The United States, therefore, has taken the lead in encouraging, facilitating, promoting, assisting and, ultimately, requiring, foreign ports to establish appropriate port and container security measures that are consistent, compatible and acceptable to United States authorities. US leadership, however, has not only contributed to the development and implementation of better port and container security policies and procedures around the world, but has also contributed to ill feelings and resentment among foreign counterparts who are offended by the imposition of US national security policies on their own port operations. Such bitterness is overcome, perhaps, by the economic necessity to engage in international trade, particularly with the United

States. But US sensitivities to global concern about programs such as 100% cargo scanning diminishes its ability to lead on this and other important security issues.

An International Maritime Security Regime Has Emerged and May Persist

Although there was international activity on maritime safety prior to 9/11, it was not until after 9/11 that the international community developed global rules, regulations and procedures that sought to prevent the use of ports and cargo containers to perpetrate violence and engage in terrorist activity. As demonstrated in Chapter 5, with the advent of international standards and guidelines, such as ISPS, and the agreements established by several international organizations, such as the WCO, IMO and G8, it is evident that an international maritime regime has emerged. States have expressed certain expectations regarding the security of the world's ports and the global transportation of containerized freight. However, it remains to be seen whether such a nascent regime will persist for the longer term. Questions have been raised by many abroad about the role of the United States in the international maritime security regime and its insistence on programs and procedures that seemingly enhance US security primarily. Counterparts abroad may very well become more reluctant to assume the costs of stronger security measures to protect US national security at a cost to their own economic security. Whether the IMSR will be a robust regime that exists for years to come remains to be seen.

Balancing Economic and National Security Is a Must, Yet Remains a Challenge

It is often the case that the economic priorities of increased profits and diminished costs would be at odds with security priorities of minimizing risk and maximizing safety. The two concerns – economic wellbeing and national security – need not be contradictory concepts. However, the increased logistics and equipment costs of implementing enhanced security measures may indeed negatively affect global business productivity and profitability. This is particularly the case if trade were to slow down due to additional security constraints. On the other hand, it may also be the case that stronger security measures to prevent terrorist attacks and enhance national security also serve to prevent fraud, theft and loss of goods, thereby contributing to better outcomes for business. Several representatives from private enterprise, in fact, suggested to us that they use stronger security measures as a marketing tool, encouraging others to do business with them as they are "safe and secure" operators. Striking a balance between economic and national security, therefore, may be difficult, but in the long term, greater security may just as well lead to increased efficiency and stronger trade relationships, thus serving the purpose of both important goals.

Specific Gaps in Port and Container Security Procedures Do Exist

Despite the number of accomplishments in the area of port and container security over the past ten years, serious gaps in specific policy, procedure and implementation are evident. Weaknesses include the lack of adequate response and redirection plans at ports around the world; the implementation of background checks for all relevant port and freight employees and officials; the issuance of TWIC cards and the necessary card readers at domestic ports; and the continued need to manage tensions between economic efficiency and national security and enhance relations between private businesses and public officials. However, although these are serious concerns, there are reasons to believe that additional progress will be made.

This study found that although response and recovery plans were often in place at ports around the world, these plans rarely included redirection arrangements in the event of a terrorist attack or some other sort of violent or traumatic event that would necessitate port closure and the redirection of shipping traffic. Lessons learned in previous incidents involving hurricanes and labor slowdowns indicate that plans for quickly responding to terrorist or other incidents and redirecting incoming ships are important for successful recovery – as are relevant tests, drills and updates of established plans. Moreover, while all ports studied for this book had some sort of response and recovery plan in place (often absent redirection), the procedures were numerous and detailed for every kind of possible of possible event, which could hamper actual implementation in times of crisis.

The US government is struggling with the implementation of the TWIC card system, which includes criminal background checks for all transportation workers that require unescorted access to port facilities and containerized freight. The slow and confused process has most likely been a result of, as well as a reason for, much criticism and debate among port officials, transportation companies, and employees who work in port operations. Implementation of the TWIC program is required by the MTSA of 2002 and the SAFE Port Act of 2006, but the DHS is considerably behind not only in developing and standardizing the appropriate biometrics to be included in the smart cards, but in issuing the universal identification cards themselves and installing necessary card readers at all ports.

Finally, the security of ports and containerized freight cannot be achieved without substantial cooperative interaction between governments and private enterprise. Although interaction among the US business community and US government officials is substantial, due in large part to the C-TPAT program, similar interactions abroad among public and private interests are lacking. Particularly in Asia, few countries have developed C-TPAT-like arrangements. In fact, such partnerships seemed extremely foreign to authorities in Asia. Europe has developed the AEO program, which is similar to C-TPAT, and is actually quite a bit more rigorous. There is, therefore, somewhat of a disconnect regarding how to best interact between business and government – the United States taking a flexible, more partnership oriented route; Europe taking a more rigorous path; and Asia not engaging in business/government partnerships at all.

Theoretical Implications

This book focuses on the development and effectiveness of port and containerized freight security policies in the US and abroad from both practical and theoretical perspectives. Each chapter, therefore, explores not only the practicalities of some aspect of freight and port security, but attempts to use relevant theoretical approaches and schools of thought to place the issues in a broader context and learn important theoretical lessons that may help us generalize from this issue to other security issues of significance. Based on our study of port and container security in a more theoretical manner, therefore, we can present a number of theoretical implications.

Capitalizing on Fear

Scholars have long known that there is a popularity "bump" for US Presidents during times of war or crisis. More recently, it has been discovered that the increase in positive opinions also extends to members of Congress who support the President during these times. The population is said to "Rally 'Round the Flag" to support their leadership. The rally that occurred after 9/11 and was extended by the early invasion of Afghanistan and then Iraq allowed the President and legislators to push through significant legislation, resolutions of war and the creation and reorganization of a major US bureaucratic agency (DHS). These activities were largely made possible by the post-9/11 environment of fear and the subsequent rally effect capitalizing on the unease of the US citizenry. External events, such as the invasion of Afghanistan for example, helped extend the rally effect, but so too did the manipulation of the atmosphere of alarm. Members of both US parties as well as the media, saw the advantages (electoral returns and media time) of highlighting fear, which served to politicize and heighten the importance of security and foreign policy – areas that in "normal" times receive little attention from the general public.

Our investigation of freight security is not only illustrative of the ways in which a rally can be used and fear capitalized upon, but it also provides significant theoretical insights. Few people, even on Capitol Hill, gave much attention to seaports or freight security prior to the terrorist attacks of September 11, 2001. Yet after 9/11, port and container security became hot topics of interest in Washington and elsewhere. When the Dubai Ports World deal occurred in 2006, much of the US population was aware of the weaknesses in our port policies and resulting vulnerabilities – based on the limited information that was being provided via political officials and media outlets. We generally expect a rally effect to last a few of months, an election cycle at best. The strength and length of the rally, the manipulation of fear and the politicization of patriotism ran much deeper than most could have imagined. Port security, though certainly an important issue and a defensive loophole throughout the last century, is not necessarily the most concerning, nor the most probable security threat – yet this issue became shrouded

172 *Protecting Our Ports*

in fear and patriotism, which informs future theoretical scholarship on the rally effect in times of crisis.

Interagency Communication, Coordination, Cooperation and Collaboration

Three primary lessons from interagency interactions on port and container security have implications for theoretical perspectives on interagency communication, coordination, cooperation and collaboration – building on past relationships and practices; developing a joint mission; and mandating from above. The newly created Department of Homeland Security and its interagency process involving, in particular, CBP, TSA, USCG, DNDO and ICE, inserted itself as the lead Department responsible for much of the port and container security initiatives being pursued. Finding pre-existing cooperative relationships in areas relevant for port and container security, such as nuclear nonproliferation policy, was an important place to begin. Multiple agencies involved in nuclear nonproliferation issues were also relevant for port and container security concerns. The US Departments of State, Defense, Commerce and Transportation, along with the DHS, built on those existing relationships to achieve even greater levels of interagency activity. However, history may also mean that interests, practices and cultures are deeply ingrained in bureaucratic mindsets. Building on the past is key, but so is establishing a joint mission that brings together all of the various and potentially competing missions of each agency. This is, of course, far more complicated and difficult and requires higher levels of interagency interaction, such as collaboration. But, with a mandate from above and oversight requirements – in the case of port and container security, from Congress and the White House – advanced stages of interagency action are more likely. Future research on interagency communication, coordination, cooperation and collaboration, therefore, would benefit from considering the impact of previous interagency relationships, the possibilities of joint missions, and the existence of interagency mandates.

International Cooperation and State Sovereignty

Because the United States determined that the key to its own security is enhancing the security of containerized freight and transportation before ever reaching a US port, the country has become reliant on foreign counterparts to implement security protocols. This interplay between the United States and foreign governments means that port and containerized freight security also tests and informs broader issues of state sovereignty. Examining the development of international maritime policy as guided by the United States, it became apparent that challenges to state sovereignty were a growing concern. We know that state sovereignty (or autonomy) is not an absolute, largely because of the anarchic international environment that does not necessarily prevent states in the international system from interfering in the affairs of other states. It is also clear that states relinquish, often willingly, some of their sovereignty through contracts, conventions, coercion or imposition. However, when agreeing to contracts or conventions, there is the possibility that the benefits of the bargain diminish and states may feel that too much of their autonomy is being relinquished, without reciprocity or collaboration.

Although the US experienced a bit of an international "rally" after September 11, 2001, during which time it was able to advance its port and container security policies and programs abroad with limited opposition, overseas partners began to express concerns about their rights as sovereign, autonomous states given what they perceived to be an ever increasing burden based on US requirements and a lack of reciprocity in the process. Most international officials were willing to make initial changes that they felt benefited their purposes as well as US goals. However, many international partners began to see fewer benefits and perceive the relationship as a one-way street. This study, therefore, offers theoretical lessons about the ways in which global leaders can and should interact with their international counterparts and the expectations they should have regarding state sovereignty and interests in cooperation.

International Maritime Security Regime Development and State Motivations

An International Maritime Security Regime (the acceptance of rules, norms and practices on a given issue) has emerged over the last several years with the United States creating, facilitating and promoting the rules of the game. Regimes often develop during times of upheaval and crisis – and port and container security in the wake of 9/11 indicates that the IMSR is not exception. In Chapter 5 we argued that US motivations to lead the International Maritime Security Regime are based on power considerations. On the other hand, international partners tend to be motivated to cooperate with the United States based on economics. States want and need access to US markets, and establishing port and container security practices that meet US expectations is required. Therefore, international officials and governments have been rather willing to assume the costs associated with US programs and policies, but largely because there have been economic incentives to do so, not necessarily because they believe (at least most of them) that terrorism is a serious threat to their ports of entry.

The power of the United States in this case is institutional in nature, whereby the US government is able to create the "game" and set the rules. US institutional power in the IMSR suggests that the US has an advantage when promoting and requiring port security measures and that US goals of national security predominate. However, it appears that the institutional power of the United States is perhaps clashing with the sovereignty claims of some overseas partners, demonstrating that institutional power is not a constant and must be flexible and actively maintained for regimes to be robust and effective. Theoretically speaking, international regimes are created at the hands of powerful actors, but they may not persist and remain healthy if regime leaders are not consciously aware of the impact of their direction and management on their regime partners.

174   *Protecting Our Ports*

Balancing Economic and National Security

The international relations literature tends to treat national security concerns as separate and different from other forms of security – whether it is economic, environmental, health or human security. Mainstream IR theories are indeed rather stove-piped and do not well address how these various aspects of security may come together, intersect or interplay. Realist theory, for example, is the dominant approach concerning national security threats – focusing nearly exclusively on war, conflict and traditional military concerns. Recognizing the weaknesses of focusing too narrowly on military security matters, neoliberalism instead focuses on the multitude of economic factors that motivate state behavior, while constructivism may be most appropriate for the study of more contemporary concerns such as human security. What this study demonstrates is that different aspects of security are not mutually exclusive. For port and container security, concerns about both economic and national security, and even human security considering the terrorism threat, must be addressed and balanced simultaneously and in tandem rather than in isolation. Future studies of important security issues, therefore, should explore the extent to which the balancing of various security concerns matters.

The Study of Terrorism

Not surprisingly, there has been incredible growth in scholarship on international terrorism in recent years. From debates about how to define terrorism, to discussions of its characteristics, funding, structure, tactics, and potential solutions, this literature has contributed significantly to our knowledge about an issue that was previously of less importance to many. Only since September 11, 2001 have ports and cargo containers been widely recognized as possible locations of and tools for terrorist activities. Understanding the means taken to secure containers, ports, trucks and vessels that transport goods around the world is tremendously important. This study demonstrates that cargo containers may be used for nefarious purposes, that ports have not been well prepared for terrorist incidents, and that the effects of a violent episode involving port and/or cargo containers could be catastrophic. From a theoretical perspective, therefore, maritime terrorism is only now getting the attention it deserves – and such attention must continue as analysts attempt to incorporate port and container security concerns into a broader understanding of terrorist activities.

Policy Implications and Recommendations

Based on the lessons learned from this study, we can outline a number of policy implications and suggest various recommendations that may hopefully enlighten and inform policy-making on port and container security issues. First, at an absolute minimum, our research suggest that the United States and its partners abroad should continue to maintain and ultimately strengthen the policies, programs and practices that have proven to be effective. Specifically, attention should continue to focus on programs such as CSI, MTSA, Megaports, ISPS, C-TPAT and AEO to further enhance port and container security procedures.

Second, US authorities should minimize the politics and prey less on fear to promote port and container security. Instead, US officials should maximize the pragmatics and practicalities of the issue to improve both domestic and international understanding and support. Similarly, the US should work to augment both domestic and international communication, coordination, cooperation and collaboration. Domestic interagency interaction has been rather positive regarding port and container security, but certainly suffers from bureaucratic obstacles. More specifically delineating the roles of agencies and mandating their collaboration will go furthest in tackling insecurity in this area. Moreover, officials should continue to work together with industry leaders, labor unions and port officials to prevent duplication, reduce costs, enhance effectiveness and provide timely and reliable security policies.

Third, regarding international cooperation, the United States needs to be more aware of and sensitive to concerns about its leadership position and its insistence on international compliance with US programs. Undoubtedly, the United States must take the lead on port and container security, but there are implications for aggressive leadership, such as feelings of exclusion and lack of motivation. The United States should continue its leadership, but it should do better to listen to, include and assist foreign counterparts wherever and whenever it can.

Fourth, as part of an effort to enhance international cooperation, the US should make a conscious effort to frame the port and container security issue in the most positive and acceptable light from the foreign counterpart's perspective. Of the foreign countries we visited, only England expressed a significant concern about terrorist activity. Of course, had we visited Israel, India or Sri Lanka, we may have witnessed additional anxiety about terrorism, but in general, many countries view other issues (theft, smuggling, human trafficking, safety) as their top port security priorities. Yet, most US policies and programs continue to focus on the terrorist threat, relying on economic incentives to encourage cooperation. This is a missed opportunity. Looking at international cooperation on non-proliferation in the 1990s, there was a concerted effort to educate and inform states and citizens about the threat that nuclear weapons posed. The United States has largely attempted to raise awareness about port and container security by highlighting the threat that terrorism can pose. Much of this framing, however, is from a US perspective, leading many of its partners to view container security primarily as a US concern. The result is that the issue fails to resonate with many abroad. Therefore, the framing needs to change. Identifying a genuinely common concern (like nuclear proliferation) unites countries and leads to positive action. New framing that highlights the collective benefits allows the United States to "sell" its cause and makes it more palatable for others to "buy."

176 *Protecting Our Ports*

Fifth, in a crisis situation, ports of entry or sea terminals may need to close for an indeterminate period of time. This could occur due to inclement weather (such as the case during Hurricane Katrina), a union lockout (such as occurred on the West Coast in 2002), or in the worse case scenario, a terrorist attack. In these instances, port employees, shippers, vessel captains, truckers, neighboring ports and security officials must have contingency plans in place. These plans should include assistance with redirection so as to limit the negative economic effects of a port closures. Moreover, plans need not just be drafted. They must also be reviewed, updated at regular intervals, and tested in training exercises with multiple partners involved.

Sixth, based on our seaport assessments, seaports around the world should maintain an emphasis on port and container security policies, infrastructure, documentation and coordination. Specifically, ports should be sure to engage in and enhance regular information sharing, research and development, verification protocols, personnel training and enhance physical security measures. Such activities have successfully heightened port security wherever they are in place, and are significant gaps in security where they are not. Official attention to these specific measures, therefore, will contribute substantially to effective, efficient and secure port and container operations.

Seventh, enhanced policy "past the port" would further strengthen the security of ports and containerized freight. It is often the case that once containers enter the US, via seaport, land border or even air, they are generally under very little scrutiny as they travel across the United States. Similar situations are apparent around the world, where the bulk of security policy is targeted on seaports. Secured parking lots, additional tracking and enhanced background checks have been introduced as possible means to mediate this apparent gap. These ideas should be further explored and new ones encouraged.

Finally, there must always be an effort to balance what former CBP Commissioner Bonner often called "the dual goals" of his agency: economics and security. Equilibrium between these two important goals must necessarily be negotiated and accomplished. Security agencies must work with business entities to help ensure the most effective balance is struck. Careful consideration of the economic effects of security policies must always be addressed before such policies are implemented. Framing is also important here, as economics and security need not conflict with one another. It is important to find the ways and means by which to show the added benefits to trade of port and container security policies. A focus on theft and counterfeit goods has to some extent encouraged shippers to embrace some of the security policies. This is an area that should be further enhanced.

Avenues for Future Research

Even when a project comes to a close, it is clear that additional work is necessary. Our attention in this book focused on port and container policies in the United

States, Europe and Asia. The economic power of the European Union and the growing imports from Asian countries made those two regions important cases for analysis. In the future, however, an exploration of port and containerized freight security policies and procedures in Central and South America is warranted. Geographically, an exploration of Latin American seaports makes obvious sense. A significant number of goods are shipped to the United States from Latin American ports, or driven across the US border with Mexico. The history of drug trafficking, violence, organized criminal activities, insurgencies, and terrorism among many of the countries in that region effect US trade patterns as well as security and must be examined. Political disputes between the United States and various Latin American countries, among other issues, complicates the matter of port and container security in the western hemisphere, such factors also make the relevant issues all the more important.

While Central America has been slightly more attuned to the issue of freight security, especially given the important artery of the Panama Canal, South American countries have generally not taken major steps to join international programs on the issue. In all of South America it is only the Port of Santos in Brazil, the Port of Cartagena in Colombia, and the Port of Buenos Aires in Argentina that have been certified as CSI ports. Therefore, Latin America presents a gap in US and international efforts to secure global containerized freight transportation. Future research should examine the reasons for this exclusion, and explore ways to bring at least some of the countries of the region into the IMSR.

In addition, researchers and policy makers should continue to engage in seaport assessment similar to that presented in this book. Analysts, government officials, private enterprise representatives and port authorities all benefit from the assessment of port and container security policies, programs and activities as regular evaluation allows us to gauge successes and identify weaknesses in global seaport operations. Similarly, detailed evaluation of specific programs, such as CSI, allows us to highlight and address implementation problems with such programs, further enhancing their value and effectiveness. Finally, an explicit assessment of data gathering and sharing activities – especially access to and protection of Automatic Identification System (AIS) shipping data that is emitted from electronic devices on board many of the world's seafaring vessels – may contribute to better information collection and sharing practices, while avoiding obstacles associated with privacy protection and state sovereignty. Without a doubt, therefore, there remains much work to be done.

Conclusion

Although much has been accomplished since 9/11 regarding containerized freight security, there remain a number of gaps and inconsistencies both within the United States and around the world. Our research suggests that more work is needed and more research is required to enhance the security of containerized freight movements at home and abroad. This book has provided an initial attempt to systematically study and understand this issue. It should not be the last. Regular and repeated examination and assessment of land, sea and air ports of entry and exit are a necessary element for maintaining and strengthening national and international security.

Index

10+2 78-79, 86, 126
100% Scanning 17, 26, 30-32, 35-39, 41-42,
  59, 82-84, 120, 127, 132, 152, 166,
  169
1948 US Information and Educational
  Exchange Act 48
1949 Amendment to the National Security
  Act 48
1998 International Crime Control Strategy
  55
1999 National Drug Control Strategy 55,
  62

Absolute Gains 92-93, 96-97, 105, 108
Accountability xi, xii, 6, 14, 25, 35, 39, 40,
  58, 83, 87, 120-121, 133, 140,
  146-147, 160, 166
Advance Manifest 30-31, 78, 119-120,
  125-126, 132-134
Advance Notice of Arrival (ANOA) xi, 30, 77
Afghanistan 21, 34, 109, 167, 171
Airport Security 8, 23, 25, 69
Al Qaida 91
American Association of Port Authorities
  (AAPA) xi, 7, 15, 29, 121-122,
  124, 135-136
America's Counter Smuggling Initiative
  55, 64
American Trucking Association (ATA) xi,
  10, 15, 122, 125
AmTrak 10
Anarchy 12, 65-66, 68, 72, 86, 89, 92-93,
  115
Anomalies 79, 132, 142, 154
Anthrax 21-23, 39
Ashdod Port 1, 91, 115
Asia Pacific Economic Cooperation
  (APEC) xi, 72-74, 143, 162
Asia xi, 3, 8, 13, 41, 68, 72-75, 80-81, 87,
  108, 114, 122, 138-139, 141, 143,

148-149, 151, 154, 162, 166, 170,
  177
Association of Southeast Asian Nations
  (ASEAN) xi, 72-74, 88, 146
Authorized Economic Operator (AEO) xi,
  76, 78, 88, 110, 111, 113-115, 155,
  170, 175
Automated Commercial Environment
  (ACE) xi, 31
Automated Targeting System (ATS) xi,
  30-31, 79, 125, 142
Aviation Security 3

Background Checks 81, 119, 145, 147,
  155-156, 159, 170, 176
Bio-data 31
Border Security 39-40, 52, 55, 64, 113
Bureaucracy 21, 61
Bureaucratic Agencies 47, 171
Business xi, 5-6, 11, 14-15, 29, 35, 40,
  54-55, 69, 70, 77-78, 89, 98, 100,
  104-105, 118, 120-125, 127-128,
  130-134, 141, 145-147, 153,
  155-156, 159-160, 169-170, 176
Business Anti-Smuggling Coalition 55
Business Community 6, 118, 123, 145,
  170
Business Executives Enforcement Team
  (BEET) xi, 55

Canada xi, 23, 29-31, 69, 73, 77, 79, 80,
  88, 91, 100, 107, 113, 117,
  121-122, 125-126, 135-136
Canadian Border Services Agency (CBSA)
  xi, 77
Captain of the Port 26, 57
Cargo Containers 1-4, 14, 23, 27, 30, 32,
  38, 61, 91, 137, 140-143, 153-154,
  156, 168-169, 174
Cargo Manifest 142, 158

Caribbean Community (CARICOM) xi, 72, 74-75, 87
Carrier Initiative Program 55, 64
Center for International Trade and Security (CITS) xi, 139
Central Intelligence Agency (CIA) xi, 46-47, 49, 62-63
Cold War 3, 8, 20, 44, 48, 49-54, 63, 96, 109, 139
Collective Action 11, 45-47, 56, 60, 137, 140, 163
Constructivism 92-93, 95, 174
Container Security Initiative (CSI) xi, 9, 70, 74, 78-79, 82-86, 88, 102-103, 107, 110, 113, 127, 166, 172, 175, 177
Containers/Boxes 1-5, 7, 9, 14, 17, 23, 26-27, 30, 32-33, 35-38, 53, 61, 65, 68-69, 76, 78-79, 81, 83, 86, 91, 98, 104, 106, 118-123, 130-131, 137, 140-145, 147, 151-154, 156-158, 163, 166, 168-169, 174, 176
Container Ports 24, 40, 68, 71, 76, 83, 87, 100-101, 108, 113, 121
Container Seals and Smart/Wired Seals 29-30, 123, 151,
Container Terminals iv
Containerized Freight iii-v, vii, 4-5, 7-10, 17, 22-28, 32-33, 37-38, 43, 44, 65, 69-70, 72-73, 80-81, 83, 86, 97, 102, 118-123, 126, 128, 130, 132-134, 137-141, 143, 145-147, 149, 153-157, 163, 165-167, 169, 170-172, 176-177
Containerized Freight Security iii-iv, v, vii, 8-9, 17, 26, 28, 32-33, 37-38, 43, 80, 83, 86, 118, 121, 123, 127-128, 132, 134, 137, 140-141, 163, 165, 167, 171-172, 177
Cooperation iv, xi, 4-5, 7, 9-10, 26-28, 37, 41, 43-47, 51, 57-62, 65-66, 69, 72-76, 84, 86-88, 91, 93-97, 99, 101-102, 104-109, 112-114, 120, 135, 143, 145-147, 151-152, 154, 156, 159, 160, 162, 167-168, 172-173, 175
Coordinating Committee for Multilateral Export Controls (COCOM) xi, 51

Coordination 9-10, 43, 45-47, 52, 56-57, 59-62, 138, 140-141, 145-147, 152, 159-160, 168, 172, 175, 176
Collaboration 5, 9-10, 43, 44-47, 53, 57, 59-61, 65, 95, 101, 123, 127, 133, 138, 147, 152, 154, 156, 168, 172, 173, 175
Corruption 3, 53
Cuban Missile Crisis 17-18, 49, 61
Customs ix, xi-xii, 5, 9, 14-15, 24, 26, 40-41, 43, 51-52, 55, 58, 61, 64, 69-71, 73-74, 77, 79, 82-83, 86-89, 99, 103, 110, 113-115, 119, 124-125, 135, 142, 150-151
Customs and Border Protection (CBP) ix, xi, 5, 9, 14, 26-27, 30-32, 34, 36, 39, 41, 43, 52, 55, 57-58, 60-61, 64, 69, 71, 74, 77-79, 82, 84, 86-87, 102, 113, 115, 119, 122, 124-130, 133, 135, 150, 162, 168, 172, 176
Customs-Trade Partnership Against Terrorism (C-TPAT) xi, 9, 69, 76-78, 83-84, 102-104, 108, 110, 111, 115, 127-129, 132-135, 145, 155, 162, 170, 175

Dirty Bombs 4-5
Documentation 8, 10, 23, 138, 140, 144, 147, 154, 158, 160, 176
Domestic Nuclear Defense Office (DNDO) xi, 35, 43, 57, 60, 69, 70, 87, 172
Domestic Politics v, 8, 17, 19, 21, 23, 25, 27, 29, 31, 33, 35, 37, 39, 41, 65, 114
Drug Trafficking 24, 53, 74, 177

Economic Security v, 10, 87, 117-121, 123, 125-127, 129, 131, 133, 135, 169
Elements of a Secure Containerized Freight System vii, 147
E-manifest Program 31
End User/Use 51, 142, 144
Enforcement xi, xii, 14, 26-27, 32, 40, 43, 48, 50, 55, 66, 72, 80, 140, 146-147, 150, 160
Europe/European xi, 3, 5, 8, 9, 15, 41, 68, 72-74, 79, 80, 81, 83, 87, 102,

Index

104, 107-115, 122, 138-139, 141, 148-149, 151, 152, 154-155, 166, 170, 177

European Union (EU)/ Commission xi, 5, 9, 15, 72, 74, 107-108, 110, 113, 115, 177,

EU Directive 2005/65 72, 87, 151

Exports 4, 55, 68, 75-76, 82, 86-87, 108, 111, 121-122, 136

Export Control xi, 51-52, 55, 63, 139, 140, 162

Export Control and Border Security Assistance Program 52

Express Delivery and Logistics Association (XLA) xii, 10, 15, 122-123

Evaluation 10, 20, 102, 124, 138-141, 148, 150, 163, 177

Federal Aviation Administration (FAA) xi, 3

Federal Bureau of Investigation (FBI) xi, 24, 39, 46-47, 51-52, 59, 62-63

Federal Emergency Management Agency (FEMA) ix, xi, 44

First Mover Advantage (Primary mover) 104, 105, 107-108, 114

Foreign Policy 13, 20, 39, 48-50, 61, 63-64, 68, 115, 167, 171

Free and Secure Trade Program (FAST) xi, 31, 76-78, 125

Freight Forwarder 28-29, 32, 118-119, 122-124, 126, 133

Global Governance v, 91, 93, 95, 97, 99, 101, 103, 105, 107, 109, 111, 113-115

Globalization 3, 13, 65, 67, 91, 99, 115

Global Security 2

Global Supply Chain 7, 9, 38, 60, 70, 76, 104, 111, 115, 138, 141-142, 165, 168

Global Trade 2, 5, 13, 68, 71, 74, 98, 101, 117-118, 121, 129, 133, 141-142

Governments ix, 5, 10, 27, 29, 37-38, 61, 66, 68-70, 72, 80, 83, 94, 100, 103, 106-108, 111, 141, 143, 145-147, 152, 156, 170, 172-173

Gross Domestic Product (GDP) xi, 48, 121

Harbor iv, 17, 54, 151

Highly Enriched Uranium (HEU) ii, xi, 51

Homeland Security ii, iv, ix, xi, 4, 6, 12, 14-15, 22, 26-29, 33, 37-41, 44, 56-57, 59, 61, 69-70, 87-88, 137, 139, 144, 153, 163, 172

Homeland Security Act 27

House Subcommittee on Border, Maritime and Global Counterterrorism 27

Hurricane Katrina 47, 61-62, 130, 152, 176

Ideas 93, 95-97, 105, 107-108, 112, 153, 176

Identification Cards 81, 124, 145, 147, 154-156, 159, 170

Illegal Trafficking 3

Illicit Trafficking 49

Immigration and Customs Enforcement (ICE) xii, 14, 26-27, 34, 40, 43, 57, 69, 119, 168, 172

Implementation xii, 4, 7, 9-10, 25-26, 29, 34, 36-38, 47, 51-52, 56, 60, 69, 73, 75, 78-79, 82-83, 86, 88, 91, 103, 106, 118, 122-123, 132, 143, 145-147, 149-150, 155, 160, 163, 168, 170, 177

Implementation Agency for Crime and Security (IMPACS) xii, 75

Importer Security Filing (ISF) xii, 78, 86

Imports 4, 68, 82, 83, 91, 98, 106, 108, 111, 121-122, 130-131, 133-134, 136, 177

India 13, 49, 51, 114, 175

Information Sharing 30, 97, 140, 146, 152, 156, 159, 160, 176

Infrastructure ix, 10, 24, 28, 31, 59, 62, 68, 70, 72, 75, 78-81, 83-83, 128-129, 133, 138, 140, 141, 147, 150-151, 157, 160, 176

Institutional Power 106-107, 111-112, 173

Interagency Committee on Marine Transportation System (ICMTS) xii, 56, 61

Interagency Cooperation 10, 26, 45, 58

Interests ii, 9, 24, 29, 45-47, 49, 66, 67, 80, 82, 92-93, 95-97, 105, 108, 112-114, 118, 120-121, 123, 125, 130-131, 134, 167, 170, 172-173

Intermodal Transportation/Trade 2, 98
International Air Transport Association
 (IATA) xi, 129
International Cooperation iv, 51, 76, 91,
 94, 99, 107, 112, 146-147, 152,
 159, 160, 168, 172, 175
International Community 51, 61, 65, 83,
 99, 139, 166, 169
International Environment 9, 92-94, 172
International Longshore and Warehouse
 Union (ILWU) xii, 28-29, 40,
 130-131, 135
International Maritime Organization
 (IMO) xii, 5, 15, 71, 72, 75, 79-80,
 88, 99, 100, 103, 115, 143, 146,
 154, 169
International Maritime Security Regime
 (IMSR) v, xii, 9, 86, 91-93, 95,
 97-99, 101-113, 115, 165, 169,
 172, 173, 177
International Organizations (IOs) ix, xii, 5,
 51, 66-68, 70, 83, 93-97, 99, 100-
 101, 112-113, 146, 154, 169
International Politics iii-iv, v, 7, 9, 10,
 65, 67-69, 71, 73, 75, 77, 79, 81,
 83-84, 87, 89, 92-93, 114-115, 134,
 136, 165
International Ports 15, 77-80, 86, 98-99,
 103-104, 148, 152-153, 167
International Port Security Liaison Officers
 (IPSLO) xii, 80, 82
International Regime Theory 9, 91, 94
International Relations (IR) xii, 9, 66, 91-
 95, 112, 114, 120, 133, 135, 174
International Security 3, 11, 47-48, 91-93,
 95
International Ship and Port Security (ISPS)
 xii, 9, 71, 75-76, 78-80, 83-84, 88,
 97, 99, 100, 102-103, 108, 138,
 142-144, 151, 166, 169, 175
International System 5, 65-68, 70, 92 167,
 172
International Terrorism 3, 21, 174
International Waterways 8
Iranian Hostage Crisis 18
Iraq 21, 23, 29, 51, 62, 67, 109, 113, 131,
 136, 167, 171

John Kerry 22, 42
Joint Training 143, 146, 154, 156,
Just in time shipping 120, 125-126, 133,

Karl Rove 22
Kuwait 51

Law Enforcement 26, 48, 51, 55
Layered Defense 4-5, 25, 28, 40, 102, 166,
 168
Lockheed Martin 10, 15, 122
Longshoremen 40, 58, 131, 135, 155

Magnuson Act 54
Manifest 22, 30-32, 76-79, 119-120,
 124-126, 132-134, 140, 142, 144,
 146-147, 157-159
Marine Transportation System National
 Advisory Council (MTSNAC) xii,
 56, 63
Maritime Administration (MA) xii, 54, 63
Maritime Domain Awareness Program
 (MDA) xii, 146
Maritime Security v, xii, 5-6, 9, 11-14, 54,
 63, 74-76, 86-88, 91-93, 95, 97, 99,
 101-105, 107, 109, 111-113, 115,
 146, 162-163, 169, 185
Maritime Trade 71
Maritime Transportation Security Act
 (MTSA) xii, 58, 76-77, 83, 97,
 100, 102, 108, 124, 144, 155, 170,
 175
Measurement 141, 149
Megaports 9, 76, 78-79, 175
MERCOSUR xii, 72, 74, 87-88
Multilateral xi, 10, 51, 137-138, 146-147,
 156, 160, 163
Murrah Federal Building 98

National Academy of Science 51
National Research Council 51
National Security v, 5, 7, 8-10, 17, 20,
 22-24, 26, 28, 34-35, 38, 41, 43-
 44, 48-50, 60-62, 69, 82, 91, 113,
 118-121, 123, 125, 127, 129, 131,
 133-135, 137, 165, 168-170,
 173-174, 178

Index 183

National Security Act 48
Neo-liberalism 92-93, 95, 120, 174
Nongovernmental Organizations (NGOs)
    6, 51, 125
Nonproliferation Disarmament Program
    Fund 52
Norms 9, 94-97, 101, 146, 173
North American Free Trade Agreement
    (NAFTA) xii, 31-32, 72-74, 77
Nuclear nonproliferation 8, 50-53, 62, 70,
    96, 168, 172
Nuclear Suppliers Group 51
Nuclear Threat Reduction 22
Nuclear Weapons/Weapons of Mass
    Destruction 1, 5, 13, 33, 49-53, 60,
    100, 139, 175
Nunn-Lugar 50, 52

Operation Desert Storm 17, 62
Organized Crime 13, 49, 98-99, 177
Organization of the Petroleum Exporting
    Countries (OPEC) xii, 68, 75-76,
    87, 108
Oversight 24, 27, 41, 69, 79, 81-82, 86,
    103, 126, 131, 142, 145, 147, 150,
    157, 159, 172

Pakistan 1, 36
Pallet 2, 12
Panama Canal 130, 152, 177
Partnerships 7, 45, 61, 64, 68, 72-74, 78,
    92, 113, 127, 145-146, 155-156,
    159-160, 167, 170
Partners in Protection (PiP) xii, 76-78
PATRIOT Act 20
Patriotism 18, 20, 171-172
Pearl Harbor 17
Pentagon 24, 43
Persian Gulf War 50-52
Piracy 6, 11-12, 99
Points of Entry/Exit 1, 17, 98, 126, 130,
    133, 150, 166
Policing 3, 21, 27, 66, 147, 160
Policy Past the Port 76, 78, 111, 176
Politics of Fear 21, 39, 167, 171
Politicization of port security 33
Port Authority 151-152
Port of Antwerp, Belgium 15, 83, 148, 151

Port of Athens, Greece 15, 83-84, 148
Port of Duress, Albania 15, 148, 150, 154
Port of Gdansk, Poland 15, 148
Port of Hamburg, Germany 15, 148, 151,
    153
Port of Hong Kong, China 15, 68, 148
Port of London, UK 15, 83, 104, 148,
    151-152
Port of Los Angeles/Long Beach (LA/Long
    Beach), USA 15, 68, 70, 122,
    130-131, 148
Port of New Orleans, USA 15, 34, 148, 152
Port of New York/New Jersey, USA 1, 15,
    34, 68, 70, 122, 148,
Port of Rotterdam, the Netherlands 15, 79,
    148, 150-151, 153
Port of Seattle, USA 15, 57-58, 68, 122,
    130-131, 148
Port of Singapore 15, 81, 83, 88, 108, 148
Port of Taicang, China 15, 84, 148, 154
Port of Thessaloniki, Greece 15, 148, 151,
    154
Port of Tokyo, Japan 15, 148
Port of Yangshan, China 15, 148, 154
Ports i-ii, iv, ix, xi-xii, 1-15, 17-18, 20,
    22-42, 44, 46, 48, 50, 52-66, 68-72,
    74-84, 86-88, 91-92, 94, 96,
    98-107, 110-114, 117-118, 120-
    124, 126-138, 140-158, 160,
    162-163, 165-178
Port Security v, vii, xii, 1, 3-13, 14, 23, 25,
    27-28, 33, 35, 38-40, 44, 47-48,
    50, 53-61, 63-65, 69-72, 74-77, 80,
    82-84, 98, 100-103, 105-109,
    112-113, 137-144, 146, 148-150,
    152, 156-159, 163, 165-168, 170-
    177
Post-Cold War 8, 49-50, 53
Power ii, 36, 40, 47, 50, 66-70, 74, 80,
    88-89, 92-93, 95-98, 105-108,
    111-115, 117, 120-121, 135, 173,
    177
President Bill Clinton 3
President George H.W. Bush 18-19
President George W. Bush 8, 19- 22, 26,
    33-34, 38-40, 42, 109, 131
President's Executive Committee
    (EXCOMM) xi, 49

Private Enterprise ix, 6, 11, 54, 122, 125, 153, 155, 169-170, 177
Private Sector 10, 122-124, 128-129, 133-134, 153
Proliferation Security Initiative (PSI) xii, 70
Proprietary Information 146, 153, 156, 160
Pushing Borders Out 9, 25, 27, 68, 70, 80, 105, 107

Radiation Portals/ x-ray/gamma ray xii, 30-32, 39, 119, 133, 143-144, 151, 155, 158
Radio Frequency Identification Devices (RFID) xii, 30, 32
Radiological Weapons 6
Rally 'Round the Flag 17-18, 33, 38, 171
Realism 92-93, 95, 135
Regime v, xii, 9, 46, 86, 91-97, 99, 100-115, 128, 165, 169, 173
Regime Cooperation 95-96
Regime Effectiveness 95-96, 101
Regime Robustness 95-96, 101
Relative Gains 92, 93, 95, 105, 107
Report of the Interagency on Crime and Security in US Seaports 2000 3, 13, 53, 63, 98-99, 114
Republican Party 20, 22
Re-routing and Redirection 129-130, 140, 144, 152, 156, 158, 170, 176
Research and Development 54, 60, 104, 153, 156, 158, 176
Response and Recovery 129, 143, 147, 151, 158, 170
Rules 9, 30, 59, 72, 84, 86, 94-95, 97, 101, 106-108, 110, 112-113, 125, 134, 140-141, 146-148, 150, 156-157, 160, 169, 173
Russia 41, 49-50

SAFE Framework of Standards 74, 166
SAFE Port Act 35-37, 41, 58-59, 78, 83, 89, 102, 106, 124, 129, 144, 155, 167, 170
Safety of Life at Sea (SOLAS) xii, 9, 79-80, 99-100, 103, 115
Seafarers' International Union of North America 28

Seaports ix, 1-4, 6-9, 11-13, 24, 30-32, 34-36, 38, 41, 53-54, 57, 63, 65, 68-72, 75, 77, 79-81, 83-84, 91, 98-99, 101-106, 111, 114, 117-118, 122-123, 126, 128, 134, 137, 140, 142, 148-149, 151-152, 156, 165, 166, 171, 176-177
Seaport Crime 3
Secure Border Initiative (SBI) xii, 58
Secure Freight Initiative (SFI) xii, 35-36, 39, 41, 76, 83, 88, 102, 106, 152, 167
Security Elements 139, 141
Security Elite 129
Security Layers 4, 25, 27-28
Select Committee on Homeland Security 12, 15, 33, 40
September xi, 2001 (9/11) 3-4, 6, 17, 19, 43-44, 53, 56-57, 77, 83, 100-101, 107, 109, 112, 117, 165-167, 171, 173-174
Shipping Container 2, 79, 91, 163
Shoe Bomber 21
Smart Border Accords 31, 73
Smuggling 14, 24, 27, 31, 52-53, 55, 56, 62, 64, 82- 84, 98, 104, 175
SOLAS xii, 9, 80, 99-100, 103, 115
Somalia 1, 6
Soviet Union/Bloc 49-51, 54, 96, 104, 139, 162
Standardization 2, 119
Stephen Flynn 6, 38, 117, 142, 165
Subcommittee on Transportation Security and Infrastructure Protection 28
Supply Chain 7, 9-10, 12, 25, 28, 36-40, 42, 55, 60, 70-72, 76-77, 81, 83, 103-104, 111, 115, 118, 121, 123, 125-128, 132-138, 140-149, 152-153, 155-157, 159-160, 165-166, 168
Surveillance 58, 120, 143, 147, 150-151, 157

Taft-Hartly Act 131
Targeting xi, 14, 30, 64, 125, 142-144, 147, 149, 153, 157-158
Technology 23, 25, 30-31, 33, 35, 50-51, 65, 78-79, 83, 87, 99, 113, 119, 123-124, 126-127, 143, 152-153, 158

Index 185

Terrorism ii, iv, xi, 3, 5-6, 9, 11-13, 20-21,
23-24, 28, 39-41, 44, 47, 49, 53,
55, 56-57, 60, 69-70, 74, 77, 82-84,
87, 98-100, 104, 115, 117, 126-127,
130, 153, 173-175, 177
Terrorists 1, 3-4, 6, 13, 24-26, 34, 50, 79,
89, 100
Theft 3, 23-24, 28, 53, 75, 82-84, 98-99,
104, 120, 153, 169, 175-176
Third Party/Trusted Enclave 70, 80,
124-125, 146, 152-153, 156, 160
Threat Assessment 142, 147, 157
Tom Brokaw 22
Tom Ridge 22, 26, 41
Trade Act of 2002 30-31
Trade Fraud 24
Transnational Crime 3, 13-14, 49
Transportation xi-xii, 2-6, 10-11, 13-15,
23-30, 34-36, 38-40, 44, 54, 56,
58-59, 61-65, 77, 81, 89, 97-98,
100-101, 113, 119-120, 123-124,
127, 129, 137, 144, 147, 155, 165,
168-170, 172, 177
Transportation Security Administration
(TSA) xii, 6, 13, 26-27, 32, 34, 43,
57-59, 69, 125, 128-129, 168, 172
Transportation Worker Identification
Credential (TWIC) xii, 12, 29,
58-59, 70, 81, 124, 155, 170
Trusted Traveler 126, 132

Union of South American Countries
(UNASUR) xii, 72, 74, 89
Unions 28-29, 54, 72-73, 131, 175
United Arab Emirates (UAE) xii, 34
United Nations Convention of the Law of
the Sea (UNCLOS) xii, 99-100
United Parcel Service (UPS) xii, 7, 10, 15,
32, 122, 127, 132, 133
United States Center for Disease Control 44
United States Chamber of Commerce 7,
10, 15, 122-124
United States Coast Guard (USCG) xii, 5,
15, 26, 34, 43, 51-52, 54-55, 57,
59, 64, 69, 71, 76-77, 79-80, 82,
88, 100, 102, 119, 121, 146, 163,
168, 172

United States Congress/House of
Representatives/Senate 5, 12, 15,
20-21, 26, 33, 39-40, 83-84, 102
United States Department of Commerce
(DoC) xi, 5, 14, 28-29, 44, 51, 54,
56, 172
United States Department of Defense
(DoD) xi, 5, 14, 28-29, 49, 51-52,
54-56
United States Department of Energy (DoE)
xi, 5, 14, 44, 51-52, 56-57, 59, 70,
79
United States Department of Health and
Human Services 44
United States Department of Homeland
Security (DHS) xi, 4-6, 14, 22,
26-29, 31, 33-36, 39, 41, 43-44,
56-59, 69-70, 73, 79, 87-88,
124-125, 127-129, 168, 170-172
United States Department of State (DoS)
xi, 5, 14, 28-29, 44, 48-49, 51-52,
56-57, 60, 70, 79, 87, 110, 129,
172
United States Department of Transportation
(DoT) xi, 3, 5, 28-29, 54, 56, 61,
63, 87, 113
United States Economy 9, 118, 134
United States Environmental Protection
Agency 44-45, 56
United States Information Agency 48
United States Navy 26

VACIS 30
Verification 144, 147, 153, 154, 158, 176
Virtual Border 25, 68, 105
Vulnerability 11, 24, 98, 104, 138, 142,
165-166

"War on Terror" 22, 109
West Coast Ports 122, 130-131, 135, 152
White House 10, 34, 53, 56, 172
World Customs Organization (WCO) xii,
5, 15, 71, 78, 89, 99, 100, 103, 119,
154
World Trade Center 24, 98
World War II 8, 17, 33, 44, 48, 71

CPSIA information can be obtained
at www.ICGtesting.com
Printed in the USA
BVHW04*0354080718
520995BV00005B/142/P